RADICAL PEOPLE'S
THEATRE

Washerwoman's Nativity

RADICAL PEOPLE'S THEATRE

Washerwoman's Nativity

EUGÈNE VAN ERVEN

INDIANA UNIVERSITY PRESS
Bloomington and Indianapolis

Manufactured in the United States of America

Library of Congress Cataloging-in-Publication Data

Van Erven, Eugene.
  Radical people's theatre

  Bibliography: p.
  Includes index.
    1. Theater—History—20th century. 2. Theater—
Political aspects. 3. Theater and society—History—
20th century. 4. Radicalism. I. Title.
PN2189.V3 1988   792'.09'047   87-46368

ISBN 0-253-34788-2

1 2 3 4 5 92 91 90 89 88

To A., J., A., and X.

The arts are political, whether they like it or not. If they stay in their own realm, preoccupied with their proper problems, the arts support the status quo, which in itself is highly political. Or they scream and kick and participate in our own country's struggle for liberation in whatever haphazard way they can, probably at the expense of some of their sensitive craftsmanship, but definitely for their own soul's sake.

Peter Schumann
of the Bread and Puppet Theater

CONTENTS

ILLUSTRATIONS

Unless otherwise credited, all photos are by the author.

PREFACE

I feel very fortunate in having gotten to know and spent quality time with the
following theatre practitioners, all of whom tremendously influenced my perspective on contemporary culture and without whom this project would not have
been the wonderful adventure that it was: Catherine Bonafé of lo Teatre de la
Carriera; Charles Tordjman of le Théâtre Populaire de Lorraine; Agnès Blot and
Albert Boadella of Els Joglars; Lilyane Drillon and Salvador Távora of la Cuadra
de Sevilla; Guillermo Heras of Tábano; Paco Obregón of Teatro Geroa; John
McGrath, Elizabeth MacLennan, and Bob Rae of the 7:84 Theatre Company;
Volker Ludwig of Das Grips Theater; Wolfgang Anrath of Theater K; Joan
Holden of the San Francisco Mime Troupe; Gloriamalia Flores and Andrés
Gutierrez of el Teatro Campesino; Elka and Peter Schumann of the Bread and
Puppet Theater; and all those wonderful and brave theatre workers of the
Philippine Coordinating Council for People's Culture. I thank them for sharing
their food, their homes and their rich thoughts, all of which opened for me a new
dimension to theatre research outside the walls of the university library when I
thought I was going to be buried inside forever. I should also like to thank the
following individuals for putting me up and putting up with me during my
research-related travels: Rob and Alice Griffiths in London; Jack and Brigitte
Bussy and Eric Vincent in Paris; Evelyne and Serge Vicens in Marignane; Lothar
Witte in Berlin; Brian and Stephanie Lewis in West Topsham, Vermont; Pablo
Gillespie in New York; Cathy Lipe in San Francisco; Christiane Bober in
Strasbourg; Cristina Menal in Barcelona; David Calvo in Bilbao; Alberto Gonzales del Tanago in Madrid; Gardy Labad, Jojo Sanchez, Jack Yabut, and the
other marvelous cultural workers of P.E.T.A. in Manila; and Beth Mondragon
and the people of Banaag in Cebu City. Inside the walls of academia, the
following friends, teachers and colleagues were responsible for keeping my
thoughts and language on track when they were in great peril of derailment: Dan
Church, who first aroused and then nurtured my interest in popular political
theatre; Hans Joachim Schulz, who taught me that, fortunately, there was life
beyond the English department; Jürgen Pelzer, who generously shared with me

his vast knowledge of East and West German theatre; Jenny Spencer and Edwin Gentzler, who are living proof that backhand volleys and political theatre are compatible after all; Jean Leblon, who kept my words in check when they needed it most. I am particularly grateful to Ana Rueda for her unfaltering support even when she was under great stress herself.

I should like to thank the following people and institutions for their financial support: Jack Batho and the French Ministry of Culture for subsidizing my trip to the 1983 Avignon Theatre Festival; Vanderbilt University's research award committee and the Ethel Mae Wilson Fund for partially financing my research in the summer of 1984; and Phillip Mann, David Carnegie, and the University Grants Committee of Victoria University of Wellington, New Zealand for awarding me a postdoctoral fellowship, generous friendship, intellectual stimulation, and a spectacular setting during the final stages of this project. Imelda Anderson and John Casey of the Victoria University's Photography Facility were also instrumental in developing and printing the greater part of the photographs that appear in this book. I also thank Moíses Perez Coterillo of El Centro de Documentación Teatral in Madrid for so generously providing me with indispensable materials on the Spanish political theatre.

Earlier versions of chapters 6 and 9 appeared originally in *Minnesota Review* and *New Theatre Quarterly,* respectively. I am grateful to Cambridge University Press and the editors of these journals for allowing me to reprint some of these materials here. A special thank you is in order for Professor Sam Smiley, who suggested I include the chapter on Spain and then generously shared with me his notes and contacts. Without his advice, I would never have gotten to know one of the most exciting examples of radical theatre in the West, nor indeed Albert Boadella's cured ham and Agnès Blot's formidable *mousse au chocolat,* which would perhaps have been an even greater shame.

E.v.E.,
Wellington, New Zealand,
25 March 1987

RADICAL PEOPLE'S
THEATRE

CHAPTER 1

INTRODUCTION

This is a book about contemporary theatre, but it will not be dealing with Grotowski, Barba, Brook, Bob Wilson, Shepard, Pinter, or Beckett. Rather, I will be tracing the rise and decline of the powerful alternative political theatre movement that developed in the wake of the turbulent sixties and that, in my opinion, forms an aspect of modern theatre every bit as worthy as the work of Brook or Beckett. The generation of theatre practitioners that emerged under the rebellious spirit of '68 is responsible for creating decentralized, antiestablishment theatre in alternative spaces for popular audiences throughout the Western world. If nothing else, the radical theatre provided its practitioners with a tough, all-around theatre training, ranging from bookkeeping, loading trucks, and sewing costumes to building sets, writing plays, and performing during rush hours in city squares. Now, as we are slowly approaching the nineties, this new wave of radical theatre, which for almost two decades provided some of the most exciting popular theatre experiments in the post–World War II era, seems to have gone into undeniable decline. The radical theatre artists of yore can now be found in national theatres, television and film studios, ministries of culture and their subsidiaries, regional art councils, or university drama departments. Others have dropped out of the theatre scene completely and, disillusioned, can sometimes be found growing grapes in the foothills of the Pyrenees and other out-of-the-way places. Most of the groups that have survived, are now openly accepting financial support from the governments and the mainstream theatres that they once so vehemently despised. The time seems ripe, therefore, to draw up the balance of twenty years of radical popular theatre in the West. What were its historical antecedents? What were the sociopolitical conditions that surrounded its birth? What were its artistic and political achievements? What were the

1

reasons for its decline? Did true popular theatre for the underprivileged lose out once more to the forces of commercialism and co-optation? Is there a future?

Although the radical popular theatre is now an integral part of the contemporary cultural scene, for a long time it refused to have any dealings with what it considered the commercial apparatus of bourgeois mass culture. Because it was not regarded as "high" culture, the radical popular theatre did not receive the general critical attention that it undoubtedly deserved. The past decade has fortunately shown a gradual increase in the number of critical articles on radical popular theatre, but most of these deal with individual groups only. In addition, a few books discuss the development of popular theatre in one country, but a full-length study of the radical popular theatre set in its international scope has yet to appear. With this work, I hope to partially fill that gap. Without pretending to be comprehensive, I will attempt to define radical popular theatre as an important international phenomenon. Focusing on selected plays created by representative troupes from the United States, France, Great Britain, West Germany, Italy, and Spain, I will test the hypothesis that these troupes share essential characteristics and ideological objectives. For this purpose, the creative methods, satirical strategies, aesthetic structures, and social frameworks of their plays will be submitted to careful analysis.

I will focus my study on the decade immediately following the pseudorevolutionary events of 1967 and 1968, for it was then that the current wave of radical popular theatre received its vital impulse, amidst Beatle tunes, antiauthoritarianism, love-ins, sleep-ins, teach-ins, sit-ins, communes, sexual liberation, emerging feminism, pacifism, and cries for Third World solidarity. Most sociohistorical commentators disagree as to the exact nature of the issues involved and the actual results of the massive, student-instigated demonstrations that paralyzed many North American university campuses and most European capitals in the fall of 1967 and the spring of 1968. The aftermath of the unrest revealed no significant improvement in the structures of the university system against which students had so passionately protested, nor had workers been able to improve substantially their economic position. However, the tumultuous events did leave a prominent and lasting mark on the arts. The performing arts, in particular, were inspired by a new sociopolitical consciousness that proved much more durable than the rather short-lived utopias of the students and more substantial than the material benefits of the workers, which were soon obliterated by inflation and tax increases.

The new social values became most evident in the increasing activities of the newly politicized young playwrights, directors, and actors who decided to place their art at the service of what they considered to be the oppressed classes. Consequently, they turned their backs on the classics and conventional theatre venues and based themselves in densely populated neighborhoods of heavily industrialized urban centers or in impoverished rural areas with the intention of creating political theatre dealing with the specific socioeconomic and political issues of the people who lived there. Most of these young artists had participated in lengthy discussions on the political function of art during the occupation of university auditoriums and theatres in the mid-sixties. Their leaders had studied the appropriate works of prominent progressive thinkers and on that basis had founded their own versions of militant cultural action. Thus they resolved to use their creative talents to raise the political consciousness of agricultural and industrial laborers and to oppose an alternative culture to what they regarded as the dominant bourgeois hegemony.

The following study, divided into a theoretical and a practical component, hopefully contains valuable bibliographic and historical information and critical analyses that are intended to benefit both the serious research scholar, the theatre practitioner, and the general public. The theoretical section is presented in chapters 2 and 3, and the practice of the generation of '68 is discussed in the remaining chapters. In chapter 2, I trace the notion of popular theatre through some of its historical manifestations and its development under the influence of socioeconomic and cultural changes. In this general chapter, I focus mainly on those ideas about popular theatre in Europe and the United States before the sixties. In chapter 3, I discuss the sociohistorical scope of the 1968 unrest and its implications for the reoriented popular theatre movement that emerged from it. In the same context, I also explore some of the cultural concepts of political thinkers like Antonio Gramsci, Herbert Marcuse, Wilhelm Reich, V.I. Lenin, and Mao Tse-tung as they relate to the discussion on the political function of art that took place at the time. In the six subsequent chapters, I analyze the creative and political activities of representative radical theatre groups arranged by country.

It is not my intention to present a complete, panoramic picture of all the radical popular theatre companies that have been operating in Western Europe and the United States since 1968. Although, undoubtedly, many others have done valuable work that merits discussion, I have limited myself, for practical reasons, to the most resilient groups. Many radical troupes that were active in the early seventies have been defunct for several years now and left little or no documentation behind. The groups that I selected for discussion have been around for fifteen years or longer and, in most cases, have gone through interesting developments that I have been able to trace by way of personal interviews, script analyses, and direct observation of performances. I prefer to divide my discussion by country because all troupes in question respond to very specific sociopolitical circumstances and search for formal elements in the popular cultural patronage of the regions in which they work. Obviously, the artistic and sociological particularities of each group must be understood before any fruitful comparison can be attempted.

Chapter 4 deals with the important work of three American radical theatre companies that started their alternative activities already well before the protest movement peaked in Western Europe. The Bread and Puppet Theater, the San Francisco Mime Troupe, and el Teatro Campesino explored forms of cultural agitation that were very close to the type of radical theatre that emerged in Europe after 1968.

Chapter 5 deals with the regional radical popular theatre in France as it is exemplified by the Thionville-based Théâtre Populaire de Lorraine and lo Teatre de la Carriera from Arles in Occitania. In chapter 6, I focus on the situation in Great Britain, where radical popular theatre has been dominated by the activities of John McGrath and the 7:84 Theatre Company. In chapter 7, I discuss the radical popular theatre in West Germany, using the example of the prolific Grips Theater from West Berlin.

In chapter 8, I explore the work of the internationally renowned Italian playwright-actor Dario Fo, whose activities, both as creator and performer, serve as an indication of the radical popular theatre's artistic and political potential. Finally, in chapter 9, I discuss the activities of the radical popular theatre in Spain, which, for many years, was engaged in a life-and-death battle against a very real fascist dictator, while its colleagues north of the Pyrenees were trying to combat a much more elusive class enemy.

Obviously, socioeconomic, cultural, and political circumstances vary from one human community to another. So far, few attempts have been made to define the radical popular theatre as a genre because it speaks to the specific concerns of regional target audiences. With this study, I hope to reveal the radical popular theatre's strong uniformity despite the cultural differences that naturally exist between its representatives.

CHAPTER 2

POPULAR THEATRE IN HISTORICAL PERSPECTIVE

Popular theatre is not a concept that is self-evident. Although in the early beginnings of drama all theatre was popular, we now require the adjective *popular* to distinguish a theatre that caters to an audience of working-class people from one that caters to the bourgeoisie. Furthermore, the term *popular* is ambiguous in itself. To some people it means "intended for the general public"— i.e., for all classes in society. To others, it has a more radical, political significance and means "of and for those people who sell their labor"; to this latter group, then, the term "popular" is generic and denominates workers, peasants, students, petty bourgeois employees, office workers, and the like.[1]

In his *Sociology of Popular Drama,* J. R. Goodlad conceives of popular drama in purely numerical terms as that drama which attracts the largest possible audiences for the longest period of time; thus he also includes "popular" television drama in his considerations.[2] My own interests, however, lie with the type of popular theatre that tries to attract traditionally nontheatregoing audiences of laborers, peasants, and white-collar workers. Before attempting to formulate a more precise definition of the aesthetic forms, the sociological strategies, and the political objectives of this theatre, I want to look at some of the major historical developments of forms, styles, and methods of the popular theatre in general as it consciously presented itself as a cultural alternative to the dominant, bourgeois theatre.

The theatre has always been a social phenomenon par excellence; it is a dynamic, simultaneous exchange of communicative signs between performers on the stage and spectators in the auditorium. Theatre anthropologists have traced its origins back to the attempts of prehistoric tribes to sublimate their existential fears through symbolic representation in dance. Most of their investigations arrive at the Ur-form of theatre in the ritual of religious celebrations.[3] Similarly, the earliest forms of Greek theatre formed part of massive religious worship. The oldest documented sources of theatre describe the Dionysian festivals of ancient Greece as gigantic, popular celebrations that united hundreds of thousands of people from all walks of life. Medieval theatre also originated in the church, initially as simple dramatizations of Biblical passages rendered in dialogue. Even when medieval drama moved out of the formal confines of the church, it remained largely a community enterprise inspired by the specific religious occasions of the church calendar. In their massive, outdoor manifestations and drawing on entire town populations for active and passive participation, the morality, mystery, and cycle plays constituted a truly popular theatre that, at times, functioned as a vehicle for social protest. Many of the pseudoreligious plays were ploys to criticize church fathers and worldly rulers, and, as a result, drama for the people and by the people was pushed more and more into the margin of society.

Several theorists of the popular theatre point to the Renaissance adoption of Greek and Roman aesthetic criteria as the cause for drama's separation from the people.[4] Formally basing themselves on the classical comedies and tragedies, sixteenth- and seventeenth-century playwrights lost touch with the popular masses in order to create theatre that would be pleasing to a small, aristocratic elite that supported them financially. Small traveling troupes continued to play for the masses at county fairs and public celebrations. But if such popular theatre became too successful and potentially dangerous in political terms, the elite quickly bought it out. This strategy was particularly evident in the case of commedia dell'arte in Italy and France. This type of improvisational farce originated as a theatre form for and by the people, but was later absorbed by the aristocracy.[5]

The tendency of theatre (and art in general) to cater to the ruling class became even more evident when the bourgeoisie took over the social and political hegemony and capitalism made art into a commodity. The twentieth century, however, has known an increasing number of theatre people who cut themselves loose from the commercial bourgeois theatre circuit in order to reach out to the so-called culturally deprived classes. The activities of the popular theatre in our century range from romantic ideals about making the classics available to all to aggressive, militant street theatre that reveals the capitalist causes of the working man's misery.

Most historical accounts of the modern popular theatre go back to the late eighteenth century to find the earliest attempts at giving the exclusive, elitist theatrical arts back to the people.[6] Denis Diderot and Jean-Jacques Rousseau are often quoted for their conviction that the theatre has an eminently social, as well as an educational, function. In their vision, the ideal theatre performance is a large, popular celebration that unites the entire population of a community. Both Diderot and Rousseau enviously looked back to Greek Antiquity when thousands and thousands of spectators would congregate in the huge amphitheaters:

> Think of the power in that great assemblage, when you consider the influence of one man on another and the immediate transmission of emotion in such a crowd . . . how vastly different is our petty theatre, wherein we amuse our audience of a few hundred at fixed times, and at fixed hours! What if we were to assemble the whole nation on holidays.[7]

As Romain Rolland mentioned in his *Théâtre du peuple* ["The People's Theatre"], the ideas of Rousseau and Diderot had a decisive influence on leaders of the French Revolution like Boissy d'Anglas, who were among the first administrators to utilize the theatre as a medium for political consciousness-raising. They conceived of the theatre

> as one of the properest instruments for furthering the development of society and rendering men more virtuous and more enlightened. . . . [We should] make it a national enterprise . . . [thereby] opening up a path along which the human mind can pursue its way to even greater heights than heretofore . . . and offer the people an ever new source of instruction and pleasure, and form the national character. [pp. 78–79]

In this early modern concept of popular theatre, then, the inseparable combination of education and entertainment already revealed itself as an essential feature. In the nineteenth century, Jules Michelet, a French historian who sympathized with the plight of the proletariat and the ideals of 1789, never tired of opposing the dominant coalition of church, king, and bourgeoisie. According to Michelet, a people's theatre should give the proletariat and the peasantry,

> their own legends, and show them their own deeds. Nourish the people with the people . . . I mean a theatre universally of the people, echoing every thought of the people, and extending to every hamlet . . . a drama simple and vigorous played throughout the countryside, where the energy of talent, the creative power which lies in the heart, and the youthful imagination of an entirely new people shall do away with mere physical adjuncts, sumptuous stage-settings and costumes, without which the feeble dramatists of this outworn age cannot take a step. [pp. 85–86]

No doubt, Michelet was correct in this harsh evaluation of his contemporary bourgeois playwrights, but more importantly he stressed the need for an alternative, popular theatre to spread its activities to rural areas. Thus he provided a theoretical basis for the decentralization and regional implantation that characterize twentieth-century popular theatre.

Acknowledging Michelet as his main inspiration, Romain Rolland was one of

the first writers to dedicate an entire book to discuss popular theatre. In his
Théâtre du peuple, he formulates three essential requirements that all popular
theatre should fulfill. His first principle is that a people's theatre should be

> a pleasure, a sort of physical and moral rest to the working man weary from his
> day's work. It will be the task of the architects of the future People's Theatre to see
> that cheap seats are not instruments of inquisitional torture. It will be the task of
> the dramatists to see that their works produce joy, and not sadness and boredom.
> [p. 113]

However, Rolland emphasizes that this rule should not be interpreted to mean
that popular theatre must consist of tear-squeezing melodramas or facile drawing-room comedies that temporarily relieve the working man's economic and
political distress. Such drama would only numb the proletarian audience—it acts
as "a soporific, and contributes, like alcohol, to general inertia . . . the theatre
ought to be a source of energy: this is the second requisite" (p. 114). Rolland's
final requirement involves the educational function of the people's theatre: "It
should flood with light the terrible brain of man, which is filled with shadows
and monsters, and is exceedingly narrow and cramped . . . he must be taught,
then, to see things clearly as well as himself, and to judge" (pp. 115–16).
Romain Rolland's initiatives were admirable attempts to reach out to the working
class, but his concept of people's theatre was too idealistic and top-down, and the
plays he wrote himself, too grandiose to be practicable. His epic-size works
never appealed to the proletarian masses as he had hoped.[8]

Romain Rolland's activities to establish a workers' theatre by no means
constituted the sole effort in this direction at the beginning of the twentieth
century. In 1895, Maurice Pottecher had already produced his first popular play
with the Théâtre du Peuple in Bussang, in the extreme eastern part of France.
Using local amateur actors, he created grandly conceived, open-air dramas of a
religious and folkloristic nature.[9] Also Firmin Gemier made a substantial contribution to popular theatre with his Théâtre National Ambulant (1911). For
several years he travelled through France, producing plays in a circus tent in
front of rural audiences. At the same time, in Paris, several small popular
theatres with a socialist or communist orientation presented plays that were
specifically designed for the proletariat. Soon, similar theatres could be found in
most industrialized cities of Europe. Typically, these small, working-class
theatres would produce naturalistic or realistic plays—Ibsen, Zola, and Haupt-
mann were the favorites—or agitprop creations that praised human liberty,
exposed the exploitation of the workers by ruthless capitalists and called for a
unified class struggle. But the best-known examples of popular workers' theatre
could be found in Berlin at the beginning of this century.

The German popular theatre can be assumed to have started at the end of the
nineteenth century when Otto Brahm and associates founded the Freie Bühne in

Berlin (1889). Brahm intended to produce predominantly naturalistic plays for the working classes, but because its membership fees were too high his enterprise failed. As an alternative, Bruno Wille took the initiative to found the Freie Volksbühne, a truly proletarian theatre that wanted to be a "source of high artistic gratification . . . moral uplift . . . and a powerful stimulus to thinking about the great topics of the day."[10] Inspired by these early initiatives, *Volksbühnen* eventually spread all over Germany, performing until they were disbanded by the Nazis in 1933. They incorporated a wide range of artistic forms and also provided such later innovators of political theatre as Erwin Piscator and Bertolt Brecht with their first experience in professional theatre.

Erwin Piscator's activities in and around the Berliner Volksbühne were of great importance for the later development of popular theatre in Europe and the United States. In 1920, Piscator created his Proletarisches Theater which, like the other independent popular theatres of the time, was financed through the contributions of individual members. Piscator's theatre distinguished itself from the Freie Volksbühne insofar as it subordinated its art to progressive political purposes: its intentions were to produce plays that would "seize on contemporary events and act politically."[11]

Throughout the twenties, Piscator remained involved in various proletarian theatre ventures that were much more militantly antibourgeois than the Freie Volksbühne, which tried to maintain a neutral stance in the class conflict. Consequently, Piscator severed all ties with the Volksbühne in 1927 and from then on cooperated much more closely with the militant Jugend Volksbühne, whose members refused "to accept the bourgeois interpretation of the neutrality of art. As the theatre is an important instrument in the working class struggle for freedom, the stage must reflect the purpose and the life of the proletariat fighting for a new order in the world."[12] Until the repressive measures of the Nazis curtailed popular theatre activities in the mid-thirties, Piscator continued to produce revolutionary plays by means of highly sophisticated stage techniques.[13]

Great Britain also had its share of proletarian theatre in the period between 1928 and 1936. During that time, the Workers' Theatre Movement (WTM) served as an umbrella organization for numerous local branches of proletarian theatre that were closely connected to the Communist Party. As Raphael Samuel assesses it, this type of popular theatre was concerned much more with agitation than with entertainment, "and addressed itself to specific issues rather than the 'social question' generally. Theatrically, it turned increasingly from 'naturalistic' drama to agitprop, in the form of sketches, cabaret, and revue, and attempted to exchange indoor performances for a theatre of the street."[14]

WTM troupes were very issue-oriented and performed before and during strikes in order to collect money for strikers' relief funds. Although their work was very limited in artistic terms, their structural organization and their uncompromising, utilitarian concept of art approached the militant popular theatre in the period after 1968.

It is generally less well-known that the United States enjoyed an active proletarian theatre movement in the twenties and thirties. Although a native American theatre had existed since colonial times, it had been of a notoriously poor quality. It can well be argued that the first major emancipatory impulse of American drama came from left-wing playwrights in the second and third decade of this century. Eugene O'Neill, Elmer Rice, Clifford Odets, and John Dos Passos launched their careers as serious playwrights with politically inspired, often expressionistic plays that were produced by various workers' theatre collectives. One of the first and most active of these groups was the Workers' Laboratory Theatre, which followed the example of Russians and Germans in using laborers as actors.[15] Their goal was eventually to establish a network of small proletarian theatres throughout the United States. These could include traveling troupes as well: "Ready one day to go to strike meetings to cheer up the strikers, just as ready another day to accompany a demonstration to inspire the workers; [what these troupes present] must be a theatre where the worker may be inspired to fight for his liberation; a theatre of class struggle—a theatre of the workers, by the workers, for the workers."[16]

Anticipating a typical attitude of the post-1968 popular theatre, the Workers' Laboratory Theatre downplayed the importance of the playwright and stressed the value of collective creations and theatrical activities outside the walls of the theatre building. Most often, it performed its impromptu sketches and revues at political rallies, at union gatherings, and in factory halls. The Theatre Union was another influential proletarian drama group in the twenties. Setting itself a clear pedagogical task, it aimed "to produce plays that all honest militant workers and middle class sympathizers can support; plays that, without compromise on questions of principle, will appeal particularly to unorganized workers who are not yet class conscious."[17] In order to create this appeal, the Theatre Union intended to produce plays, "that deal boldly with the deep-going social conflicts, the economic, emotional and cultural problems that confront the majority of the people."[18] The Theatre Union also established a policy of low ticket prices in order to attract as large a working-class audience as possible.

As Sam Smiley points out in his *Drama of Attack,* the emergence of the American radical theatre movement was clearly related to the economic crisis of the thirties:

> In April of 1931 a call went out from prominent socially concerned theatre people for plays to dramatize the social issues and for a theatre to play to the vast "oppressed" masses. Subsequently, leftist theatre developed. Small troupes who performed agitprop plays to "awaken the workers" began appearing at labor meetings, rallies, and strike demonstrations. On June 13, 1931, representatives from no less than 244 workers' cultural groups in New York City and vicinity attended a conference to form a federation of workers' theatres.[19]

Ultimately, the radical theatre in the United States organized itself in several professional and amateur organizations that coordinated activities throughout the country. The New Theatre League, for example, "held conferences, sponsored publications, and operated a script bureau. Its membership included not only such New York organizations as Theatre Collective, Negro People's Theatre, Theatre Advance, Labor Stage, Forum Theatre, and Negro Theatre Guild, but also many groups from other cities, such as the Rebel Players of Los Angeles, the Blue Blouses of Chicago, and the Solidarity Players of Boston."[20] Even Broadway started producing a great number of political plays.

The radical theatre in the United States culminated with the unique activities of the Federal Theatre Project, which, during its four-year existence employed over 10,000 performers, set-designers, stagehands and other theatrical technicians who, due to the Depression, were out of work. Under the executive directorship of Hallie Flanagan, in the mid-thirties the project came closer than any other theatrical enterprise in American history to establishing a national popular theatre. It included an unprecedented effort to decentralize the Broadway-dominated theatre industry, encouraging a great range of regional dramatic activities. Under its sponsorship, important topical plays were produced in New Orleans, Miami, Atlanta, Chicago, and San Francisco.[21] The Federal Theatre Project was also responsible for the development of an exciting new form of political theatre: the Living Newspaper, which presented the latest socioeconomic facts and their effect on the personal lives of the workers in a radically new form of documentary drama.[22]

In the first three decades of this century, then, the native American theatre was dominated by an ideal of popular theatre that bore strong European characteristics. American playwrights were particularly influenced by Expressionism and Realism, and the various types of workers' theatre were organized on the same principles as the European ones: membership fees, low general admission prices to attract a working-class audience, and a repertoire consisting of accessible plays with themes involving the social and political problems of the average working man.[23] However, most of the original plays created by the various popular theatres in Europe and the United States were, generally speaking, of a relatively poor quality. It was not until the sixties that a more recognizable and respected form of popular theatre began to emerge.

The anticommunist witch hunt of the McCarthy period effectively prevented any continuation of radical popular theatre in the United States. Many theatre people, including Hallie Flanagan, were accused of having been involved in "unamerican activities," and subsidies for the Federal Theatre Project were permanently cut. Also, many of the best actors and authors of the radical theatre movement were drawn to Broadway and Hollywood with promises of fame and fortune. Meanwhile, the European theatres were only very slowly recovering from the tremendous shock suffered in World War II.

In the late forties and early fifties, several measures by the French and British governments proved very important for the development of decentralized popular theatre in these countries. The newly founded British Arts Council encouraged initiatives to create drama outside the commercial West End theatre district. Joan Littlewood's Theatre Workshop was the most outstanding popular troupe to emerge in this period. Founded in 1945, the Theatre Workshop still forms a guiding example for many popular theatre groups in the eighties. As Kenneth Tynan recalls, the troupe was

> run on a completely egalitarian basis: actors, director, designers and stage staff all got an equal share of the takings. . . . [The company] spent eight penniless years on the road, touring Germany, Norway, Sweden and Czechoslovakia as well as England before coming to rest in 1953 at the Theatre Royal, Stratford-atte-Bowe, a shapely Victorian playhouse deep in East London. Here Joan's actors toiled and fasted, many of them so poor that they slept in hammocks slung across the boxes and dressing rooms.[24]

For over a decade, the Theatre Workshop delighted working-class audiences with entertaining but pertinent plays told and sung in the working man's dialect. Their productions drew on music-hall elements and other forms of popular entertainment. Their most famous creation was *Oh What a Lovely War,* which became such a commercial success in the mid-sixties that it ultimately corrupted and destroyed the troupe. However, the Theatre Workshop had a lasting impact on the young actors and playwrights who started making political theatre in the late sixties.

In France, governmental measures—particularly the creation of a ministry of culture—had a much broader effect than in Great Britain. They amounted to the most sustained initiative by any country in Europe to establish a well-organized, state-supported, decentralized theatre. Although in the late sixties many radical actors and playwrights came to realize that a popular theatre subsidized and therefore controlled by a bourgeois regime may be a contradiction in terms, it cannot be denied that Jeanne Laurent, André Malraux, and their many coworkers installed a valuable cultural infrastructure. Their ideas and efforts paved the way for more radical developments in the popular theatre. The diffusion of bourgeois culture with a progressive coating by the decentralized *Centres Dramatiques* formed a necessary prelude to the shaping of more militant, antibourgeois ideas about regionalist culture in the post-1968 era.

The period between World War II and 1968 in France was characterized by a grand effort to perform old classics and new plays for audiences that had never been to the theatre before. This "nonpublic" or nontheatre audience could be attracted to newly built, nonintimidating playhouses by means of low ticket prices, convenient curtain times, abolished dress codes, and appealing performances of the great examples of world drama.[25] Furthermore, the pedagogical element was not forgotten: strongly influenced by Bertolt Brecht's ideas on political theatre, many of the classics—and Brecht's own plays—were presented not for their timeless values but for their connection to an identifiable historical period. Bernard Dort, one of the principal French Brecht critics, argued that the great plays should be produced in such a way that they would show the social conditions in which they were set as belonging to the past. Such a presentation, in turn, would lead today's spectators to interrogate their own society and would make them understand that their society is also changeable and that they possess the power to transform it.[26] Such optimistic notions of the theatre's political effectiveness were, however, quite simply invalidated by the cold fact that the working class continued to refuse to frequent the beautiful new cultural centers that had been conceived primarily for their benefit. Even the most positive statistical analyses of theatre attendance in the post-World-War-II period never estimated the proletarian portion of the audiences to exceed 5 percent.[27]

Jean Vilar, the father of the Avignon Theatre Festival and longtime director of the Théâtre National Populaire in Paris, never equated popular theatre with proletarian theatre.[28] His ideas were much closer to André Malraux's insofar as he wanted to make the greatest dramatic works available to the largest number of people. In his opinion, theatre should receive state subsidy as a public service like water, gas, and electricity.[29]

Already well before 1968, the populist main stream of France's popular theatre encountered heavy criticism from such radical thinkers as Jean-Paul Sartre and Emile Copfermann. Sartre's main objection to Vilar's type of popular theatre was that the latter refused to take an outspoken political stance and catered to the petty bourgeoisie and the upper middle classes as well as to the proletariat. For Vilar, a popular audience consisted of all Frenchmen without distinction of class; for Sartre it consisted of the workers only. Sartre criticized Vilar, then, for failing to create a genuine popular theatre in the political sense and for accepting state subsidy, which, in turn, forced him to play a bourgeois repertoire.[30]

Dedicating an entire book to a critique of French popular theatre, Emile Copfermann basically made the same point as Sartre: because popular theatres are supported by the state, they necessarily spread the state's ideology. Thus, several years before the outbreak of the student riots, Copfermann already pointed to the cultural and political conformism of the popular theatre as it existed in the early sixties. Rather than producing a critical, political consciousness, popular theatre had become "an element of social adaptation, of acquiescence to the values of a repressive society."[31]

Two main types of popular theatre emerged, then, in the twentieth century. The first conceives of the theatre as a place of communion where all social groups meet to receive their regular dose of the national cultural heritage through the designated classics. As such, it is a theatre of integration and unification. The second type of popular theatre is more Marxist in orientation; it sees the theatre as a place where the oppressed classes in society are made conscious of the injustice of their predicament. As such, it could be seen as a theatre of class struggle that uses cultural means to prepare the upset of the bourgeois hegemony. In the two decades following the Second World War, popular theatre was predominantly of the first, conformist kind. Only a few incidental attempts were made to create a more radical popular theatre of the kind that had prevailed in New York and Berlin earlier in the century. The widespread revolts of 1967 and 1968 gave the essential impulse to a radical reorientation of the popular theatre in Western Europe and the United States.

CHAPTER 3

THE EVENTS OF 1968 AND THEIR RADICAL CULTURAL CONCEPTS

The radical movement of the sixties constitutes one of the most interesting social phenomena of this century. Many accounts of it have been written during and after the events, by insiders and outsiders, and what emerges is a confused picture in which elements of pacifism, civil rights agitation, anti-Vietnam sentiments, sexual liberation, feminism, and other forms of antiauthoritarianism are chaotically thrown together.

The protest movement was inspired, fanned, and led by students, from the early beginnings in the southern United States to the fierce battles in the barricaded streets of the Quartier Latin in Paris. Protests evolved from peaceful, civil disobedience to violent opposition to the often brutal police actions. The protests had been initiated in the period between 1960 and 1962 when, following Martin Luther King's lead, thousands of students demonstrated for civil rights and racial equality. These demonstrations were followed by the unrest at Berkeley in the fall of 1964, when students, who had demanded elaborate university reforms, were clobbered by riot police. From that point on, the war in Vietnam became more and more the essential issue, although it continued to share center stage with protests against racial discrimination and calls for reforms in higher education. For example, the 1967 riots at Columbia University had to do with the institution's segregation from nearby Harlem as well as its intellectual contributions to the Vietnam war through its Research Program for Defense Analysis.

In Europe, the protests had started in the mid-sixties with huge demonstrations against the war in Vietnam. Berlin's Freie Universität formed a conspicuous center of radical activities. As Stephen Spender mentioned, this university had been conceived in 1948 as a model for progressive education and as a showcase of the West's liberty as opposed to the Eastern bloc's repression, but severe overcrowding soon forced a reinstallation of conservative bureaucracy.[1] Protests followed, which were countered by the authorities with a ban on demonstrations, an act of repression that was bloodily underlined by the police's shooting of a student during a demonstration against the visit of the shah of Iran to Berlin. In most other European cities, student protests were also originally provoked by the Vietnam War and the outdated structures of higher education, and violence escalated through unnecessarily brutal police actions.

This is not the place to accuse or to judge the authorities or the protesters. But the question as to what actions and issues eventually had an effect on the evolution of the popular theatre is of obvious interest in the context of this study. Whatever the confusing facts, the events of 1967 and 1968 politicized many previously apathetic people, including artists, who started questioning the uncontested structures of society. Also, cultural institutions were carefully scrutinized; art was brought down from its ivory tower and its media were used to express the young people's discontent. University walls were painted with eye-catching slogans and colorful revolutionary signs. Protest singers sang "What are we fighting for?" and theatre groups took spontaneously to the streets to shock passersby out of their complacency with improvised, highly topical sketches. Apart from the often spectacular and bloody clashes with the "keepers of the peace," the cultural reawakening formed the most visible and enduring aspect of the protest movement.

The cultural protests were mainly directed against the repressive nature of late capitalist, technocratic society. This repression could take the form of international imperialism (American-dominated multinationals securing new markets and natural resources in South America, Vietnam), or ideological manipulation (through educational institutions and the mass media). As Alain Touraine correctly remarks,

> corporate capitalism masks the ideology of its technocratic control behind a mask of objective neutrality . . . [likewise] it masks the violence of its repressive domination behind a mask of liberal goodwill towards all . . . it has been very difficult to understand the anti-liberal aspects of the student-movement. This is because "liberal" has been so intricately associated with the advertised image of corporate capitalism. We have a liberal democracy, although Vietnam, racism, abject poverty and technocratic centralization are bipartisan policy, and thus not open to political challenge.[2]

The young countered the system's demands for adaptation and integration with exuberant forms of self-expression and demands for sexual liberation. Spontaneity in cultural expression and in personal relationships were typical of the young people's attempts to counteract the pervasive organization of advanced industrial society. They also voiced their strong feelings of solidarity with the struggle of the people in underdeveloped and colonialized regions of the world who are oppressed and exploited to provide the Western centers of industrialization with cheap raw materials, labor, and lucrative consumer markets. Thus, the events of 1967 and 1968 had a strong impact on the fights for regional emancipation in Western nations, for which a revitalized, militant regional theatre provided the cultural framework.

Despite the claim of some sociologists and historians that the events of the mid-sixties had, at best, only a short-lived effect, they did influence people's mentality in the ensuing years. It is true that the wage increases obtained by the French workers in May 1968 were annulled by the higher tax rates announced in October, but particularly in West Germany and the Netherlands universities underwent important structural reorganization. Socially the events initiated a vigorous feminist movement and a revival of militant regionalism. Culturally they triggered developments toward a new type of popular theatre.

During the "hot" spring of 1968, heated discussions took place in theatre circles about the political function of art in general and of drama in particular. The repertoire and the authoritarian structure of many European theatre companies were questioned—which resulted, in some cases, in gradual democratization. Several dictatorial theatre directors were ousted, and henceforth artistic decisions were made more collectively.[3] Outside the established theatres, and particularly among students and recent graduates of the performing arts academies, strong sentiments against the commercialized bourgeois theatre existed, and, influenced by the cultural concepts of Mao Tse-tung, Antonio Gramsci, and Herbert Marcuse, many of them resolved to dedicate their creative talents to the liberation of the working class.

Although it is now impossible to document exactly when and where theatrical artists read and talked about the revolutionary potential of drama, playwrights like John McGrath, Dario Fo, and Claude Alranq readily admit the importance of Gramsci, Mao, and Marcuse to their work. During the occupation of the Odéon theatre in Paris, these names were often mentioned. From 15 May 1968 on, striking actors and students debated there about the possibilities of revolutionary theatre. Young actors came to realize that they too were underpaid workers with very little creative input in their roles. In the wake of this newly gained consciousness, striking actors went to perform plays in occupied factories, and, as Emile Copfermann wrote, through the comical sketches and the political montages they performed, they developed "a new position with regard to the theater, its capacity to intervene in the class struggle, its agitprop side."[4]

Jean-Jacques Lebel, one of the most vocal participants in the Odéon discussions, later that summer continued his crusade against bourgeois culture during the renowned Avignon Theatre Festival. This most prestigeous of all

French performing arts festivals was taken to represent a global system of social repression: " . . . with minor variations, the universities of Rome, Paris, Madrid, New York, London and Tokyo all function according to the same principle. There, where the academic industry manufactures the future specialists of capitalism, cultural industry manufactures a false collective consciousness and conditions public opinion."[5]

Thus, in 1968, radical theatre artists in France, England, Italy, West Germany, and elsewhere in Europe and the United States came to see their fundamental task as opposing an alternative culture to the dominant one, which, in their eyes, was nothing but a framework for bourgeois ideological manipulation. For these militant actors, directors, and theatre technicians, to stay within the existing subsidized or commercial theatre structures would be "selling out" to the authorities; therefore, they stepped out and created a new, marginal theatre circuit. Many of them implanted themselves as theatre collectives and communes in working-class neighborhoods or went back to their native regions in order to create an uncompromising theatre of protest and consciousness-raising for the working class at large.

The ideas that inspired the actions of radical young theatre artists all over Western Europe and the United States by no means originated in the mid-sixties but had been around in some form or other since the beginning of the century. Shortly after the October Revolution in Russia, Lenin started making public speeches about the importance of culture and education for the successful continuation of the revolution. Lenin clearly recognized the power of the bourgeois ideological apparatus and the necessity to instill a revolutionary class consciousness into the peasantry and the proletariat if the insurgence was ever to be effective and enduring: "We must overcome resistance from the capitalists in all its forms, not only military and the political spheres but also ideological resistance which is the most deep-seated and the strongest. It is the duty of our educational workers to accomplish the re-education of the masses."[6] In Lenin's view, literature had a very important task in the education of the masses. To him, culture was much more than a luxury product of a successful economy; it was "a necessary prerequisite for the attainment of a consummate socialist culture, for the stabilisation of political gains and the successful building up of a socialist economy in our country."[7]

Even more than Lenin, Antonio Gramsci is often mentioned as one of the chief inspirators of the popular theatre that emerged after 1968. In one of his early articles, "Socialism and Culture," he emphasized the indispensability of a cultural revolution before a successful political revolution could take place. In this respect, Gramsci mentions the example of the French Revolution, which, in his opinion, could not have occurred without the preceding cultural revolution of the Enlightenment that gave all European bourgeois a unified class consciousness. Gramsci thought that a similar process of consciousness-raising should be implemented in the proletariat and that art could fulfill a seminal task in the building of a unified consciousness of the workers and their allies.

Throughout his career, Gramsci remained interested in developing what he called a counterhegemonistic thrust that should be opposed to the bourgeois hegemony. Only through a process of education and cultivation that avoids the traditional bourgeois machinery could an alternative, proletarian culture be created. Thus Gramsci expressed the need for "prefigurative institutions," preliminary nuclei of the future socialist society, which, in the form of workers' councils and cultural associations, could build an alternative to the hegemonic culture. For Gramsci, culture forms the cement that fuses the individual, idiosyncratic sensibilities of the workers into one unified class consciousness; it also links the proletariat with its allies, the peasantry and the petite bourgeoisie.

Being a linguist, Gramsci was thoroughly aware of the importance of language and literature in the creation of a counterhegemonistic culture. Gramsci realized that, in the hands of the ruling class, language and literature reinforce social and moral codes of the dominant culture. But in the hands of the ascending class, they can be powerful instruments for the diffusion of new values. Knowing this, throughout history the ruling classes have suppressed popular forms of cultural expression or reappropriated them for their own purposes.[8]

In his "Critique of Italian Literature," Gramsci criticized Italian literary artists and critics for being too far removed from the people and, therefore, indirectly protecting the interests of the bourgeoisie through their elitist literary activities. In order for literature to become the basis for a new culture, it should first become popular. In this context, Gramsci emphasized the significance of folklore which contains

> a conception of the world and of life—for the most part implicit—of temporally and spatially determined social groups that are in opposition (also most often implicitly, mechanically and objectively) to the "official" conceptions of the world (or, in a larger sense, to the historically determined cultivated social groups) that succeed each other in the historical development.[9]

Like Gramsci, Wilhelm Reich held that the development of a political consciousness of the working class was essential to an effective class struggle. Before the fight for social and political hegemony can take place, the oppressed groups must become aware of their potential as a collective force. Reich occupied himself mainly with the psychological aspects of political consciousness. He came to recognize the family as the central social institution through which the bourgeois value system was perpetuated.[10] Furthermore, Reich identified sexual repression, often dictated by some religiously inspired moral code, as the chief cause for submission to an authoritarian social order. Thus, Reich's importance to the protest movement of the sixties is closely related to his analyses of the authoritarian personality. His notion that social and sexual liberation must go hand in hand was extremely popular among European students.[11]

Reich is often discussed in conjunction with Herbert Marcuse, who, more than any other intellectual, inspired the youth movement of the sixties with a thorough analysis of authoritarian repression in the contemporary Western society. His *One-dimensional Man* was widely read as the single most authoritative book on the subject. In it, he convincingly reveals the profound contradictions of our presumably free Western world:

> Its productivity is destructive of the free development of human needs and faculties, its peace is maintained by the constant threat of war, its growth dependent on the repression of the real possibilities for pacifying the struggle for existence—individual, national, and international . . . the union of growing productivity and growing destruction; the brinkmanship of annihilation; the surrender of thought, hope, and fear to the decisions of the powers that be; the preservation of misery in the face of unprecedented wealth constitute the most impartial indictment—even if they are not the *raison d'être* of this society but only its by-product: its sweeping rationality, which propels efficiency and growth, is itself irrational.[12]

Marcuse's was one of the most uncompromising expositions of the subtle totalitarianism in Western society dominated by corporate capitalism. He pointed out the dangers of mass communication that manipulates the working classes into thinking that they have the same access to material happiness as their bosses. According to Marcuse, the proletariat does not realize that its "private space has been invaded and whittled down by technological reality, mass production and mass distribution that claim the entire individual."[13]

The general availability of luxury goods in advanced capitalist societies imposed a general feeling of contentment, a pattern of "one-dimensional thought and behavior," against which a "counter culture" cannot be easily established.[14] This may be the reason why the issues of the protest movement of the sixties were so vague and multifaceted: the technocratic enemy was omnipresent but nowhere identifiable. Only in some blatant, isolated cases like the Vietnam War did he show his real face. In all other instances, the protesters turned against faceless institutions of technocratic manipulation like the university systems or the mass media.[15]

In the mid-sixties, the Communist societies of Eastern Europe were hardly the ideal example for the protesting European and American youths. Che Guevara and, more particularly, Mao Tse-tung were regarded as the heroes. The Cultural Revolution in China served as a ready example for the countercultural activities of the newly committed young theatre artists. In the case of Ernesto "Che" Guevara, it was the romantic appeal of a frail young man dedicating his life to the liberation of the oppressed people on this earth that attracted the Western protesters. His ideas on guerrilla warfare also had some effect on the attitudes and techniques of street theatre in general and radical regional theatre in particular: guerrilla warfare and "guerrilla" cultural agitation are both intent on the eventual overthrow of the ruling class, and both start from the premise that a successful guerrilla operation cannot be executed without the friendship and the conscious political commitment of the local population.[16]

Although the Great Proletarian Cultural Revolution in China from 1966 through 1969 was very chaotic and bloody in itself, it had a strong impact on the young Western demonstrators and, specifically, on several militant popular theatre groups. This was the time when Mao's thoughts, collected and distributed in little plastic-coated red books, gained enormous popularity among European and American radicals. They particularly admired China's capacity for self-analysis and self-criticism, as well as its attempts to install a new educational system designed to eliminate the differences between urban and rural societies. The Chinese Cultural Revolution had the objective to purge from the Communist society all remnants of bourgeois mentality and bureaucracy in one massive action.

During the period of the Cultural Revolution, Mao's thoughts on literature and art were frequently reprinted in official Chinese publications. Originally formulated at the 1942 Yan'an Conference on Literature and Art, these ideas had been virtually ignored for over twenty years until they were suddenly recycled and revalidated in the mid-sixties. In his speeches at the Yan'an conference, Mao had stressed the relationship between authors and audience and the importance of popular forms of literature. Both points were of extreme interest to Western popular theatre artists, for Mao denied the general assumption that popular forms of art are technically and stylistically inferior to the "sophisticated" forms of art: "Rich deposits of literature and art actually exist in popular life itself: they are things in their natural forms, crude but also extremely lively, rich and fundamental; they make all processed forms of literature pale in comparison, they are the sole and exhaustible source of processed forms of literature and art."[17]

Mao was pragmatic enough to realize that wars are won not with words, but with fists and guns. Nevertheless, he also knew that physical action alone could not effect and sustain a revolution: "We still need a cultural army, since this kind of army is indispensable in achieving unity among ourselves and winning victory over the enemy."[18] Literature and art to him formed integral parts of the overall revolutionary machine and served primarily to raise the political consciousness of workers and peasants and to provoke them to rebellion against the class enemy.

Mao also recommended a new attitude for literary artists. He suggested that they go live among peasants and workers in order to comprehend their sensibilities and problems better and to learn about the richness of their language and their folklore:

> We encourage revolutionary writers and artists to develop positive contacts with workers, peasants and soldiers, we give them complete freedom to create genuinely revolutionary literature and art, we give them complete freedom to go among the masses. . . . We must use what belongs to workers, peasants and soldiers themselves, and, therefore, the task of learning from workers, peasants and soldiers comes before the task of educating them.[19]

In response to this Maoist advice, many popular theatre workers in Western Europe and the United States resolved to incorporate an extensive period of direct contact with their target audience in their creative process and to thoroughly research specific social problems in the preparation of plays on pertinent topics.[20] Therefore, many of them decided to move to working-class neighborhoods and rural areas in order to live with the people, win their trust, and learn about their culture.

In their dealings with politically naive popular audiences, most of the post-1968 popular theatre groups were involved in what Paolo Freire termed "Cultural Action." Freire, a Brazilian educator of Marxist leaning, has been very influential among radical artists since the late sixties. Predominantly concerned with the education of the illiterate masses in the Third World, Freire's ideas also apply to the non-class-conscious proletariat in the West, who, even when able to read and write, have never learned to demystify the power structure of the society that they have been taught to accept as the only one possible. Like the illiterates, workers and peasants are representatives "of the dominated strata of society, in conscious or unconscious opposition to those who, in the same structure, treat them as a thing."[21]

Cultural Action helps the oppressed to expel the myths—including the one that makes them believe in their own natural inferiority—that have infiltrated even into their deepest inner beings. Echoing Gramsci, Freire argues that this interiorization of the dominator's cultural models can only be countered by the creation of a new culture. Freire distinguishes between two types of cultural action: "Cultural action for freedom is characterized by dialogue, and its preeminent purpose is to conscientize the people. . . . [It is opposed by] cultural action for domination [which] . . . serves to domesticate the people."[22]

In line with Freire, militant popular theaters assist in what the Brazilian called the "conscientization" of the oppressed—i.e., "the process in which men, not as recipients, but as knowing subjects, achieve a deepening awareness both of the socio-cultural reality which shapes their lives and of their capacity to transform that reality."[23]

The radical popular theatre that developed after the social upheaval of the mid and late sixties associated itself very clearly with the contemporary radical intellectual climate. Explicitly advocating social change and declaring solidarity with the oppressed people in society, the post-1968 popular theater originally committed itself to a type of cultural agitation that had a solid foundation in socialist ideology. Through most of the seventies, radical popular theatre groups opted to stay out of the commercial venues in order to attract ever larger numbers of traditional nontheatergoers. At the same time, it should be noted that communion-type popular theatre did not abandon its activities. In France, for example, Jean Vilar and his successors continued the Festival d'Avignon, and the new *Centres Dramatiques* did not fundamentally change their outlook despite what looked like a militant manifesto published in Villeurbane in 1968.[24]

The radical popular theatre that forms the focus of this study distinguishes itself sharply from the less controversial activities of the communal popular theatre. Perhaps its main distinctive feature is that the artists involved see themselves as creators of *Kampfkultur,* culture that is useful for the class struggle. Most of the groups involved, be they in central California or southern France, want to help develop the political consciousness of the working class. Considering itself an integral part of the counterculture, the radical popular theatre recognizes the existence of class differences in society and the oppression of those who sell their labor by those who control the capital. The radical popular theatre sees itself in opposition to the dominant, bourgeois culture, which it regards as mystifying and perpetuating the exploitation of the workers. As a countermeasure, the contemporary radical popular theatre creates drama that does not distract or beautify, but which demystifies, politicizes, and struggles in solidarity with the oppressed for a more just social structure. According to radical British playwright John McGrath, the militant popular theatre is primarily concerned with "the social, political and cultural development of the working class towards maturity and hegemony."[25] He therefore defines the radical popular theatre as "a form of theatre which is searching, through the experience and forms of the working class, for those elements which point forward in the direction of a future rational, non-exploitative, classless society, in which all struggle together to resolve humanity's conflict with nature, and to allow all to grow to the fullest possible experience of life on earth."[26]

The radical popular theatre groups discussed in the following chapters all more or less share (or used to share) the same objective.

CHAPTER 4

REVOLUTIONARY VOICES IN THE AMERICAN POLITICAL THEATRE

As I indicated in chapter 2, the first wave of radical popular theatre in the United States was a rather short-lived enterprise that quietly expired with the termination of the Federal Theatre Project. The twentieth-century European drama had a much longer and more continuously productive tradition of alternative, political theatre. It must therefore be considered surprising that a major impulse for the new wave of radical popular theatre in Western Europe after 1968 came from several American troupes. Most of these radical theatre companies had started their activities well before the period of intensive contestation that had characterized the late sixties. The most conspicuous and spectacular push came, undoubtedly, from Judith Malina and Julian Beck's exiled Living Theatre. Forced to leave the United States because of insurmountable tax problems, they exported their anarchistic theatrical call for revolution to Europe's streets and stages, creating controversies and riots wherever they went. Among other things, they were instrumental in occupying the respectable Odéon theatre in Paris in May 1968, and they stimulated animated discussions there. Later that summer, *Le Living,* as the Living Theatre was fondly called by its supporters, caused a major riot at Avignon's Theatre Festival when their license to perform in the streets was revoked by the municipal authorities because of alleged public obscenity and disturbance of the peace.[1]

However, the Living Theatre's radical, anarchistic *attitude* formed a greater inspiration for the ensuing attempts at radical popular theatre than did their rather esoteric, mystical theatrical creations.[2] The Bread and Puppet Theater and el

24

Teatro Campesino also made their first European tours in the spring of 1968 and were directly involved in some of the large student protests. Their organization, creation, and acting proved much closer to the style of the European radical popular theatre groups that developed in the wake of the events of 1968.

In the seminal year of 1968, Ron Davis, artistic director of the San Francisco Mime Troupe and uncrowned leader of what he considered to be a grass-roots American radical theatre movement, organized a Radical Theatre Festival at San Francisco State College. This event, which took place from 25 through 29 September, included workshops, films, and performances by radical troupes that Davis regarded as the avant-garde of the American radical popular theatre. One of the most significant activities of the festival was a panel discussion between Ron Davis, Luís Valdez of el Teatro Campesino, and Peter Schumann of the Bread and Pupper Theater.[3] In this forum, Davis, Valdez, and Schumann drew the balance of their many similarities and their political and aesthetic differences.

What emerged most strongly from the Radical Theatre Festival was the tremendous respect that Davis, Valdez, and Schumann had for each other's work. Their sense of cooperation was extraordinary; often, actors who found themselves burnt out in one troupe were warmly welcomed in another. The three troupes also borrowed theatrical techniques from each other. Both the San Francisco Mime Troupe and el Teatro Campesino created puppet plays that were clearly inspired by the work of the Bread and Puppet Theater. Likewise, Luís Valdez, who worked with the Mime Troupe in the summer of 1965, admits to the strong influence of this troupe's style of commedia dell'arte in his *actos* and subsequent creations. All three American radical troupes are militantly opposed to the cutthroat capitalist consumer society, its imperialist excesses, and the commercialized bourgeois culture that upholds it. All three troupes, at one point or other, were deeply involved in anti-Vietnam demonstrations and created plays that advocated American withdrawal from imperialist fronts. All three troupes are collectively organized (although they all have outspoken, identifiable leaders), avoid stardom and commercialization, take their plays to people who do not habitually attend the theatre, perform in streets as well as indoors, are committed to changes of social structures and mentality, and employ traditional and contemporary elements of popular culture. Brechtian techniques, comedy, and satire constitute their main aesthetic elements. All these factors place the San Francisco Mime Troupe, el Teatro Campesino, and the Bread and Puppet Theater in a direct, continuous line with the Western European alternative theatre. Yet, each troupe emphatically maintains its distinct artistic style and political motivation.

THE SAN FRANCISCO MIME TROUPE

The San Francisco Mime Troupe—founded in 1959 as the R.G. Davis Mime Studio and Troupe, a subsidiary of the San Francisco Actors Workshop—is the oldest of the active radical theatre companies in the United States. It is also the most consistent troupe in its political aims. Related to the leftist factions of the civil rights movement that developed in the pseudorevolutionary events of the mid and late sixties, the Mime Troupe evolved from a purely aesthetically oriented movement theatre performing for an elitist audience to a full-fledged theatre company that employs its special blend of commedia dell'arte and political satire to expose the negative aspects of modern American corporate capitalism.

Ron Davis, originally a professional dancer who studied mime with Paul Curtis and Etienne Decroux, started doing avant-garde mime improvizations while an assistant director at San Francisco's main professional theatre company, the Actors Workshop. Growing politically more conscious and increasingly disgusted with the bourgeois theatre, Davis and his mimes broke with the workshop and "drifted toward an alternative culture or a cultural parallel to the powerful middle class."[4] The first major production of the newly formed San Francisco Mime troupe was a Brechtian version of Alfred Jarry's presurrealist classic *Ubu Roi*.[5] But the Mime Troupe did not start reaching out to an alternative audience until it adopted the style of the sixteenth-century Italian commedia dell'arte.

The Mime Troupe defended its adoption of the commedia form with the argument that "the intrinsic nature of commedia dell'arte is its working-class viewpoint."[6] It was originally a form of improvizational street theatre performed in market places and on street corners for the masses of the lower social strata. With songs, mime, satire, and stereotyping it poked fun at the dominant upper class. As happens so often with political or cultural expressions of subversion, commedia satire was brought into the cultural mainstream and henceforth became entertainment for the aristocracy and, thus, politically impotent. The commedia form itself, however, did develop further with the contributions of such literary geniuses as Molière and Goldoni.

It was one of the Mime Troupe's primary intentions to reinstate the commedia's working-class essence.[7] Furthermore, commedia dell'arte, with its broad gestures, easily recognizable stock characters, music, loud voices, farcical situations, and comic suspense produces highly effective theatre that is perfectly suited for performance in the open air. Also, the flexibility of the plot and the space for improvization left sufficient room for continuous updates and adaptation to everchanging political circumstances.

The clear character structures and relationships made the commedia easily accessible to popular audiences unfamiliar with the theatre. Although the presence of stereotypes usually makes sophisticated critics uneasy, it should not be forgotten that stock characters form part and parcel of popular culture. Also, they were perfectly acceptable in medieval drama, and even today they are inherent in such elevated cultural forms as opera and ballet. Stereotypes are indispensible for clarifying social and economic human relations.

Good humor and conviviality are two essential aspects of the Mime Troupe's performance style. Apart from being overtly political, their productions always provide good old-fashioned fun. On more than one occasion they challenged the municipal authorities with their unauthorized outdoor performances in San Francisco's parks. Time and again the troupe won official court rulings for permission to play in the open air, mainly because they had so much popular support. Although the professional standards of the Mime Troupe are high, the performers do what they can to break down any social or psychological barriers between themselves and their audience. The shows are always preceded by clownery and singing while the makeshift stage is constructed. Actors do physical warmup exercises, and musicians play rhythmic music, inviting the audience to clap or sing along. Often, after exiting, actors emerge from backstage to watch the performance with the public until they have to "go on" again. The Mime Troupe's enthusiasm carries over into postperformance discussions that are indispensable for solidifying the relations with its audience and for improvement of the troupe's future work.

Most radical popular theatre companies have a comic temperament, and the San Francisco Mime troupe is no exception. For them, comedy and satire are conscious choices. Everybody loves to laugh, and, if the laughter of the popular classes is louder than that of the sophisticated bourgeoisie, that does not necessarily mean that popular humor is of a lower intellectual quality. It is often based on colorful language, puns, and grotesque situations. Humor is further necessary to attract the working classes to the theatre and to keep them there. Humor is also ultimately optimistic; it presents a potentially tragic situation in a somewhat distorted manner and makes fun of it. Humor in political drama is never gratuitous, though, and therefore often assumes the form of satire. Ron Davis explains, "Our comedies were bound by real politics, thus satire was our forte, not slapstick. We always related our jokes to something tangible, rather than developing comedy from fantasy."[8]

Although satire and comedy may coexist in the same play, they are essentially different in nature.[9] Satire causes rage and provokes pensive laughter, as opposed to the pleasing, uncommitted merriment produced by comedy. Both satire and comedy rely on wit and humor, but, as Northrop Frye argues, comedy always works toward social resolution and a happy outcome from disorder, whereas satire presents that disorder without the resolution.[10] Satire exposes folly and ignorance without curing and eventually removing them, as comedy does. As a result, satires have no happy endings, and, if they contain positive resolutions, these are either transparently accidental, fantastic, or obviously artificially imposed. The true happy endings of satires must of necessity be created outside the theatre by the audience's actions.

In order to keep the audience aware of its fictionality, the radical popular theatre is, essentially, a self-conscious theatre. To emphasize its theatricality, it often relies on techniques derived from Brecht's epic theatre. Actors step out of their role to address the audience directly, painted signs break the illusion and suspense by announcing what is happening next, and songs com-

ment on the action or provide narrative connections between one scene and
another.

A Minstrel Show or Civil Rights in a Cracker Barrel (1964), was the Mime
Troupe's first major self-made production. As the title indicates, the show was
cast in the form of a black and white minstrel show, a traditional popular
entertainment indigenous to the United States. *A Minstrel Show* was not really a
play with a continuous plot, but a collage of satirical sketches that were designed
to shock the public in the deepest of its racist attitudes. In this respect, the San
Francisco Mime Troupe hooked up with the concerns of civil rights activists that
were prevalent in the mid-sixties: "We would get right into the problem of
racism—ours and everyone else's—by unearthing those stereotypes, clichés,
cornballs and all that Uncle Tom jive."[11]

The fast-paced minstrel show shared many elements in common with commedia dell'arte. It contained masked stereotypes, broad gestures, and quick
gags. The many jokes themselves were often updated versions of original ones
selected from some three hundred old minstrel shows. They were presented in
rapid exchanges between the "straight" interlocutor and a stereotypical black,
and served as transitions between the self-contained sketches.

The San Francisco Mime Troupe not only carefully researches the popular
cultural forms it adopts for its shows, it also extensively investigates its themes.
Thus, the short dramatic scenes of *A Minstrel Show* sharply satirize specific
aspects of racial prejudice. The "Chick-Stud" scene, for example, deals with
miscegenation and forms one of the most shocking parts of the show. In this
piece, a white girl and a black male viciously tear at their races' cultural
prejudices, revealing both to be irreconcilable and cliché-ridden. However, the
black and white actors also ridicule the artificial cordiality of exaggerated racial
tolerance. In the "Bathroom" scene, for instance, a middle-class black and a
white man are so polite that neither wants to urinate first. Finally, a third
character wearing a sign saying "Nigger" pushes them away yelling: "I don't
know what you came in here for, but it sure wasn't for pissin'. . . . Shit,
man—you need an education to learn to piss more than one in a commode?"[12]

In the first six years of its existence, then, the San Francisco Mime Troupe
performed many satirical comedies that were inspired or directly taken from the
commedia dell'arte repertoire. In the mid-sixties, the troupe also went more and
more in search of a truly popular audience in the city's public parks. These
outdoor performances were always free; only at the end were the spectators asked
to make donations according to their means. From 1965 on, the Mime Troupe
extended its activities to the Midwest, where performances at colleges provided
the group with a ready source of income that was necessary to support the
nonsubsidized activities in San Francisco. These college tours also involved the
Mime Troupe in nontheatrical political activities like the huge demonstration in
Madison, Wisconsin, against the Dow Chemical plant for its involvement in the
Vietnam War.

The Mime Troupe's disgust with the imperialist war in Vietnam was clearly expressed in their next major production, an adaptation of Goldoni's *L'Amant Militaire*. This play was created collectively in 1967 after Ron Davis had considerably cut down the size of the company from approximately fifty part-time members to fifteen full-time actors. The direction of the play was shared among four people with a great deal of input from the actors. Joan Holden wrote most of the text, making changes whenever actors and directors requested them. The actor who played Punch, the puppetlike narrator of the play, wrote his own text and had the liberty to respond to the audience's reactions.

Punch was conceived as a Brechtian distancing device. Like the singer in *The Caucasian Chalk Circle* he comments on the action and points out the specific parallels with the audience's contemporary situation. Furthermore, comically presented as a puppet box with legs, he constantly reminds the public of his own theatricality. His comical physique and the farcical acting of the masked actors in the actual play made it easier for the politically unsophisticated audience to digest the show's radical undercurrent.

Everything in and around *L'Amant Militaire* expresses a playful atmosphere. In the play's outdoor version, the stage and the set were erected while some actors stretched, danced, and sang in an attempt to warm up both themselves and their audience. Throughout the performance proper, the illusion was constantly broken by the actors' burlesque exaggerations and their willingness to respond to comments by the spectators. The plot of the play involves the love affair between Rosalinde, Pantalone's daughter, and Alonso, lieutenant in the Spanish forces that are occupying Italy. In Carlo Goldoni's original script the love intrigue is central, but in the Mime Troupe's version it is overshadowed by the dealings between Pantalone, Italy's largest arms manufacturer, and Garcia, commander-in-chief of the Spanish army. It is obviously in Pantalone's interest that the war continue, and he pleads with Garcia to maintain his forces in Italy:

> I got a lot in this war. I own 51 percent of the shares. I got munition plants in Milano, I got weapon labs in Torino, I got banks and pawnshops outside of every base—when you end the war you end the war industry! You murder my markets— you assassinate my economy—you expose me to recession—to depression—to suicide.[13]

Pantalone's exaggerated New York Jewish accent and Garcia's Spanish lisp help to add a satirical twist to their words. The parallels between the play's sixteenth-century Spanish imperialism in Italy and the American involvement in Vietnam are made apparent by clear, topical references to bombing and chemical destruction of dense forests. Furthermore, Garcia idealistically defends "Spain's" intervention in "Italy" in a discourse pronounced with a fake Lyndon B. Johnson accent, while the song "America" plays in the background and he prepares to mount a human horse consisting of two actors covered by the Stars and Stripes:

> In the struggle for men's minds, no weapon can be ignored. Señores, the enemy is all around us—they're ruthless, sneaky and uncompromising: and we won't be safe, your children and mine, until every last one of them is wiped out. We are not fighting for Spain alone, señores. We are fighting for the very lifeblood, I say the very lifeBLOOD, of our civilization. [p. 177]

And if there could still be anyone in the audience who thinks that the play is no more than a comic melodrama about a conservative wop who prohibits his daughter from marrying a spick, Punch comes on stage to erase any remaining doubts: "Bravo, Pantalone, bravo! Pantalone's a cutie, isn't he, folks? Put Lyndon behind a pushcart and you'd love him too. But you'd never vote for him. Go ahead, Pantalone—sell your daughter. She's worth about 50 cents in the backroom of any Saigon bar" (p. 181).

The play's humor is mainly based on the exaggerated ethnic accents of the characters and joking references to their cultural particularities. Thus the Italians and the Spaniards become their American immigrant counterparts and are explicitly referred to as spicks and wops, and in one instance Pantalone shuts Alonso up by telling him: "Shove it up your guacamole, buddy!" (p. 180). But the humor does more than simply capitalize on popular concepts of ethnic minority behavior. It also seriously criticizes the relatively large percentage of minority recruits that joined the U.S. army for simple-minded reasons: "For them the army represents a step upward—decent pay, respect, the adoration of women" (p. 181). With these silly visions of instantaneous glory and social ascent, they are partly responsible for maintaining American imperialism. Again, the puppet-narrator gives extra punch to this political message by commenting: "Powerful! Devastating! Good old hard-hitting *realism!* Dig it: the system forcing that poor slob into the army" (p. 184). But he also proposes an alternative, explaining that nobody has to go into the army if he does not want to. He lists several ways to get out and ends the act by leading the audience in chanting, "Hell no—We won't go!"

L'Amant Militaire is, then, pedagogical as well as satirical. It reveals the ridiculousness of the political discourses by the American leaders. It explains the business interests in perpetuating the war, and it suggests ways to do something about all this. Part of the solution lies with the young. They must, first of all, refuse to join the army, and, secondly, they must convert their capacity to love into a capacity to act. The play clearly portrays a generation conflict as well as a class conflict. The young are pitched against the old, and the servants are exploited by their masters. The young are represented by the dreamy, naively patriotic Alonso, Rosalinde, her quick-witted maid Corallina, and her lover, the dumb Italian army recruit Arlecchino. Rosalinde and Alonso show that human love can overcome cultural and political differences, but that in its naive manifestation it is not going to change the world and risks resulting in the ultimately powerless and absurd stance of the flower-power movement.

Corallina is the true heroine of the play. Her love for Arlecchino is down to earth and unstained by unrealistic, romantic lyricism. She represents the positive force of the enlightened proletariat and, converting herself into an Italian-American papa ex machina, provides the fictional world with a happy ending. In true commedia dell'arte fashion, that fictional world had complicated itself to such a point that only an outside force could untie it. First, Pantalone wants his daughter to marry the generale in order to get lucrative arms supply contracts wherever he goes. But instead of sensual words, Rosalinde gives Garcia an antiwar lecture. When Alonso hears about his lover's "malicious" intentions, he runs to Pantalone's house to save his commander from the foul, pacifist rhetoric. But the generalissimo sees Alonso as an accomplice and has him and Rosalinde taken to the stockades to be executed. Meanwhile, Arlecchino tries to get out of the army by dressing as a woman. But he gets into trouble as the other soldiers take him to be a whore. Finally, Espada, the pot-smoking black soldier, recognizes Arlecchino and drags him off to be executed as well. Just as the firing squad aims, Corallina appears in a pope's outfit and declares: "I'ma da Pope, dope!" and saves her friends by declaring peace. She tells everyone to quit the army and orders Pantalone to convert the production of his factories from arms to olive oil.

The play's pedagogical essence becomes particularly evident in the final scene when "da Pope" explains why "he" stopped the war: "We stop it because there's nothing in you to stop it with. You empty, and you country's empty. And you try to fill it up by expanding into other people's countries. You can't fight yourselves by destroying other people . . . the real enemy, mi bambini, is *ignorance*" (p. 192). *L'Amant Militaire* tries to take away some of that ignorance. The San Francisco Mime Troupe does not believe in passive, theoretical lessons only, however, and with clear Brechtian overtones it communicates to the audience that the play itself is not going to change a thing. Before the show ends, Corallina steps out of her role and tells the spectators that, if they want something done, they should do it themselves.

The practice of the Mime Troupe in the "Davis period" (1960–1970) and after has been oriented by the very Brechtian ideal of instruction through entertainment. The company wants to contribute to social change by means of didactic comedies that will amuse its "found" audience with highly professional theatre and teach them the hidden mechanics of the hegemony's power structure. The radical actors are acutely aware that if their performance is poor their audience will leave and their message will be lost in the wind. Particularly in the first ten years of the Mime Troupe's existence, commedia dell'arte was considered a very useful medium for its radical themes because of its "open and colorful form . . . masks, music, gags, and [because it is] easily set up with a backdrop and platform."[14] It is a theatrical form that is supposed to be loud because it was originally designed to compete with the cacophony of street noises. It is a brief, fast-paced form that is not likely to bore popular audiences quickly. But commedia dell'arte is by no means the only possible theatrical medium for popular political theatre. Davis suggests that morality plays, burlesques, rock and roll, vaudeville, and the circus all provide useful forms for political outdoor theatre.

One of the first creations that appeared after Ron Davis left the Mime Troupe in 1970 was a parodic melodrama called *The Independent Female or a Man has his Pride,* a controversial play about feminism. Ron Davis left the San Francisco Mime Troupe on 12 March 1970, after what seems to have been an ideological and organizational dispute. Joan Holden, the company's present artistic director, recalls: "There was a big fight over how much authority the director should have. People wanted more democracy. Davis made all the artistic decisions, and people wanted to have a lot more to say."[15]

The San Francisco Mime Troupe reorganized as a theatre collective with actors doubling as bookkeepers and publicists. The post-Davis Mime Troupe also radicalized its politics: "The strong Marxist foundation existed most firmly in the early collective days. Davis's theoretical foundation was much more aesthetic. He was interested in experimental theatre in the sixties. In the seventies, we belonged to the Marxist movement. We wanted to serve the people in their critical ideas. But it sort of cooled off like the entire revolutionary fervor cooled off."[16]

After *The Independent Female,* a satire of narrow-minded machos who dominate modern society and of submissive women who see it as their duty to uphold the status quo, the revitalized Mime Troupe continued with *The Dragon Lady's Revenge* (1971), a play that reveals the CIA's involvement in the drug trade of Southeastern Asia. This action-filled drama, based on the popular medium of the spy-adventure movie and the comic strip, is set in the fictional city of Long Pinh (i.e., "there where the heroin needles are long"). The plot basically records the adventures of Clyde, the U.S. ambassador's son, who discovers that his father is the leader of a drug gang. The Mime Troupe uses the extremely effective tool of self-incriminating satire when the U.S. dignitary tries to defend himself in front of his son:

> AMBASSADOR: Please son, I know this looks bad—but don't judge me too quickly. . . . The drug trade is exceedingly profitable. Our government, as you know, encourages profit.
> CLYDE: But it's criminal!
> AMBASSADOR: Can anything that makes billions "really" be called criminal?[17]

The Ambassador, appropriately named Mr. Junker, explains how his crackdown on Long Pinh's drug trade has only been a cover for his rerouting the drug traffic to the American mass market where the drugs are used to counter the potential subversion of the hundreds of unemployed and the ethnic minorities.

The humor of *The Dragon Lady's Revenge* is not as persuasive as that of previous Mime Troupe creations. It consists mainly in rather silly puns on the characters' names. Thus the puppet president of the Asian country is called Rong Q, which, aside from sounding Vietnamese, is an allusion to the theatrical playfulness of the show. It also provides the basis for such gratuitous wordplays as "That's right, Rong." However, the parody of the spy movie is more than a simple mockery of this popular item of Hollywood culture. The American authorities and their CIA bulldogs are presented as comic-strip caricatures, and, consequently, their invincibility is dramatically deflated, and their eloquent defense of their involvement in the drug trade for the purpose of safeguarding the freedom of Western democracy is revealed to be mere political rhetoric. Through parody and deflating satire, the capitalist oppressor is shown to be fallible like everyone else; the imperialist empire that they have constructed is human made, and, the play suggests, it can therefore be destroyed by humans and replaced with a more equitable society.

The purpose of *The Dragon Lady's Revenge,* as of so many other contemporary radical popular plays, is to uncover the true face of the capitalist oppressor in all his apparently benevolent manifestations. This procedure of unveiling is most commonly and most effectively executed by means of satire. The words with which the capitalist politician presents his greed as selflessness turn against him as his actions betray his speech, and the dignified upholder of our Western civilization is caught with his pants down. For the oppressed to become aware of their predicament they must, first of all, be made to realize that the "democracy" in which they think they live is far from democratic and only perpetuated by means of criminal excesses like the CIA protection of fascist rulers in the Third World. Secondly, the oppressed must be made conscious that their class enemy is very well organized and slyly manipulates public opinion in his favor. Radical popular dramatic satire insists that the oppressor is by no means unbeatable and suggests ways to overcome him. In all this, the radical popular theatre never forgets its own theatricality. The Mime Troupe's self-consciousness is, then, more than just playful mockery of popular cultural traditions; it adds an indispensable epic quality to its theatre that constantly reminds the audience they are only watching a performance and that the real social changes must be made by them.

San Fran Scandals (1973) employs vaudeville forms to explain the intricate manipulations of hegemonistic forces in San Francisco's local politics. The specific occasion for the play was the projected destruction of a large area of low-rent housing for the construction of a prestigious performing arts center dedicated to opera and ballet and financially inaccessible to the popular masses. Frank and Stella, two unemployed vaudeville artists, are evicted from their apartment but, with a comic ruse, manage to make Harold Smellybucks, the millionaire patron of the performing arts center, renounce his project. Their strategy is reminiscent of that of the traditional lower-class impostor or harlequin who, through his actions, reverses the dominant social order.

The satiric victims of *San Fran Scandals* are Harold Smellybucks, who invests his dollars in the perpetuation of bourgeois culture, and the snotty prima donna Carlotta Snotta, who sells her art as a commodity. It is hardly surprising that Smellybucks wants to contract the diva Snotta for the inauguration of his arts center. In the Western world, opera is the most pretentious form of bourgeois culture. This time, however, the most elevated of the performing arts is outsmarted by vaudeville, the most vulgar and popular of the performing arts. In a way, then, *San Fran Scandals* dramatizes a class struggle in terms of the social hierarchy of cultural forms.

Vaudeville is a type of theatre that used to be very popular with the working classes. It was characterized by farcical sketches interspersed with song and dance. *San Fran Scandals* is a parody of this form of performing arts; its heroes, Frank and Stella, are sixty-two and fifty-eight, respectively, and have been unemployed vaudevillians for the past twenty-seven years. All the large vaudeville theatres of yore have been razed and replaced by office buildings and parking lots. Only occasionally do Frank and Stella practice their old routines in their living room.

The play is laden with typical vaudevillian one-liners that are injected with topical political references. At one point, Stella delivers the following vicious invective against Richard Nixon:

> Isn't it great the way President Nixon took crime off the streets and put it in the White House? You know the motto of the Republican Party used to be "Four More Years," today it's "Five to Life." Ah, but I shouldn't be making all these jokes about the President; why, he had to go into the hospital for brain surgery. Really. To remove all his hemorrhoids. No, I was just pulling your leg, or anything else I could find; President Nixon never had hemorrhoids and never will. You know why? Cause he's a perfect asshole.[18]

Presented as a mere rehearsal of an old vaudeville act, the play-within-a-play derivative provides the Mime Troupe with a time-tested foil for its sharp attacks on public authorities. Mr. Harold Smellybucks, who has made his fortune in the toilet paper industry—indeed a "smelly" business—is the play's main object of attack. He is famous because his name is in every toilet. He is shown to have absolutely no concern for those he calls "the little people" who have to vacate their homes to make place for the cultural complex. Yet, this pedantic, French-speaking man who prides himself on being the architect of the "New San Francisco" by evicting four hundred families, is mercilessly deflated by the Mime Troupe's stinging satire.

In the second scene of the play, Smellybucks is waiting for Carlotta Snotta's arrival so he can have her sign the contract for her recital at the opening gala for the new arts center. He has never met Carlotta and mistakes Stella, who has come to complain about the eviction, for the diva. A hilarious comedy of errors ensues in which the ex-vaudeville star ruthlessly unmasks the capitalist villain. The plot thickens when the real diva enters, asking if "thees [is] the office of meester Smallpox?" Fortunately for Frank and Stella she travels in disguise because, like Smellybucks, she hates "the little pipple": "They touch me, they ask me things, they want me to sing. That's disgusting. I don't sing for nothing" (p. 106). With the unexpected assistance of Miss Farquhar, the tycoon's secretary, the vaudevillians manage to lock the prima donna in a trunk and change the contract into a document in which Smellybucks "agrees to resign from the Art Commission and to turn the Commission over to the artists and the people of the neighborhoods." He also promises "to destroy no more houses, and to build new housing, inside the city, for all the poor people he has dislocated. . . . Finally, and last but not least, if the rich people of this city desire a complex for their artsy activities, let them build it with their own smellybucks. They will not touch a penny of the public taxes, which will go to the people who really need it" (pp. 110–11). The fake Carlotta blackmails the toilet paper magnate into signing by threatening to sue him for having chafed her sensitive buttock skin with his tissue, which, according to the "victim," felt like "ground glass" (p. 111). The play ends in true vaudeville fashion as the secretary, who turns out to be Frank and Stella's long-lost daughter, and her parents dance together in political and family union to the refrain "Don't let them screw us anymore."

After *San Fran Scandals,* the Mime Troupe came out with a long-winded, naturalistic play called *False Promises/Nos Engañaron,* which dealt with the successful, unified strike of Anglo-Saxon and Mexican copper miners in the West at the end of the nineteenth century. This was followed by the much better received *Hotel Universe* (1977), with which the company made its first appearance in Europe.[19] Wrapped in a comic plot, *Hotel Universe* attacks the plans of the San Francisco city government to raze a number of cheap downtown hotels inhabited by the elderly poor in order to "manhattanize" the inner city. In 1979, the Mime Troupe did a play called *Squash,* which was about struggle and resources. The premise is that three gods give a poor neighborhood in Los Angeles an eternal gasoline pump. In that year, the company also produced Dario Fo's *We Can't Pay! We Won't Pay!*[20]

In the election year 1980, the San Francisco Mime Troupe dedicated itself to the demystification of the New Right:

> We were showing the people what had happened: deregulation, right-wing moral crusade, cuts in education programs. It was an extremely conservative platform. . . . We were looking for a format to deal with all these different issues, and so we came up with the idea of a superhero of clarification, someone who could set

The San Francisco Mime Troupe. In *Hotel Universe* (1980) the mayor and a real estate speculator have to deal with an irate tenant. Photo by Tom Copi.

people's minds straight. The model of Superman is that in real life he is the opposite: a wimpy office clerk who wears glasses—a weak, uncertain, and confused person.[21]

Joan Holden wrote *Fact Person* while basing the heroine on herself: "I have often felt frustrated with not having the right information at my fingertips when I needed to prove an opponent wrong. You know that you're right and they're wrong but you can't prove it because the facts have slipped out of your mind. And afterwards, when you're alone, you can prove it. Our Fact Person had the magic power to have all the facts present at will."[22]

Fact Person and its sequels *Factwino Meets the Moral Majority* and *Factwino vs. Armageddon Man* were summer shows performed in the parks from 1980 through 1982. They were based on the comic book form, which, in many respects, is the popular art form par excellence. In the meantime, in 1981, the

The San Francisco Mime Troupe. Publicity shot for the musical comedy *Factwino: The Opera* (1985). Photo by Michael Bry.

Mime Troupe created a full-length show on Central America called *Last Tango in Huehuetenango*.[23] This musical play, full of Latin and Caribbean rhythms, essentially deals with how the historical dialectic has left Central America and how, through the fault of the United States, a peaceful path is no longer possible. *Last Tango* was performed through 1983. In that year, the Mime Troupe also presented *Secrets in the Sand* in the parks. This show had to do with a scandal about the movie that killed John Wayne and Susan Hayward. This movie, *The Conqueror,* had been shot in the radioactive sand in Utah one year after an A-bomb test there. An enormous percentage of the cast got cancer and died, and the Mime Troupe turned this subject into a mystery play.

In 1984 the San Francisco Mime Troupe, in its twenty-fifth year, was still alive and well. During the spring and summer it toured through the parks and public squares of the Bay area with *1985,* a satirical play that explicitly instructs its audience to vote against President Reagan. This political goal is pursued with many of the same dramatic tools that have given the Mime Troupe its reputation as America's most successful and consistent radical popular theatre group. The play contains easily recognizable stock figures—some of them based on prominent political personalities—farcical situations, comic suspense, and catchy songs. The main device by which the Mime Troupe tries to convince its audience to vote against the incumbent president is a dramatized view of the future that is reminiscent of Charles Dickens's "A Christmas Carol." The protagonist, a black lawyer called Ebenezer Jones, is visited on election night by the spirits of the past, present, and future. They help to awaken him from his conservative bourgeois complacency. But when at the play's conclusion Jones is finally convinced that voting can make a difference, he discovers to his horror that he is not registered to vote. However, the play was performed well in advance of the 6 November elections, and, jumping out of the play's fictional framework, the actor playing Ebenezer Jones led the other unregistered voters in the audience to a nearby registration table.

Before Ebenezer reaches his moment of revelation, *1985* takes its audience through a comic review of what has happened to radical America since the late sixties and presents a grim picture of what will happen to the world if Mr. Reagan gets reelected. Ebenezer represents that large group of militant minority students who loudly called for revolution in 1967 and who, in 1984, have fallen victim to political apathy.

The play opens with a scene set in the law offices of Baker, Baker, Baker, and Bunz on the afternoon of election day. The law firm is immediately established as a right-wing enterprise defending the capitalist interests of multinationals and other large corporations. Ebenezer is introduced as a very useful link in this organization. With his Black Power background and his charismatic voice, he is able to convince community workers of the benefits of constructing a huge office building in a housing project. Baker, Jr., the senior partner's wimpy son, admiringly describes Jones's thrilling performance in court:

> It was Africa in there! The witnesses, the judge, the city attorney—I was the only white man in the room— except Jones. . . . The judge turns to us with a scowl on his face. My knees are shaking as I start to rise. Jones grabs the portfolio and strides to the bench! The crowd pulled back with a hushed roar at the sight of his Wilkes Bashford suit. . . . Jones was magnificent. As he melodically delineated our inflated figures on the number of jobs the project would create, you could see some of the old women start to hum and sway.[24]

Baker, Jr.'s brief testimony efficiently reveals the shady intentions of the law firm and Jones's greater concern for his own career than for the people. As a result, he cannot even be bothered by the racial prejudices that inadvertently slip into the words of his superiors. Self-contented, he drives his Mercedes Benz to his luxury condominium home.

The San Francisco Mime Troupe. The ghost of the past in the shape of Richard Nixon disturbs Ebenezer's peaceful nap in *1985*, produced in the Panhandle of Golden Gate Park (1984).

The ghosts of the past, present and future appear to Jones when he dozes off for a short nap at quarter after six in the evening. The first ghost enters in the shape of Richard Nixon, convincingly portrayed by the same actor who played Baker, Jr. Wearing a full mask and imitating Nixon's accent with authenticity, he enters with rolls of audio tapes sticking out of his pockets. But the tapes turn out not to be of Watergate but of Jones's own radical past. Nixon is quick to point out the similarities between Jones's present predicament and his own: "We grew up together. We went through the sixties together. . . . I am your president. Now we are here again. You're not voting, and I'm not running, and we both say bullshit to the whole thing, right brother?" (p. 8). But Nixon's fraternizing attitude brings out the old radical in Ebenezer and he requests to see the tape of the university takeover.

The scene presenting Ebenezer as the well-spoken Black Power leader is not devoid of satire. Jones delivers his charismatic speeches still dressed in his designer silk pajamas, and his audience includes a selection of caricatures of revolutionary characters ranging from Maoists to Che Guevara followers. The scene shows how Jones prevents an armed uprising and manages to obtain important concessions from the university's administration. But his victory is immediately undercut by the next flashback in which we see Jones cheerfully accept a full-time job at the university's newly created Third World and Minority Institute. Nixon, who plays the role of epic narrator between flashbacks, summarizes Jones's dream of the past as follows: "So you grew up. In '72 you were too radical to vote for McGovern. By '76, you were too turned off to vote for anybody. Thank you Eb!" (p. 14).

The second dream sequence involves the ghost of the present who enters in the guise of Nancy Reagan. The first lady takes Jones on a holiday to Central America in reward for his "hard work, dignity, fierce independence [and his] plain good sense" (p. 15)—in other words, for never having interfered with her husband's policies. She introduces Jones to her intimate friends Marcos, Mobutu, and Pinochet. To welcome their American guests, this trio performs a cabaret-type song called "Best of Friends," in which they relate how they had come to power by ousting (or killing) their progressive predecessors with the assistance of the CIA. The song ends in a satirical comment on Reagan's human rights record:

> PINOCHET: Jimmy Carter he was some kind of red,
> MARCOS: Always worry about the tortured and dead.
> MOBUTU: But with this administration things are better than before:
> ALL: We don't even have to say we're sorry anymore! That's why we're glad to see ya, American guy. We're the best friends that your money can buy. We're fighting for freedom and getting paid! We're Marcos, Mobutu and Pinochet. [pp. 17–18]

The inhuman nature of the three dictators is shown through their physical aggression of the indigenous waitress and their greedy devouring of a dish of barbecued baby limbs. Furthermore, Nancy Reagan's sensual flirtations with them suggests the U.S. support of fascist dictatorships throughout the world. At the end of this scene, *1985* moves to the brink of the future as Jones is forced to watch the preparations for a U.S. invasion of Central America. For the first time in the play, the protagonist protests: "I didn't think it would be this soon! Nobody asked me! I never voted for any invasion!" But the dictators dismiss his remark by cynically pointing out that he never voted against it either.

With *1985*, the San Francisco Mime Troupe seems to argue that those who vote for a particular government are no more responsible for its crimes than those who abstain from voting. The vision of the future, presented by Ebenezer's new wave daughter Lakisha, shows the kinds of excesses apathetic citizens will be blamed for it they do not vote. Lakisha leads her father to the postelection

The San Francisco Mime Troupe. Mobutu, Pinochet, and Marcos (l. to r.) in *1985* (1984).

Supreme Court, now reorganized with Reagan faithful Mr. Baker, Sr. as chief justice. A quick sequence of court cases indicates the new, conservative pattern that is likely to emerge if Reagan, in his second term, is allowed to appoint three new members to the Supreme Court: ecologists lose their battle against offshore drilling, workers will lose their right to union representation, and under the new antiterrorist act of 1985 Jesse Jackson will be convicted as a subversive for having visited Nicaragua. Screaming and bathed in sweat, Jones wakes up to this nightmarish vision: it's a quarter to eight and he still has fifteen minutes to cast his vote. He runs to the polling station only to discover that he is not registered.

Inspired by the depressing statistic that the United States has the second worst record for voter turnout of any democracy on earth, *1985* managed to convince thousands of Bay area residents to register in the summer of 1984. This success strengthened the Mime Troupe's determination to continue their outdoor performances. But over the years, their more sophisticated indoor performances have become just as indispensable to them. In 1984, the company's indoor season featured *Steeltown*, a musical tragicomedy about unemployment, manipulation, and exploitation in the steel industry. In 1985, the troupe performed *Factwino: The Opera* in theatres around the Bay area and *Crossing Borders* in the parks. In the spring of 1986, the Mime Troupe attracted 11,000 spectators to the Los Angeles Theater Center for its five-week run of *Spain/'36*, an elaborate multimedia show with masks and dancers. And in the rainy summer of that same year, it performed *The Mozamgola Caper* and a new version of *Hotel Universe* on eight weekends for an estimated 10,000 people. To emphasize its solidarity with the Nicaraguan people, the company also traveled to Managua in November 1986 to perform *Hotel Universe* in both English and Spanish. The Mime Troupe's immediate objective for the future is, then, to be active indoors as well as outdoors. As in the case of other radical troupes that started in the sixties, there seems to be, in Joan Holden's words, a desire for legitimization:

> If you are an artist, you want to mount bigger and bigger shows, unless your ambition is strictly to play and be folk. As a writer, I have been writing plays for fifteen years only to be shouted by actors into the wind. I also want to write plays that are produced indoors, under lights, where there are more technical possibilities. And I can only do this if we get more money. The same goes for the actors. It is the logic of artistic development.[25]

Thus, in 1986, the San Francisco Mime Troupe is considerably less radical than in the early seventies; it even found itself accepting a major grant from the National Endowment for the Arts. Yet, it claims that it is not selling out to the bourgeois cultural power structure:

> There are contradictions in capitalism that one learns to live with. The fact is that the enemy has the money. If you want to do anything at all you have to get the money from them in one way or another. . . . It's impossible to live in this society and remain pure. Right now, we're much more willing to make certain compromises than in the seventies. But we know what we want to get out of it; which is not to be rich and famous but to have access to a bigger forum.[26]

The San Francisco Mime Troupe is not about to cut itself loose from its grass roots. And even indoors, the company's main concern is to reach a popular audience. There is a large popular crowd that is not prepared to sit in the grass to watch an outdoor show: old people, ethnic minorities, and, particularly, black people go much more easily to the theatre than to the park. In the second half of the eighties, then, the company continues to be inspired by a radical philosphy. The San Francisco Mime Troupe remains committed to the idea that there will never be justice, plenty, and peace until the present social and economic systems are changed.

El Teatro Campesino

El Teatro Campesino cannot be considered to have maintained such a consistent political focus over the years. Starting out as the cultural branch of César Chavez's Mexican-American farmworkers union, el Teatro Campesino is still based in the state of California but is much less Marxist oriented than the San Francisco Mime Troupe. Whereas the Mime Troupe reaches out to all the exploited classes in American society (including students and the petty bourgeoisie), Campesino identifies itself with the political and cultural struggle of the oppressed Mexican-American Minority. The militant beginnings of el Teatro Campesino have been well documented, both by critics and by its founder, Luís Valdez. In several interviews, Campesino's artistic director and chief playwright proudly speaks of his childhood days in a family of Mexican migrant workers and how, at the age of twelve, he used to entertain friends and relatives in the fields with his homemade puppets.[27] Valdez wrote his first play while a student at San Jose State. His *Shrunken Head of Pancho Villa* was performed in San Francisco in 1964. This was also the year that Valdez went to Cuba to learn about the revolution in practice. This experience contributed considerably to the development of his political consciousness, whereas his internship with the San Francisco Mime Troupe in the summer of 1965 showed him a type of popular theatre in which politics could fit perfectly: "I figured if any type of theatre could turn on the farm workers it would be that type of theater—outside, that lively, that bawdy."[28] When Valdez started performing agitprop sketches for the striking Mexican farmworkers in the Delano Valley in the fall of 1965, he made sure to include commedia dell'arte elements, slapstick, and dramatic satire.

As the cultural affiliate of union organizer César Chavez, Luís Valdez started touring with a company of amateur actors recruited from among the strikers to convince the farmworkers to join the union and the Huelga (the Delano grape pickers' strike). Impromptu dramatic sketches were developed collectively in sessions led by Valdez, during which Mexican migrant workers acted out the types of exploitation they had suffered themselves. Hardly subtle, the early *actos,* as these short pieces were called, were designed to crudely convey a political and economic truth, and they served as a simple artistic form for the *Raza's* self-expression.

The nine *actos* that were published in a mimeograph edition in 1971 indicate the evolution that this indigenous Chicano dramatic form underwent over a six-year period. Structurally, the pieces developed from one-dimensional characters and agitprop temperament to much more complex story lines and characterizations. Thematically, after 1967 the *actos* moved away from union recruitment and strike propaganda to other sociopolitical and historical concerns involving the Mexican-American population. They started dealing with ethnic discrimination in high schools, Mexican-Americans in the Vietnam War, and imperialist aspects of Cortez's conquest of Mexico. This broadening of el Teatro Campesino's aesthetic and thematic perspective was partly due to the troupe's separation from Chavez's union and its move from Delano to Del Rey and, later, to Fresno.

Las dos Caras del Patroncito ("The Two Faces of the Boss") is one of the first *actos* created by el Teatro Campesino. It premiered on the picket line during the Delano grape strike in 1965. This comic agitprop sketch was intended to show the fake alternating intimidation and friendliness of the ranchero. The boss was represented by an actor with a pig mask, a borrowing from commedia dell'arte. The humor of *Las dos Caras del Patroncito* is predominantly visual and based on mime and broad acting. In true agitprop fashion it shows how the proletarian underdog gets the better of the capitalist pig. The *acto*'s basic objective is to satirize the ranchero. It shows that his fake friendliness and toughness are only adopted poses that hide a weak person. He needs his mask to better exploit his Mexicans. The play's satire, then, proceeds to strip the patroncito of his mask. Subsequently, the *acto* indicates that the oppressed farmworkers should adopt the boss's power tactics for his own purposes: the rancheros will only listen to the workers if they are spoken to in the same rough tone with which they address their workers. Therefore, the intrigue of *Las dos Caras del Patroncito* revolves around an exchange of identity. The ranchero gets so involved in convincing the farmworker how beautiful the life of a grape picker is that he exclaims:

> Sometimes I sit up there in my office and think to myself: I wish I was a Mexican. . . . Just one of my own boys. Riding in the trucks, hair flying in the wind, feeling all that freedom, coming out here in the fields, working under the green vines, smoking a cigarette, my hands in the cool soft earth, underneath the blue skies, with white clouds drifting by, looking at the mountains, listening to the birdies sing.[29]

To make his farmworker feel even better, the ranchero tells him about all the financial problems he has to deal with. To emphasize his point, the boss hangs the Patroncito sign on the farmworker's neck and sighs that he wishes he could be a Mexican. He further adorns the Chicano with a cigar, a Western hat, a whip, a mean look, and, finally, the pig mask. But suddenly the farmworker *is* the Patroncito, and the boss starts seeing the exploitation through the eyes of a farmworker:

> PATRONCITO: You're nuts! I can't live in those shacks! They got rats, cockroaches. And those trucks are unsafe. You want me to get killed?
> FARMWORKER: Then buy a car.
> PATRONCITO: With what? How much you paying me here anyway?
> FARMWORKER: Eighty-five cents an hour.
> PATRONCITO: I was paying you a buck twenty-five!
> FARMWORKER: I got problems boy! Go on welfare!

PATRONCITO: You know that damn César Chavez is right? You can't do this work
for less than two dollars an hour. [pp. 17–18]

So, at the end of the *acto* the roles have been completely reversed. The
patroncito cannot convince the farmworker to give him back his clothes and the
latter has the former boss dragged off by Charlie, the bodyguard. *Las dos Caras
del Patroncito* ends, then, with the exploited exploiter crying, "Help! Where's
those damn union organizers? Where's César Chavez? Help! Huelga! HUEL-
GAAAAA!" (p. 19). It convinces the farmworkers that joining the union is the
natural thing to do; even their boss would join if he had to live on their wages.

La Quinta Temporada ("The Fifth Season"—1966), another *acto* from Campesino's union period, is already more complex. It has the same farcical tone, but
its cast of characters now includes ten people, several of whom are allegorical.
The four seasons—so important to the outdoor laborers—are personified and a
fifth season (*la quinta temporada,* in Spanish) embodies "union solidarity." The
acto dramatizes the double exploitation by ranchero and labor contractor (*contratista*). The main dramatic action involves the contratista's luring the naive
farmworker into working with promises of instant wealth: "You go to work for
me and you'll be rich. You'll have enough money to buy yourself a new car, a
Cadillac! Two Cadillacs! . . . You'll be middleclass! You'll be anglo!" (p. 25).
El Teatro Campesino not only satirizes the ruthless exploitation by the bosses and
their associates; it also mocks the näiveté and mistaken bourgeois values of the
farmworkers. They do not prepare themselves properly for the harshness of the
winter, and the gentle springtime has to explain that they have to fight for their
rights. So when the summer comes, fatly dressed in green dollar bills, the
farmworker goes on strike and the patroncito loses his crop. However, when fall
appears, the farmworker is starving and almost prepared to accept the contratista's job when spring comes rushing to his assistance, "dressed as a nun
representing the churches." She feeds him and gives him some money as the
summer enters dressed as "unions" and the fall "dressed as a mexican revolutionary representing *la Raza.*" All of them express their solidarity with the farmworker and encourage him to pursue his struggle. They also help him fight off
the cruel winter; they surround the farmworker as winter charges at him, and, in
playful dance, they push the cold season toward the patroncito. The boss,
subsequently pushed and beaten, shivers with cold, and, in the end, is forced to
call in the help of the union, *la Raza* (the united Mexican-American ethnic
minority), and the Church, who force him first to sign a labor contract. At the
closing of the *acto,* winter reveals herself to be *La Quinta Temporada,* or "Social
Justice," and, in accordance with commedia dell'arte tradition, kicks the contratista off the stage.

Satiric humor is essential to Campesino's drama.[30] Despite the often tragic
circumstances, the language of the Mexican immigrants and Chicano farmworkers is full of jokes and wordplays and rich in humoristic imagery. Luís Valdez

explains that his plays are full of this humor and slapstick. "But," he specifies, "it depends on who is slapping who."[31] Obviously, in the *actos,* the farmworkers and the union do most of the slapping, and the patroncito and the contratista receive most of the blows. A theatre that considers its main task to be the generation of energy for social change must lift the spirits of its public allies and must show the potential vulnerability of the oppressor.

Luís Valdez is fond of talking about el Teatro Campesino's liberating laughter, a reference to the company's humor that has clear Brechtian overtones.[32] The radical popular theatre's commitment to social change naturally affiliates it with Brecht's political theatre, and, as a result, many contemporary radical troupes employ adapted forms of the epic theatre. In the case of el Teatro Campesino, Brecht is most conspicuously present in the acting style and much less in the structure of the plays. Nevertheless, the use of narrative songs and signs that announce the contents of scenes and identify characters is related to Brechtian aesthetics. Valdez openly admits that Campesino's self-conscious acting is inspired by Brecht. Campesino alternates between showing and telling to "keep the spectators perpetually conscious of what is happening."[33] Campesino does not want the audience to get completely wrapped up in the action or the plot, nor does it want them to identify emotionally with the characters. Particularly in the *actos* el Teatro Campesino realized that it was essential to "clearly express the issues, openly, without falling back on a plot or characters."[34]

The *acto Vietnam Campesino* (1970) has no plot to speak of; it is a comparison between the Mexican-American campesino and the Vietnamese farmworker. It is expressive of Campesino's broadened perspective, which has moved from specific strike agitation to the dramatic expression of the worldwide ramification of imperialist oppression of farmworkers. In five brief tableaux, *Vietnam Campesino* sketches the intricate relations between the rancheros, the Pentagon, and the Vietnam War. The *acto*'s main objective is to show that thousands of Chicanos are dying in Vietnam in a war against Vietnamese peasants, who are exploited just like them. After a Piscator-like sequence of slides showing Vietnam, farm labor, crop dusting, and corpses, *Vietnam Campesino* concludes with the voice of a young Mexican-American soldier who is killed in Vietnam: "The war in Vietnam continues, asesinando familias inocentes de campesinos. Los Chicanos mueren en la guerra, y los rancheros se hacen ricos, selling their scab products to the Pentagon. The fight is here, Raza! En Aztlán!" (p. 130).

In the beginning of the seventies, the concept of Aztlán and corresponding Mexican-Indian symbols and myths began to characterize the dramatic creations of el Teatro Campesino. This new direction indicated Campesino's desire to move away from the issue-oriented *actos* to a more ambitious style of cultural agitation. It wanted to concentrate on making Mexican-Americans aware of their rich cultural heritage. Besides, many of the traditional concepts and deities still survived in the barrios and provided the troupe with a readily available frame of popular cultural reference. The Nahuatl word *Aztlán* means "Land to the North" and refers to the southwestern part of the United States, from which the Aztecs had come before they settled in central Mexico. Since World War II, Mexicans have started migrating back to this "Land to the North" for economic reasons. Strongly influenced by the movement for civil rights of minorities in the mid-sixties, the Mexican-American started becoming more aware of his political identity: Chicano nationalism, or *La Causa,* was born. From 1969 on, Chicanos started claiming Aztlán as their national territory, arguing that it "belongs to those who plant the seeds, water the fields, and gather the crops, and not the foreign Europeans."[35]

El Teatro Campesino became very much involved in this nationalist movement and regarded itself as performing the essential task of shaping the Chicano's national character. As a result, since the early seventies it has placed more emphasis on the purely artistic and cultural aspects of its theatre work than on the topical political aspects. El Teatro Campesino was largely responsible for the foundation of the Teatro Nacional de Aztlán (TENAZ) and inspired the formation of new Chicano theatre groups all over the country. In 1971, Campesino had moved its quarters to San Juan Bautista, the site of an old Spanish Mission, where, on a terrain of forty acres, acquired by Luís Valdez and his wife Lupe, a biodynamic commune was installed. There, Valdez and his associates also founded the Centro Campesino Cultural, a community center for Chicanos that offered theatre workshops and music courses and organized related cultural and political activities.

In the early seventies, Campesino developed the so-called *corrido.* A *corrido* is a traditional Mexican folk ballad that Campesino used as a narrative framework for a fast-paced collage of dramatic scenes. In this way, the action was built on continuous music that gave the dialogue a metric quality and turned movements into dance. According to Nicolás Kanellos, "the Corrido is designed to depart from realism; for the Corrido is lyrical, satirical, lightly philosophical and somewhat reminiscent of ballet . . . but it is in no way comparable to the directness of the agitprop Acto. The Corrido wins over the audience with the use of familiar songs, aesthetically attractive costumes and acting style, and the creation of easily recognizable scenes and situations."[36] The dramatic action of the *corrido* is linked together by the Corridista, or folk singer, who, like a Brechtian narrator, provides commentary and, like a cabaret performer, adds political lyrics to the tune of well-known folk songs.

La Gran Carpa de la Familia Rasquachi ("The Big Tent of the Rasquachi Family"—1972) is Campesino's most successful *corrido.* The work *rasquachi* is used both generically (meaning "the wretched") and as a proper name: the play's hero is called Jesús Rasquachi. He is an example of the stereotype known in Mexico as the *pelado* ("the rascal," or, literally, "the peeled one"). A *carpa,* apart from being a tent, is also a form of Mexican folk theatre that was very popular in the twenties. According to Roberto J. Garza, the *carpa* was a "short, musical revue" that lasted approximately one hour and was updated every week.

Carpas were usually performed by travelling vaudeville groups.[37] Campesino's *carpa* consciously maintained that popular, folk atmosphere and thus complied with one of the major requirements for creating successful popular theater. According to Roger Copeland, el Teatro Campesino emphasized the creation of a convivial atmosphere surrounding the play:

> The evening begins with the creation of a playing pace. One by one, the jaunty, good-natured company members introduce themselves to the audience, and even solicit help in erecting a backdrop of burlap bags and potato sacks stretched between volleyball poles. I have no way of knowing whether or not the actors are really as friendly as they appear; but clearly this slowly-evolving rapport is no facile waving of peace-signs or distribution of plastic flowers, no push-button brotherhood created on cue.[38]

The play tells the life story of Jesús Rasquachi, from his crossing of the border to his pathetic death as an invalid. Jesús represents the unskilled Chicano laborer. In the thirty brief scenes that make up the play an epic picture is painted of the plight of all Mexican-American immigrant workers. Death and the devil are Jesús's main opponents; they exploit him in many different shapes. They appear as the owner of the vineyard, the landowner, the contratista, and the social worker. But Jesús himself is also considered to be partly responsible for his predicament: his ignorance, his refusal to learn English, his machismo, and his materialistic consumer habits make him an all too easy victim for capitalist exploitation.

La Gran Carpa de los Rasquachis is a pivotal play in Campesino's artistic and political development. Its first version downplayed the political elements in favor of a metaphysical solution which one critic ironically terms a "Quetzalcoatl-ex-machina."[39] The original play was filled with metaphorical characters, and Jesús Rasquachi's secular adventures almost became meaningless in relation to the omnipotence of the deities and evil forces that confronted him. As a result, the more progressive circles of the Chicano movement criticized *La Gran Carpa* and the subsequent *mitos* for their heavy concentration on metaphysical solutions for the social and economic problems that afflicted the Mexican-Americans. Ignoring these attacks, el Teatro Campesino continued to create plays full of Mexican-Indian and Catholic symbols, convinced that this was the only meaningful way to a true cultural identity of the Chicano. But under pressure from most other Chicano groups, Campesino returned to a more concrete political involvement after the mid seventies. In 1977, *La Gran Carpa* was radically updated and, this time, salvation did not come from the combined white Christ and Aztec godhead but from the United Farm Workers Union.

The ideological conflict between el Teatro Campesino and many of its former admirers came to an emotional confrontation at a Latin-American theatre festival in Mexico City in the summer of 1974. At this gathering of progressive theatre companies from the entire Latin world, Campesino performed a dramatized religious ceremony from the Chortí Indians, a tribe living in southeastern Mexico.[40] Many Latin-American troupes, most of them living and working under political and cultural repression, violently opposed Campesino's insistence that "the cause of social justice becomes tied to the cause of everything else in our universe and in the cosmos."[41] The radical Latin-American troupes rightly felt that, if one searches for the causes of social injustice in the metaphysical domain, one adopts the capitalist mystification process.

Although it can be argued, then, that el Teatro Campesino removed itself gradually from immediate political concerns, in terms of the radical popular theatre in general it continued to develop interesting forms. The *mitos* period is important because it is expressive of Campesino's concern to find symbols and references with which its nontheatre audience could identify. After all, what symbols and narratives are more popular than religious ones? Furthermore, history teaches that religion can be much more effective in moving the masses than any political dogma because it appeals to humanity's profoundest emotions: fear of death, desire to be eternally happy, and confusion about the origin of creation. *Bernabé* (1973) is a good example of how the thematic interest in religious symbolism led to the partial obliteration of political contents. In the play's preface, Luís Valdez explains that the protagonist, Bernabé, symbolized Man's lost love for Earth. He is also the "prototype of the proverbial village idiot [who symbolizes] . . . purity, truth, innocence and love."[42] These words are hardly indicative of a desire to raise the political consciousness of the oppressed Mexican-American populace. Bernabé is not a typical Chicano exploited by an Anglo boss. The only character with specific political significance is the bar owner and contratista Torres, but he plays only a minor role in the play. The dramatic focus is on Bernabé and his mystical love affair with Mother Earth.

Bernabé wastes much time and action in getting to the point. The majority of the play is taken up by the protagonist's silly dealings with his unfeeling mother and his cousin Eddy, who is convinced that Bernabé is not really crazy but only behaving strangely because at age thirty-seven he is still a virgin. The first five scenes of the play consist of Eddy's attempts to cure his cousin by coaxing him into sleeping with the local prostitute Consuelo. At the last minute, however, Bernabé escapes from her embrace, knocks over pimp-capitalist Torres in the process and rushes to his true lover, Mother Earth. He has an instinctive understanding that it is just as evil to sell the love of a woman as to sell Earth.

Scene 6 forms the true climax of the play. Here, Moon, Earth, and Sun recognize Bernabé as the pure, uncorrupted Chicano. He is the only one worthy of marrying Earth because, as the Sun explains:

> You are the first one and the last. The last descendent of a long and noble lineage of men that I knew in ancient times; and the first of the new race that Earth will

inherit for all of us. Your face is cosmic memory, Bernabé: you remind me of an entire humanity in your eyes, your skin, your blood. They also loved Earth and honored their father above everything else. [p. 55][43]

The humanity that the Sun refers to is, of course, the Aztec tribe who worshipped the sun as the primary godhead of their pantheon. To avoid any further doubt about this point, the stage directions inform us that the Sun enters to the sound of Indian flutes and "rises in the guise of Tonatiuh, the Aztec sun god" (p. 53).

Bernabé is contrasted with the corrupted Chicanos. The greatest concern of his mother is that he will be sent to a lunatic asylum and that she will then lose the potential income from his labor. His uncle is an unemployed wino who lives off the charity of his relatives. Eddy has a good heart, but he has also been corrupted by working with the arch-exploiter Torres, whose main sources of income are the sale of alcohol, women and land. In the play's vision, the corrupt behavior of Bernabé antagonists has become the norm in the present-day Chicano environment. Motivated by the Aztec philosophy that everything is solar energy, Bernabé's fusion with Mother Earth should serve as an example to the Chicano population that harmony with nature and with other human beings is necessary if they want to become a resilient people again. Lack of such harmony only leads to the exploitation of one human being by another and to internal division and destruction of nature.

Bernabé is indicative of el Teatro Campesino's gradual departure from radical popular theatre. It stands at the beginning of a development toward more complex stage designs that require more and more sophisticated sets and lighting schemes. Increasing theatrical sophistication made Campesino's performances much less suited for makeshift theatrical spaces. With the commercial success of Zoot Suit, a realistic musical play dealing with the Blue Lagoon murders and Chicano riots in Los Angeles in the forties, el Teatro Campesino ceased to be a full-fledged radical popular theatre company and became a production company.[44] It no longer performs in found theatre spaces but in established playhouses on extended runs. Although the plays it puts on still contain Mexican-American elements, they are performed before large, more conventional theatre audiences rather than farmworkers and barrio residents. In 1986, Campesino was no longer a street theatre collective; headquartered in the Teatro Campesino Playhouse in San Juan Bautista, artistic director Luís Valdez selects Mexican-American plays that he finds interesting and hires professional actors on an ad hoc basis for productions in commercial theatres of California's largest cities. Since the enormous success of Zoot Suit in L.A.'s Mark Taper Forum, which featured current Miami Vice star Edward James Olmos and which also ran, less successfully, on Broadway and was turned into a movie, Luís Valdez has produced only two more plays of his own.[45] The first, Bandido, was only performed for a short run at the opening of the new Teatro Campesino

El Teatro Campesino. The Broadway poster for *Zoot Suit*.

Playhouse.[46] Since then Valdez has divided most of his attention between writing film scripts, doing video work, completing construction of his theatre building, and producing plays by others under the Teatro Campesino label.[47] All plays produced by Campesino fit into a thematically arranged repertoire called "The Miracle, Mystery and History Cycle of San Juan Bautista."

Every year, at Christmas, Campesino has been performing religious folk operas based on ancient miracle and mystery plays. *La Pastorela* is based on the traditional shepherd plays that Franciscan missionaries brought to Mexico from Europe in the sixteenth century. And each December since 1971 Campesino has presented a stage version of *La Virgen del Tepeyac*. This play is a popular dramatization of the four miraculous visits that the Virgen de Guadalupe paid to Juan Diego, a humble Indio who had only recently been converted to Catholicism. Luís Valdez explains: "The Cycle will continue to grow in the next few years with a Passion Play as an annual Easter event . . . and our annual calavera extravaganzas on the 'Dia de los Muertos,' All Souls Day. Interspersed with the Cycle plays, we will produce a series of original dramas and comedies."[48]

El Teatro Campesino, then, sees itself in the eighties as a regional popular theatre implanted in the Central Coast region of California and developing "a body of work based on the history and heritage of Hispanic Americans."[49] At the same time, Luís Valdez wants to prove that Chicano theatre can compete with the best in the American professional theatre world. Thus *Soldier Boy,* a play about Mexican-Americans returning home from the Second World War only to fight again—this time for their human rights—featured several Mexican-American star actors known from movies and television.[50] Likewise, *Los Corridos,* a reworked version of the musical plays Campesino created in the early seventies, was presented in an expensive commercial production for San Francisco's Marines Memorial Theatre in an extended run from 16 September through 31 October 1983.[51] Valdez's big-time ambitions have become most clear with his latest play, *I Don't Have to Show You No Stinking Badges,* which opened in February 1986 at the Los Angeles Theatre Center. It is a Chicano family comedy aimed at the largest possible audience and features a cast of Chicano Hollywood extras. In a recent newspaper interview Valdez claimed, "I'm determined to make it as a professional artist. I'm going to make movies that make money. I'm going to make plays that are critical and commercial successes, just to prove to the forces that be that what goes on in San Juan Bautista must be funded."[52]

Supported by an annual grant of $300,000 from the National Endowment for the Arts and the California Arts Council, el Teatro Campesino seems to have "sold out" to bourgeois cultural standards. Gloriamalia Flores, the company's administrative director, disagrees:

> The teatro has grown older, its reputation, and the standard of aesthetics has grown—demands for quality on the part of the audience also. It gained responsibilities. It can't go back and do the same kinds of things it did in the beginning. When the teatro was young it travelled and didn't mind roughing it. But as you grow older you simply can't continue traveling. Also, the teatro was born in the grape strike, and in the beginning its sole purpose was to educate the farmworkers, performing on flatbed Fords. But a couple of years following that, talking about the farmworkers issue no longer was the entire story. That's when

the teatro went into student unions and started tackling civil rights issues. At that time it felt no longer appropriately placed in farmworkers circles and needed to find a new home. The original core of actors followed Luis and established a commune-type situation. They shared everything, and they were receiving something like sixty dollars a month in salary; five dollars extra for people with kids. It was very difficult for them to survive., But they believed in what they were doing, and they continued. Then the teatro started getting invited for tours, not only in the U.S. but in Europe as well. Gradually they started being asked at more and more legitimate playhouses, performing arts centers, etc. With this new response, new responsibilities came. You simply can't go back to what it was before.[53]

It should not be forgotten that before el Teatro Campesino no other Mexican-American company had ever been able to gain any kind of recognition in professional arts circles. Campesino's commercial success and even its penetration into Hollywood must, then, be considered a revolution of sorts and an enormous boost for Chicano cultural respectability and social dignity.

THE BREAD AND PUPPET THEATER

The Bread and Puppet Theater can be regarded as having undergone a mystical development similar to that of el Teatro Campesino, but it has never been interested in commercialization. A good twenty years after its foundation, it continues on the fringes of the established theatre world, respected but poor. The Bread and Puppet Theater occupies a somewhat awkward position among the international company of radical popular theatres. Its theoretical political foundation is rather vague; led by Peter Schumann, a sculptor and dancer, it has little patience with the spoken word, preferring instead to express its perspective on modern civilization with stark visual images in motion. Its organization, its creative processes, and its performance style, as well as its regional implantation, however, bear the distinct markings of popular theatre. Furthermore, Peter Schumann considers Bread and Puppet's work to be strongly political:

> In a year we do dozens of different shows and the majority of them are politically natured. Most of what we do is performed outside; a much smaller part of our repertoire goes inside. In what way are we a political theatre? Well, there are two aspects of political theatre; one is to work on political themes, and the other is to get in a political way to the audience, which could mean different things. It could mean that you support the existing political movement or that you confront the general status quo, or stupidity, or whatever you want to call it, of a general, normal audience.[54]

Peter Schumann, Bread and Puppet's founder and artistic director, declares that he was not familiar enough with the works of thinkers like Gramsci and

Marcuse to be seriously influenced by them, but through the twenty years of his theatre's existence he has always considered it to be in opposition to the capitalist hegemony that rules the United States. "We don't like it," says Schumann, "and we don't want to be dependent on it. It's impossible to avoid the thought that Mr. Reagan supports you when you play a show against his policies in Nicaragua and do it on the basis of a grant that comes from Washington."[55] In this respect, the Bread and Puppet Theater is considerably more consistent in its political focus than allegedly more radical companies such as the San Francisco Mime Troupe. True to its principles, Bread and Puppet prefers to be poor and independent rather than selling its art as a commercial product to Broadway entrepreneurs or accepting government support.

Throughout its colorful career, the Bread and Puppet Theater has always maintained a strong political commitment that carried over into its art. In the early sixties it started out performing social protest plays in the slums of New York City—plays directed at bad housing, rats, and high rents. In August 1964, when President Johnson ordered the bombing of Vietnam, the Bread and Puppet Theater started its lifelong struggle against mass killings of innocent people in the name of patriotism and imperialism. From then on its masks, puppets, and street plays became part of every major anti-Vietnam demonstration in the eastern United States.

Fire was Bread and Puppet's first major production that was conceived for performance indoors. It is a solemn theatrical ceremony for the Vietnam dead and is dedicated specifically to three Americans who burnt themselves to death in protest of America's crimes in Vietnam.[56]

Bread and Puppet took *Fire* to Europe in 1968 and have returned there almost every year since then. These European tours and the indoor performances in the northeastern United States (mainly at colleges, community centers, and churches) form the troupe's main source of income. When in the United States, the troupe travels in a colorfully painted old schoolbus, which makes the company members more than just a touch reminiscent of wandering medieval puppeteers. Tour revenues fund the other, nowadays mainly regional, activities of Bread and Puppet. In 1970, after the troupe returned from Europe, it found itself expelled from its rehearsal space in New York City and decided to move to Plainfield, Vermont, where it had been invited to become "theatre-in-residence" at Goddard College. While at the college, the company developed a piece called *Stations of the Cross*, a serene piece created for concentrated, indoor performances to accompany the Easter period.[57] The Bread and Puppet Theater remained in Plainfield until 1974, when several company members decided to go their own way and Peter Schumann moved with his wife and children to nearby Glover. In 1986, the theatre was still headquartered on the Schumann farm there.

The troupe's move from New York City to Vermont also meant exchanging one of America's most sophisticated and politicized audiences for a very con-

servative, rural public. Consequently, Bread and Puppet found itself forced to
tone down its radical political messages:

> In New York we were really . . . more politically involved than we were up here.
> When we moved to Vermont, and we came into village parades with our anti-war
> ideas, and were telling them what we think about Cambodia or Laos or what have
> you, we made a lot of enemies there, very fast. And it changed our ideas about
> how to get to people a little bit . . . it didn't make too much sense to push a
> political point too much.[58]

Initially, the troupe had to fight against a negative reputation ("Commies,"
"subversives") that had preceded them from New York. Gradually, however, the
puppeteers became aware that their political effectiveness was contingent on
their popularity in the region. By responding favorably to invitations to enliven
all kinds of public festivities with their larger than life puppets and stilted
dancers, the Bread and Puppet Theater has by now become an ineffaceable
element of Vermont life. No Vermont community celebration or public parade is
complete without Bread and Puppet's participation. Vermonters are particularly
fond of the annual Bread and Puppet Domestic Resurrection Circus, a theatrical
event lasting two days in late summer and attracting thousands of New England
residents to the Schumann's farm.

Peter Schumann explains the rationale for the creation of Our Domestic
Resurrection Circus:

> When we moved from New York City to Vermont in 1970, it became necessary to
> see and learn and listen in a new way, to invent animals and to understand how to
> move in a landscape in order to become part of it. We thought that we could
> produce a cyclic event that would be representative of life in general and of our
> distinct political environment in particular. We called this event Our Domestic
> Resurrection Circus and have performed it almost every year since then.[59]

In the Domestic Resurrection Circus project, Bread and Puppet reveals itself to
be a truly regional popular theatre enterprise. Puppetry and circuses are arguably
two of the most resilient forms of traditional folk culture, and both form essential
components of Bread and Puppet's art. It uses these forms to convey its political
commitment in accessible theatrical forms to nontheatre audiences. Peter Schumann explicitly insists that "the best audience is the audience which never goes
to the theatre."[60] The Bread and Puppet Theater searches for its audience in
streets, churches, and community centers, and, once a year, lures the masses to
its show by presenting it as a circus. To many, the circus still represents the
epitome of popular entertainment: a fast-paced show packed in glitter and filled
with exotic animals and artists from countries where the average spectator has
never been. It shows the awed spectator challenges to the limits of mortality in

daredevil stunts relieved by slapstick humor and the elegance of a bareback rider. This variety show is punctuated by the catchy and sometimes dramatic music of a group of musicians that can best be characterized as a mixture of a marching band and a Dixieland group. All these elements are delightfully represented in Bread and Puppet's weekend-long circus—an immense, larger-than-life parody of the real thing, complete with forty-foot dragons, camels with human humps, clumsy clowns, tamed horses, and obnoxious ringmasters.

The Domestic Resurrection Circus emphasizes *Domestic Resurrection* as much as the *Circus*. The event has the chaotic but friendly atmosphere of a medieval country fair with side shows, music, and drama going on simultaneously in different locations of the vast, gorgeous setting of meadows and forests that form the natural backdrop for the circus. People walk from show to show and are encouraged to bring their own picnics. All day long Peter Schumann provides the spectator with his homemade rye bread baked in an outdoor oven that he constructed himself. Bread and Puppet's explanation of its generosity is reminiscent of Jean Vilar's ideas: "We sometimes give you a piece of bread along with the puppet show because our bread and theatre belong together. For a long time, the theatre arts have been separated from the stomach. Theatre as entertainment was meant for the skin. Bread was meant for the stomach. Theatre is more like bread, more like a necessity."[61]

The Bread and Puppet Theater does not concern itself simply with providing free entertainment, aesthetic beauty, and wholesome bread. One of its chief occupations is its fight against the end of the world. From 1980 through 1983, the Domestic Resurrection Circus treated the possibility of atomic warfare as its main theme. To counteract the destructive tendencies of the modern world and its power-hungry leaders, Schumann proposed the resurrection of our domestic values. The only way to make people aware of the disastrous course on which our elected and appointed politicians have embarked is to show unambiguously that nuclear war will irrevocably wipe out all those little things in life that we love so dearly. Peter Schumann is a master in evoking the rich but delicate beauty of the simple things in life with the cheapest of materials: a cardboard cow grazes while ten little white clouds, held by puppeteers dressed in white, float gently overhead. Such peaceful scenes are often cruelly destroyed by some black, evil force, as when a small white dove is mercilessly devoured by a ten-foot vulture or thirteen baby boys are torn from their desperate mothers by huge armored soldiers and killed in a bloody ritual by a gigantic, ugly King Herod. Of course, Bread and Puppet's animated images could be interpreted as yet another version of the eternal battle between good and evil, but there are clear implications that its shows refer to something more specific than simply a symbolic conflict: if we want to save our domestic values for future generations, then we had better get serious about stopping the madmen who are ordering the construction of ever larger and more destructive arsenals of nuclear weapons.

From 1984 onwards, the Bread and Puppet Theater has turned its attention to

The Bread and Puppet Theater. To the accompaniment of live percussion, an arm beckons to a group of Central American women in *The Door* (1985).

Central America. The company created an indoor show called *The Door,* with which it toured the college circuit. This play, animated by life-size dolls and oversize, two-dimensional cardboard villains, tells the story of the massacre of Guatemalan and Salvadorian Indians and the plight of refugees trying to escape through a diabolically opening and closing door to the North. *The Door* also exposes, in no uncertain terms, the responsibility of American big capital for these atrocities.

Bread and Puppet also dedicated the 1984 and 1985 Resurrection Circuses to Central America, and in January 1985 the company went on tour in Nicaragua. Several puppeteers workshopped and produced *The Nativity, Crucifixion, and Resurrection of Archbishop Oscar Romero of El Salvador* with thirty-five Nicaraguan volunteers. The play, which was taken to all the major cities of the country, is an homage to the archbishop of San Salvador, who was murdered by the military in 1982. The Romero pageant also is an attempt to fuse theatre and liberation theology into a kind of theatre of liberation. The central scene of the piece is Romero's resurrection, in which the prelate puts down the Bible he was reading, which was obstructing his view of the surrounding misery.

Myths and legends (other than Indian) are largely absent in the United States, and therefore the Bread and Puppet Theater often employs biblical themes and characters to provide its nontheatre audience with the necessary popular cultural points of reference. Every child born in the Western world can be expected to be familiar with the major biblical stories and their protagonists. Schumann refers to these traditional stories, not to convert his audience into devout Christians, but to show that man's cruelty toward man still persists today and has, in fact, brought us closer than ever to the brink of total annihilation.

Together with the Bible and the circus, puppetry constitutes the troupe's main link with folk tradition. Puppet theatre has been around for a long time, and its portability makes it extremely suitable for performance in the streets by traveling companies. Throughout the ages, puppetry has made a simple and fundamental type of theatre that is naturally close to the people. From its beginnings in the Middle Ages, puppet theatre has always responded to political issues with improvised satires. Peter Schumann claims that he has been influenced much less by the theories of Marxist thinkers than by the various forms of puppet theatres that are "traditionally more radical than those sixties radicals, because they did protest as a tradition in society."[62]

To go in search of a theatrically unsophisticated audience is nothing new for the puppeteer, and the Bread and Puppet Theater considers itself to be in direct lineage with the colorful political jokesters of Punch and Judy shows and European puppetry in general. Like them, Bread and Puppet tries to respond with accessible art to the pressing issues of the time. The occasion may be of regional interest—like the construction of a huge powerline coming from Canada that was to have a disastrous effect on Vermont ecology—or of national or international interest: "So when something happens in Central America or on the television with one of Mr. Reagan's foul speeches or anything like this, then the opportunity and the necessity arises to respond to that. Or if branches of the peace movement call us and ask for our participation."[63] Thus Bread and Puppet made its presence very conspicuous in the March for Nuclear Disarmament in New York City on 12 June 1982 (with a thousand volunteers who helped carry the huge puppets) or in London to help prevent the U.S. deployment of cruise and Pershing missiles in Western Europe.[64] And the 1986 Resurrection Circus had "The Hunger of the Hungry and the Hunger of the Overfed" as its main theme, while *The Daily News Nativity,* the company's Christmas play for 1985, fused the traditional Bethlehem story with the plight of the urban homeless and the slaughter of thousands and thousands of innocent recent war victims.

Large puppets with grotesque faces figure prominently in Bread and Puppet's parades and indoor shows. Their creation is inspired by the inflated, caricatural heads of notables that dominate carnival floats in Germany and the Low Countries. Particularly the villains of the Bread and Puppet shows fall into this category: King Herod and Uncle Fatso, the arch-capitalist/exploiter. The giant puppets with their ugly features allow us to take a fresh look at previously familiar faces. Furthermore, one need not be steeped in literature or the formal developments of theatre art to become enchanted by the large, sketchy images evoked by the enormous masks and fifteen-foot puppets in motion: theirs is a crude, primordial effectiveness unmarred by corrupted cliché-ridden language.

The Bread and Puppet Theater. The original papier-mâché mask for Uncle Fatso
in the Bread and Puppet Museum.

The Bread and Puppet Theater. *Washerwoman's Nativity* (1983).
The curtain before the opening.

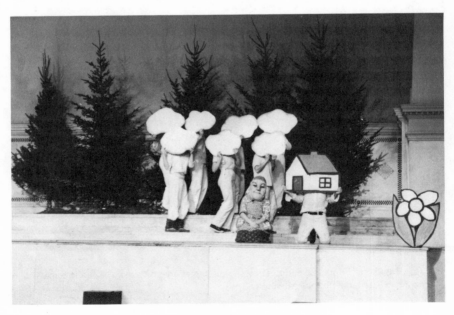

A washerwoman sits peacefully in front of her house.

Washerwomen chattering away.

An evil bird takes away the domestic bliss of a washerwoman.

The pieces created by the Bread and Puppet Theater are collective variations on original conceptions by Peter Schumann. They seldom contain extended dialogues or predetermined, beautiful speeches. Bread and Puppet conveys meaning beyond the contaminated channels of verbal communications. The choreographed motions of the puppets speak to their audience in a semantics of images that are punctuated by a large variety of mainly percussion and wind instruments (the most primitive of musical instruments). "Our everyday language is silly and does not tell the truth," Schumann declares. Did he then lose faith in the power of words? "To some degree, yes! But mainly it's my private gear. I'm a picture maker. In a picture you grasp something in a different way than in words. In a picture you grasp an idea in one instantaneous image. With words you grasp it through logic, through reason, and it's just a different process in the mind."[65]

The emphasis on nonverbal sight and sound explains why the Bread and Puppet Theater is so well suited for street performances. Conventional theatre based on dialogue is unfit to halt passersby. Disturbed by bothersome street noises, people usually have little patience to hang around and decipher speeches they can only half hear. Heavy drums and blaring trumpets that announce the arrival of a towering Uncle Sam on stilts or giant puppets dressed in bright colors, however, much more effectively attract the attention of the masses in the street.

The activities of Bread and Puppet comprise the loud, hilarious, and easygoing, easily accessible outdoor shows and the indoor performances derived from the outdoor extravaganzas, but made compact and fully utilizing the potential of electric lighting, the concentration of limited space, and the silences that are possible in a large, enclosed auditorium. Yet, even the more concentrated indoor shows are preceded by colorful puppeteers on stilts halting the traffic in front of the playhouse and by a cheerful Dixieland band playing in the street, trying to attract spectators who had not originally planned on going to the theatre. A festive and relaxed atmosphere surrounds the relative intensity of the indoor performance. Entrance charges are minimal, never obligatory and are called "contributions."

All Bread and Puppet shows rely to a large extent on the assistance of local volunteers, thus establishing an organic link with the population of the neighborhood or region where the troupe performs. In the December 1984 production of the *Washerwoman's Nativity* at the Judson Memorial Church in New York City, for example, only six professional puppeteers formed the nucleus of a company of fifty. The majority participation by nonprofessionals adds a quality of amateurism and impermanence to Bread and Puppet's art. The troupe does not strive for perfection. The audience feels close to the performance because the majority of the company has no extraordinary skills and yet, together, creates something of undeniable beauty. Consequently, there is nothing of the distance one experiences when watching the streamlined performances of Broadway. The awe for Schumann's sculptures remains, but their beauty is made more human by the delightful, imperfect movements of the amateur company that sets the masks and puppets in motion. It is extremely hard to form an idea of what Bread and Puppet's repertoire consists of if one has never actually attended a show. Since the pieces themselves are not plays in the conventional sense but virtually textless collages of images brought to life through choreographed movements, they are not reproduceable in print. Over the years only some newspapers and even fewer theatre magazines have published extracts and eyewitness descriptions of particular productions.[66]

Apart from a few scattered mimeographed stage directions and sketchy scenarios, no other materials are available to form an objective view of past creations. Luckily, the Bread and Puppet Theater likes to travel and Peter Schumann's energy seems to show no indication of waning, so chances of tasting a slice of the sourdough rye bread and experiencing one of their future puppet shows are good. It is an adventure not to be missed. The force of Bread and Puppet's art as well as Schumann's personal vitality and purity stand out as a shining example for theatre practitioners throughout the world.

In this chapter I have concentrated my discussion predominantly on the work of the San Francisco Mime Troupe, el Teatro Campesino, and the Bread and Puppet Theater. That does not mean that there are (and have been) no other activities in the American radical popular theatre. There are numerous radical companies in New York, Boston, Chicago, and throughout California. From an international viewpoint, however, the Mime Troupe, Campesino, and Bread and Puppet have proven to be most important in terms of cross-fertilization, visibility, and productivity.

CHAPTER 5

RADICAL POPULAR THEATRE IN REGIONAL FRANCE

At the beginning of the preceding chapter, I hinted at the importance of the three major U.S. radical troupes for the development of alternative theatre in Western Europe. Within the United States, Ron Davis and the San Francisco Mime Troupe were, undoubtedly, the leaders. But el Teatro Campesino and the Bread and Puppet Theater must be credited with the first exportation of the American brand of radical popular theatre. Since the spring of 1968, both troupes have made numerous appearances in Europe; the San Francisco Mime troupe did not go to Europe until the summer of 1977, although, in all fairness, it should be mentioned that a considerable reputation preceded them.

The Bread and Puppet Theater went on its first European tour in the hot spring of 1968. They had gone primarily to perform their powerful anti-Vietnam piece *Fire* at the Nancy World festival of Young Theatre, but afterwards they also played in "streets, factories, schoolyards, plazas, housing projects, community centers, theatres, universities, art galleries in and about London, Paris, Amsterdam, Utrecht, and finally Berlin."[1] All the large European cities were in uproar and it was with a clear political intention that Bread and Puppet decided to perform its provocative play in well-known seats of radical ferment. The troupe wanted to be actively involved in the massive wave of contestation. Bread and Puppet played in the barricaded streets of Paris during the eventful May demonstrations and, later that spring, performed *Fire* on the night that students took over the Free University in Berlin. Finally, Bread and Puppet did a short antiwar play in front of the U.S. Army PX in West Berlin. El Teatro Campesino paid its first visit to Europe in the spring of 1969, when the most violent protests had subsided but radical feelings were still strong. They also performed at the Nancy Festival and, as Françoise Kourilsky suggested, made an enormous impact there with their *actos,* "which are going to be the very model for a radical agitational theatre."[2] Campesino's art, then, represented not merely the plight of some faraway ethnic minority; it struck a responsive note because it succinctly expressed in effective popular terms the struggle of oppressed people all over the world.

Both el Teatro Campesino and the Bread and Puppet Theater showed European radicals how—building on a traditional popular-culture patrimony—a simple, but not simplistic countertheatre could be created with a minimum of financial resources. In the late sixties, these American troupes presented an advanced and sophisticated style of radical popular theatre to young and enthusiastic European theatre artists searching for effective ways to use their artistic talents for political action.

Along with the radical intellectuals, young artists had become aware—in the light of revolutionary developments in the streets—that politics and art could no longer be kept in separate compartments. As Jean-Jacques Lebel, who organized the Odéon occupation, later testified, "The May uprising was theatrical in that it was a gigantic fiesta, a revelatory and sensuous explosion outside the 'normal' pattern of politics."[3] There were many impromptu street theatre performances during the mass demonstrations. Groups of young actors went to occupied factories with political skits or adaptations of Brecht's plays. And there was a great sense among newly committed theatre people of the necessity to oppose the established cultural machine. They saw the bourgeois theatre as the bastion of hegemonistic culture that suppressed equally valid forms of popular art.

Writing in 1969, Jean Jacques Lebel stated that several groups of students and actors were interested in making radical political theatre:

> Nobody had actually seen any "guerilla theatre" though. Some were familiar with the Living Theatre but criticized it as too "arty" or "not directly political enough" or "non-violent" (the company was admired more as an anarchist community than as a theatre group). Actually no one had a definite idea of how or where to start and it took some time to work up the idea of theatrical cartoons on the subject of imperialism.[4]

In the wake of the massive politicization, a necessity for satire and stark theatrical images was created, and it did not take long before newly formed French radical popular theatre companies started responding.

Several energetic young actors and playwrights, shocked into activism by the 1968 rebellion, decided to return to their native territory with the determination to create political theatre dealing with the specific socioeconomic and cultural issues that affected its population. They felt that the work force and the natural resources of their region were being unscrupulously exploited by the central government and local entrepreneurs. To expose these abuses, the repatriated theatre artists started creating their own satirical plays. Two regional companies in whose works this satirical tendency is particularly evident are le Théâtre Populaire de Lorraine and lo Teatre de la Carriera.

Le Théâtre Populaire de Lorraine

Jacques Kraemer, founder and main playwright of le Théâtre Populaire de Lorraine, or TPL as it is commonly referred to, is an obvious inheritor of the artistic revolutions propelled by the events of 1968. As an aspiring young actor at the *Centre d'Art Dramatique* in Paris, he had idolized the glamorous star actor Gérard Philipe. At the beginning of the sixties, however, Kraemer discovered the productions of Jean Vilar's Théâtre National Populaire and became impressed with Roger Planchon's renderings of Bertolt Brecht's works. With idealistic dreams about reaching out to the working-class masses, Jacques Kraemer impulsively broke off his studies in 1963 and returned to his native Metz. There, together with other ex-students of the drama academies in Paris and Metz, he founded the workers' cooperative TPL. Six months after its foundation, on 28 September, TPL premiered its first show before eight hundred spectators: Arthur Adamov's *Paolo Paoli*. From the very beginning of its activities, TPL met with stern opposition from local authorities. Despite severe financial problems, TPL pursued its objective of performing classical and contemporary plays in Lorraine's cities and villages.

The events of May and June 1968 erupted while TPL was touring with Corneille's *Le Menteur*. When word reached the troupe of the Parisian uprising, the actors immediately formed a strike committee and, based on the events in Paris, created two impromptu skits that they went to perform in occupied factories. This was TPL's first great encounter with a massive workers' audience.

Under the influence of the 1968 disturbances, TPL's repertoire underwent a radical change. The classics were stored away, and TPL resolved henceforth to create original satirical plays that dealt specifically with the cultural and economic problems besetting the Lorraine region. Jacques Kraemer explains how TPL conceived its first original play:

> Together with René Gaudy we got the idea to do a satirical-poetic play on the problem of iron mining and the steel industry. We made a pun with the name *Minette*, which refers to iron mining but is also a proper name that is close to Jeannette, the nickname of Joan of Arc, Jeannette the good woman of Lorraine. Thus, Minette transformed into a young girl became the heroine of *Splendeur et misère de Minette, la bonne Lorraine*.[5]

Splendeur et misère de Minette, la bonne Lorraine ("Splendor and Misery of Minette, the Girl from Lorraine") is in many ways paradigmatic for the plays TPL created in its early radical popular period. Although Jacques Kraemer considers pure collective playwriting to be impossible, he does acknowledge the indispensability of close collaboration between the target audience (in *Minette's* case the Lorraine miners) and the artists. More than any other art form, the contemporary radical popular theatre is firmly rooted in the socioeconomic soil of its time. TPL selects a topic for a play because there is a political or an emotional demand for it. In the case of *Minette* and many subsequent productions, the groundwork consisted of gathering and carefully studying all available documentation on the subject in question. Concurrently, interviews were conducted with appropriate groups of the population. While *Minette* was being developed in a workshop context, short impromptu *spectacles d'intervention* were performed throughout the region. These often improvised, agitprop playlets, were designed to establish a close contact between actors and unsophisticated spectators who had little or no prior experiences with theatre. Further objectives of the *spectacles d'intervention* were the advertisement of the upcoming full-length play on the same topic and the gathering of important feedback from the target audience. The success of *Splendeur et misère de Minette* was overwhelming. It was the first and only time in TPL's history that the auditorium was filled with 90 percent workers. Charles Tordjman, TPL's current artistic director, asserts that *Minette* was written without a specific theoretical basis:

> I don't think that Mao, Gramsci, and Marcuse had anything to do with it. *Minette* was spontaneously created, although influenced by ideas that were in the air. And, of course, the play's ambition was to deconstruct the mechanisms of capitalism. There was, then, a transposition of sorts of Marxist theory. Althusser and Brecht are more likely to have influenced the creative process—because *Minette* was somewhat based on the idea of Brecht's *Aufhaltsame Aufstieg des Arturo Ui*.[6]

With *Minette,* TPL expressed its serious commitment to serve the working class with its art. In retrospect, Charles Tordjman believes that in that early period of original creations TPL was operating very much in the tradition of the Russian agitprop theatre groups around Mayakovsky that were active some ten years after the revolution. Nevertheless *Minette* can hardly be accused of excessive simplicity. On the contrary, it contains subtle satire couched in poetical and visual theatrical sophistication.

Splendeur et misère de Minette, la bonne Lorraine is divided into two parts. The first half deals with the *splendeur* period of iron-ore mining in Lorraine and ranges from the discovery of iron in the late nineteenth century to the unfounded optimism of the 1950s that the region would become *le Texas français*. The second part of the play deals with Lorraine's *misère*, which was the result of the growing exploitation of the region's work force, the ensuing labor unrest, and the ultimate dissolution of Lorraine's steel industry in favor of the exploitation of more profitable foreign ore. The rise and fall of Lorraine's economic fortune is effectively satirized in a low burlesque dramatic allegory that is obviously inspired by Brecht's *Arturo Ui*. Like this play, *Minette* uses the framework of a gangster story set in a Chicago-like underworld to describe the history of Lorraine's exploitation. Low burlesque satire consists of describing the object of attack in terms of animals or human beings of a vulgar social status, with the obvious intention of deflating the magnified image that the satiric victims have created for themselves. Thus, in *Minette*, the capitalist entrepreneurs who own the iron mines and steel factories are represented as greedy and ruthless pimps operating brothels that feature Minette as their chief attraction. A pimp is, of course, the symbol of criminal exploitation par excellence, and the presentation of Minette as a prostitute is particularly appropriate because of the horizontal position in which both whore and miner make their living.[7]

The essence of *Minette's* low burlesque satire is not only to expose the true nature of the capitalists dominating the Lorraine economy (i.e., ruthless exploiters of the population, which is forced to submit because "il faut bien subir pour ne pas mourir de faim" ["there is no choice but to submit if one doesn't want to starve to death"], p. 43), its essence is also to ridicule them. Clownish acting highlights the exaggerated possessiveness of the often infantile bosses, resulting in their exposure as insignificant, weak, and derisible men. This deflating presentation has the additional militant objective of decreasing the audience's awe for their "superiors," inviting them to take action against them.

The prostitution metaphor for the activities of the ruthlessly exploitative capitalists is not only restricted to the Lorraine region. The Parisian central government, with which Lorraine's entrepreneurs are corruptly linked, is described in similar terms. The president of the Republic is satirically presented as a gangster boss called "le Corse" or "the Corsican," who controls, instead of the French House of Representatives, the Parisian prostitution center, Pigalle.

Although the dominant satirical method of *Minette* is low burlesque, high burlesque is also used. High burlesque typically presents the satirical victim in exaggerated, inflated terms—that is, as a stronger or more benevolent human being than he or she really is. Thus the chief villain of the play, Monsieur Joseph, the owner of several *maisons* in the Lorraine Valley and the theatrical incarnation of the president of the de Wendel Steel Corporation, is presented as the greatest humanitarian the region has ever known. His inflated picture is shown through excerpts from *Vallée-Magazine*, a satirized version of *Lorraine-Magazine*, a monthly publication financed and edited by the management of the steel industry and an obvious indoctrination tool. The publication, which is distributed free to the homes of the workers, presents Monsieur Joseph as a humane and generous being who has only the benefit of the region in mind. Two of the headlines, displayed on large, Brechtian signs, read: "Thanks to his insistent initiatives, Monsieur Joseph will virtuously support many families" and "The virtuous Monsieur Joseph, always selfless, sacrifices his free time for the development of our valley" (p. 22, p. 37).[8] The function of this high burlesque satire is twofold: it serves as an effective attack on *Lorraine-Magazine's* reprehensible manipulation of its readers, and it mocks Monsieur Joseph and all that he represents, for in the scenes following the excerpt he is shown to be a ruthless crook. The low burlesque of the dramatized scene results, therefore, in a deflation of the high burlesque of the newspaper excerpt.

Preceding the *Vallée-Magazine* excerpts at the beginning of each scene, headlines from *Spécial-Scandale,* a Lorraine version of the *National Enquirer,* appear. These give a running commentary that continues throughout the entire play. The *Scandale* headlines focus on Monsieur Joseph's dealings with Minette as a sensational, jet-set love affair with Cinderella overtones: "Shocking! An idyll develops between Joe and a poor young girl: Oh yes! Princes still marry shepherdesses" (p. 13).[9] *Spécial-Scandale* is, then, also justly satirized for throwing dust in the eyes of the workers by presenting the heinous behavior of the industrialists in a glamorous light.

Splendeur et misère de Minette, la bonne Lorraine maintains three different fictional levels in order to satirize the true workings of the socioeconomic mechanisms of everyday reality. All three levels are sufficiently exaggerated to make the irony perceptible. Furthermore, the play has several built-in safety devices that effectively prevent any interpretation of the play merely as a dramatized gangster story. First of all, the newspaper excerpts are clearly separated from the dramatic action: they are presented as projections or large signs in the fashion of Brechtian *Verfremdungseffekte*. Secondly, the acting style, as the stage directions indicate, must be consciously clownish to preclude any possibility of mistaking fiction for reality.[10]

Jacques Kraemer and company are too well versed in Brechtian aesthetics not to want to point to their plays as self-conscious artifacts. In addition, the set design also "undermines" the theatrical illusion and emphasizes the intended frame of reference: "In M'sieur Joseph's castle, a bar and stools are structured like the supports in mine pits. . . . " And "an easy chair evokes association with the two main types of machinery that can be found in iron mines" (p. 17, p. 22).[11]

Lastly, direct textual references are made to the techniques of iron mining and processing. Thus, when in the beginning of the play Minette shows herself to be uncooperative and unwilling to prostitute herself, she is submitted to a series of treatments that are similar in name and method to the enrichment procedures applied to Lorraine iron ore in order to eliminate its phosphorus content and to enable its profitable exploitation.[12]

Minette, thus not only reveals the true workings of capitalist exploitation in a historical perspective, it also attacks the popular cultural phenomena—like the gossip press—that help perpetuate it. At the same time, the format of the gangster story is helpful in providing an accessible cultural framework for TPL's nontheatre audience. And although music is not inherent to TPL's theatrical temperament, the company recognizes the appeal that songs have to unsophisticated theatre audiences. *Minette* contains a few songs that comment on the action, like "La Chanson de Minette" and "l'Hymne des Mineurs."

Two other shows following *Minette* are also inspired directly by TPL's implantation in the Lorraine region. *Les Immigrés* (1972) deals with the oppression and exploitation of immigrant workers from Italy, Spain, and North Africa.[13] This dramatic satire also contains parodies of popular cultural forms: it employs the format of the exotic Hollywood adventure movie and the animated cartoon.

The satirical object of *Les Immigrés* is the racist, bourgeois attitude toward immigrant workers. The play mercilessly satirizes the hypocritical morality of middle-class people in seventeen scenes. It appeals to the working classes for solidarity with the oppressed foreign laborers. Like *Minette, Les Immigrés* adopts a historical perspective, linking the present predicament of the immigrant workers with the bestial treatment of the African slaves in the sixteenth and seventeenth centuries. Both were lured away from their native lands with false promises. Likewise, both the actions of the slave traders and their twentieth-century successors were condoned by Christian middle-class morality. Thus, in the scene entitled "Traffic et Crucifix," we see a religious French colonialist bless the departure of a group of slaves whom he has "reluctantly" sold to a "humane" slave trader who, in turn, promises them a comfortable voyage and good treatment.[14]

The essence of the satiric method is the transposition of a recognizable reality into a distorted, often fantastic fiction undercut by irony for the purpose of criticism. *Les Immigrés* contains one dominant grotesque species called Anthropomorphs, which are defined as "hybrid creatures, neither men nor beasts [yet human], who have been discovered in a faraway country" (p. 9).[15] These "Morphs" obviously represent the immigrant workers. This time, their bestial appearance should not be interpreted as low burlesque satire: it reflects the inhuman way in which they are abused by the citizens of the so-called civilized industrial societies.

The first five scenes of *Les Immigrés* constitute a chronicle depicting the historical discovery of the Morphs in the virgin forests of some exotic country, their "comfortable" voyage and their arrival in an industrialized nation closely resembling France. As the introduction to the play explains, the importance of the immigrant workers in France is enormous. Four million foreign workers earn the lowest wages, hold the dirtiest jobs, and live under the worst possible conditions.[16]

Although the primary objective of this dramatic satire seems to be, then, to create more tolerance among the Lorraine population for the immigrant workers, the play's topic applies to the whole of France and to those northern European countries where foreign laborers form a sizeable portion of the working force.

Les Immigrés consists of a collage of artistically stylized, stereotypical examples of narrow-minded, bourgeois attitudes toward immigrant workers. The satiric method used in this play is not high or low burlesque but, rather, satiric irony. Unlike the characters in *Minette,* those of *Les Immigrés* are not fictionally transposed. But their words are presented with a clearly recognizable ironic twist. In scene 11, for example, two landlords talk about the great advantages of renting living quarters to Anthropomorphs:

> LANDLORD I: Tell me, you who know them well, they don't make too much of a mess, do they? 'Cause I'm proud of my villa, you know.
> LANDLORD II: Oh, not at all, you know, you hear so many bad things about them, but in reality, they are really very calm. Moreover, when they get home they can only think of sleeping. They lie down on their straw mattresses and sleep . . .
> LANDLORD I: And how do they keep warm?
> LANDLORD II: Animal heat. [p. 67][17]

Les Immigrés has no sustained story line. Although the invisible, nonindividualized Anthropomorphs form the subject of every dramatized dialogue, no character appears in more than one scene. Thus, *Les Immigrés* essentially remains a collage of cabaret sketches, held together by the Morphs as recurrent objects of abuse; the play never quite develops into a full-fledged play. Furthermore, *Les Immigrés* suffers from the fact that its satiric victim is an entire social class, which can only be attacked in a general manner. In an attempt to achieve a comprehensive satiric vision, Kraemer was forced to aim too quickly at too many targets at the same time. Consequently, his satire of the discrimination against immigrant workers lacks sharpness. Jacques Kraemer is a much more effective satirist when he clings with indignation to one limited topic.

All this time, TPL's existence had not been without problems. There was no question about the company's popularity, but in the 1970–71 season the little subsidy allotted it was cut by the municipality of Metz. Thus forced into exile by the cultural and political establishment, TPL relocated to Villerupt where, on an even smaller budget than before, it managed to produce three minuscule shows with two actors, Jacques Kraemer and René Loyon. Despite the popular success of TPL's performances, France's Ministry of Culture continued to refuse to normally subsidize the company, and at the beginning of 1972 it was faced with imminent bankruptcy.

The members of TPL creatively reacted to their impending downfall with *La Liquidation de Monsieur Joseph K. (1971),* a play about the disappearance of small businesses and, by extension, TPL's own liquidation. Just as the small neighborhood grocer Joseph K. is forced out of business by the superstore

"Gobkoloss," TPL was forced to stop its activities by a political system that fears any cultural expressions that undermine the status quo. TPL elected to use Joseph K. as the play's hero because through Franz Kafka's novels he has become the symbol of the little man crushed by an absurd and all-pervading system. The literary references to Kafka's work are not meant as intellectual injections but as a general criticism of the absurdist genre. As the program booklet indicates, "One can interpret it as a criticism of the metaphysical theatre, of the theatre of the absurd. In the stage directions one will find the indispensable prop for these kinds of plays: the garbage can."[18] In this respect, TPL expresses itself to be in line with the general Marxist rejection of absurdism as a metaphysical justification for man's misery.

La Liquidation de Monsieur Joseph K. is typical of the creative strategy at TPL at the height of its popular implantation. It never has engaged in pure collective creation; Jacques Kraemer clearly stood out as the artistic leader and chief playwright who created the basic text of the plays. His texts were criticized by actors and director, and propositions for alterations were incorporated in subsequent versions. Likewise, there was only indirect audience participation in the creative process. However, it must be stressed that all forms of direct and indirect collaboration with the target audience are indispensable for an effective popular theatre production. In the case of *Joseph K.*, TPL's actors performed scenes for union gatherings and solicited explicit comments and suggestions from its audience. Neighborhood grocers were also invited to a dramatic reading of the play, and the spectators informed TPL about aspects it had not considered: sales taxes, retirement, social security, and the fact that many grocers are also small employers. All this information was incorporated in later versions.

La Liquidation de Monsieur Joseph K. consists of thirty-one brief tableaux that dramatically present different aspects of his daily exploits as a grocer, his increasing financial problems, and his ending up as an employee at "Gobkoloss." Although the pervading atmosphere is absurdist and Joseph K. seems to fight a battle that cannot be won, the play does not comment on the absurdity of existence but on the absurdity of the capitalist system. Consequently, Joseph K. is more reminiscent of the Charlie Chaplin of *Modern Times* than of the original hero of *The Trial*.

The popular cultural references of *Joseph K.* mostly lie in cabaret, silent movies, and popular song. It is no coincidence that most of TPL's protagonists are passive, Charlie Chaplin-type characters who are subjected to long series of systematic abuses. Charlie Chaplin is a recognizable exponent of popular culture. He was also one of Brecht's favorite actors. TPL rationalizes Joseph K.'s character structure also in purely Brechtian terms:

> Instead of having to follow in relative intellectual comfort the consciousness-raising of the hero, the spectator finds himself forced to remain at a distance with respect to the nonevolution of the character. . . . This form finds application in

some of Brecht's greatest works. . . . It aims at creating a new consciousness in the spectator. *La Liquidation* tries to pursue a similar objective. The play shows a blind and mystified consciousness—a man still incapable of reaching the understanding of political causality and the necessity of a collective strategy. [p. 80][19]

Joseph K. does not learn anything from his accumulated sufferings. Like Charlie Chaplin he presents himself in such a way that the audience sees his blindness and his performance. In this respect TPL bases itself on the idea of Roland Barthes that to watch someone not seeing is the best way of intensely seeing what he does not see.[20]

The songs in *La Liquidation de Monsieur Joseph K.*, as in most other TPL creations, have a definite Brechtian flavor. They either serve a narrative function or put Joseph K.'s predicament in a larger political context. Obviously, in performing the songs the actor playing Joseph K. steps out of his role and comments on his character with complete political lucidity:

> Little Song by Joseph K. on Big and Small Business
> I was a small businessman.
> I had to go out of business.
> One of the 6,929
> Who in the year 1969
> Saw the end of their firms
> Devoured by the Gobkolosses.
> How could the small shopowner
> Avoid liquidation? [p. 52][21]

La Liquidation de Monsieur Joseph K. made its point, and the general public rallied in solidarity. As a result, the new municipal government of Metz invited the company back and even provided a small, permanent theatre in the university district: the Théâtre du Saulcy. With increased subsidies, TPL enthusiastically pursued its goal of producing works that refer directly or indirectly to the region of its implantation. Led by Jacques Kraemer, René Loyon, and Charles Tordjman, TPL received national acclaim, and the Ministry of Culture seriously considered changing the company's status to that of a *Centre Dramatique National*. But the project was shelved following the scandal that surrounded TPL's creation of *Noëlle de Joie*.

Noëlle de Joie, though less successful than *Minette*, is undoubtedly TPL's most controversial production. If *Minette* succeeded in arousing the animosity of Lorraine's steel barons with all the nasty political and economic repercussions that ensued, *Noëlle de Joie* resulted in an all-out war between the conservative regional press and Kraemer's troupe.[22] The play itself is a dramatic satire directed at the *Républicain Lorrain*, an important daily newspaper that camouflages its commercial interests with a hypocritical Christmas charity campaign.

During this fund-raising campaign, the newspaper solicits money from simple, poor people in order to distribute it in the form of material gifts to the even poorer. During a flashy, highly publicized gala festival called Noël de Joie ("Christmas of Joy") only the more spectacular gifts are presented to the *déshérités* ("underprivileged") in order to provide big merchants with effective advertisement. The greatest winner in all this is the *Républicain Lorrain* itself, which every year receives a great deal of favorable exposure for free because the cost of the Noël de Joie campaign is absorbed by the collected fund.

Hypocrisy and exploitation for personal gain have incited satirists to denunciation since ancient times. TPL clearly belongs to that same tradition. Like its illustrious predecessors, TPL is moved to expose and, indirectly, to correct society's flaws through ridicule. The laughter it evokes is always thoughtful— and activating, in the best Brechtian sense of the word. It has the capacity to sharply analyze a particular, corrupted social phenomenon, tearing its false mask off and exposing its true, ugly face.

Satires always contain fantastic elements that tend toward the grotesque. Since the stylistic experimentations in the theatre of the early twentieth century, dramatic satires often resort to expressionistic techniques.[23] In *Noëlle de Joie,* as in *Minette,* we find expressionistic dream sequences. In one of them, Noëlle, the play's heroine, is freakishly tortured by the editors and directors of the newspaper.[24] In fact, the entire plot is characterized by a fantastic, nightmarish progression in which the increasing exploitation of the two young heroes by the profit-minded newspaper executives is expressed physically in their progressive mutilation. At the beginning of the play, Noëlle, a young beauty queen aspiring to be a singer, and her friend Nicolas, a young painter, present themselves at the newspaper office to offer their talents for the Noël de Joie campaign. From that moment on, they become the property of the mass media: reporters and photographers cover every significant moment of their lives. Thus, Noëlle's and Nicolas's wedding becomes front page news and so do the birth of their first child and their gruesome, mutilating accidents. At the end of the play, they have themselves become "beneficiaries" of the "Grand Crusade." The dramatic satire culminates in a highly ironic scene in which the editor-in-chief of the "generous" newspaper presents the now blind Noëlle with a top-of-the-line color television. Nicolas, who has lost his legs in the cylinders of a high-speed printing press while watching his favorite painting being turned into a mass-produced commercial poster, receives a seeing-eye dog.

Undoubtedly, TPL's dramatic satires are socio-politically as well as artistically valid works, but over the years they started showing an undeniable esoteric tendency that contributed to the loss of a truly popular audience. Charles Tordjman frankly admits, "The proportion of working-class spectators has diminished. We are at 10 percent now, which is not all that bad, actually. We have abandoned a little bit the idea that we should try at all costs to reach a working-class audience."[25]

The inclination toward eclecticism and a gradual departure from truly popular concerns started becoming more and more evident in the period following 1976, particularly in the rewritten version of *Minette* and a play entitled *Le Retour du Graully* which applied *nouveau roman* techniques to the theatre. Also in this period, Jacques Kraemer started making distinctions between truly popular audiences—for whom the *spectacles d'intervention* were intended—and a so-called *avant-garde populaire* to which he could cater with his aesthetically more complex creations.

Together with the *splendeur et misère* of the title, *Minette's* new version, called simply *Minette la bonne Lorraine,* lost much of its freshness and clarity in exchange for questionable improvements in form and style. Minette has become "a fantastic creature, subject to all kinds of metamorphoses, receptive to all kinds of symbolisms: the earth, the mother, fertility, the splendor of the flesh, decrepitude, death. . . . Minette will be like a character from an Adamovian nightmare and will undergo all possible mutilations."[26] Thus Kraemer explicitly reveals his aspirations to attain universal dimensions for his play through the mythification of his Minette. He changes the main allegorical character of his play into an ambiguous aesthetic image, virtually emptying it of all its political topicality in the process.

In the new version of *Minette,* Kraemer no longer parodies for political reasons but for the sake of gratuitous playfulness: the highly pertinent newspaper clippings have been replaced by a parody of minor literary manifestations like police stories, fantasies, pornographic magazines, science fiction, and comic strips. Similarly, the new version's language has become much more cryptic and poetic, making it less accessible to a popular audience: "Down there gushes an unheard melody, a sysmic sound from sylvan depths. . . . Attractive appeal, maddening, agonizing. . . . Blade of the depth, crack of the shadows. Foam. The interplay of time and of matter."[27] Only the more surrealistic episodes of the original *Minette* were recycled for the revised version.[28]

The updated *Minette* has been devalued as political theatre due to a loss of allegorical dimensions and of satirical bite. Minette has lost most of her prostitution aspect and Monsieur Joseph is no longer an outright gangster.[29] Many of the same objections could be raised against *Le Retour du Graully* and most of the subsequent productions. It is clear that since 1976 TPL's repertoire has tended toward a subjective and much more poetic artistic expression. In addition, other authors have been produced. Interestingly, TPL's departure from militant cultural agitation coincided with its permanent move to Thionville. In 1976, the Communist mayor of that city offered his municipal theatre and a comfortable subsidy that the itinerant theatre company eagerly accepted.

In 1984, TPL received an annual subsidy of one and a half million francs from the central government, 660,000 francs from the city of Thionville, and approximately one million francs from ticket sales. It continues to tour in the smaller towns of the region and maintains a policy of affordable ticket prices. In that year

TPL no longer had a permanent company of actors. Instead, three permanent members run the company's administration, three others are in charge of all technical aspects of the productions (set design, lighting control, tour organization), and Charles Tordjman does most of the directing and original writing. For each new production, TPL hires actors for a period of four or five months, depending on the length of the play's run.[30]

Over the past three years, TPL's repertoire has absorbed more and more bourgeois classics. In November 1983 it produced Feydeau's drawing-room comedy *Léonie est en avance;* in December it had Brecht's *Threepenny Opera* on its stage, and in the springtime it featured an Italian opera and Beckett's *Waiting for Godot.* In May 1984, however, TPL reestablished part of its popular ties with its production of *La Fiancée de l'eau* by the Moroccan playwright Tahar Ben Jelloun. This play formed the climax of a large project called Voice of Maghreb, a cultural homage to North African immigrants. Particularly in recent years, Arab workers have been subject to all kinds of racist abuses in France.[31] Although *La Fiancée de l'eau* attracted Arab immigrants to the theatre who had never even seen a play in their entire lives, the production was hardly created with the same means and objectives as TPL's repertoire of the early seventies. The play is highly poetic and mythical and not at all based on information gathered from direct investigation of the target audience's concerns. Yet, despite the changed creative process and form, Charles Tordjman thinks that TPL may have made an important step with *La Fiancée de l'eau* toward recruiting a new popular audience:

> I have never seen anything like it, I have never seen people enter the theatre dressed in djelabas and sitting down next to a Frenchman and starting to talk about their country. I really feel that we managed to make a step forward with this project. In some significant way this was real popular theatre. We played Ben Jelloun's play for one month, but we could have played it three months. Because I felt that we had found a new implantation in the public.[32]

LO TEATRE DE LA CARRIERA

At the height of its radical popular activities, TPL never intended to revive regional folklore and never used regional dialects in its plays. Lo Teatre de la Carriera, a radical popular theatre group operating mainly in southern France, uses Occitanian patois in about 50 percent of its dialogues and consciously emphasizes regional cultural traditions in its plays. Lo Teatre de la Carriera started out as an agitprop street theatre group called Théâtre de la Rue ("Theatre of the Street") in 1968. After two years of impromptu appearances in and around Lyon, the troupe, artistically and politically led by playwright Claude Alranq, decided to emphasize the politics of its Occitanian cultural tradition and moved to the Midi. From then on, the dialogues of their plays became a mixture of French and Occitanian, and their dramatic forms and themes, although inspired by contemporary issues, were henceforth based on the Occitanian cultural patrimony. Since 1970, lo Teatre de la Carriera has produced eighteen original plays and has given more than twelve hundred performances, the majority of them for rural Occitanian audiences that do not habitually attend the theatre.[33] Although la Carriera is now a full-time professional troupe, its preferred acting space is still the public square of Occitanian villages on warm summer nights.

Lo Teatre de la Carriera creates a theatre that is socio-educational in tendency and militantly regional in spirit. It tries to maintain a dialogue with labor unions and left-wing parties to convince them that Occitanian culture is indigenous to the region and not merely a variant of French culture. Until 1978, Claude Alranq was the troupe's main writer. When he left, the writing was taken over by several other members of the troupe, predominantly women. Since that time, the woman's position in Occitanian society has become one of la Carriera's main concerns, culminating in 1980 with the publication of *Ecrits des Femmes* ("Women's Writings") and, most recently, with the production of *Miracle! Miracle!*, a play for two actresses based on thirteenth- and fourteenth-century Provençal texts.[34] Since 1975, lo Teatre de la Carriera has been headquartered in an abandoned cinema in the southern city of Arles. Also since that year, the troupe has been receiving small local and state subsidies which supplement the limited income from ticket sales and donations. La Carriera works predominantly in the Provence and Languedoc regions, but it regularly tours through the other parts of Occitania and the major cities of the rest of France.

La Pastorale de Fos ("The Pastoral Play of Fos"—1975), *Mort et résurrection de M. Occitania* ("Death and Resurrection of Mr. Occitania"—1970, 1976), and its sequel *La Fille d'Occitania* ("Occitania's Daughter"—1978) are three of the most successful creations of the Alranq period and serve as useful examples of the Carriera style. *La pastorale de Fos* typifies the troupe's intention to make its audience conscious of the specific Occitanian character of its present-day socio-economic predicament. The prominence in the play of well-known local legends, folklore symbols, and traditional cultural structures like the Provençal pastoral play draw the topicality of the dramatized events into a historical-dialectic perspective. Thus, the audience's attention is directed to the fact that the present industrialization of Occitania is only the latest instance of ages of Parisian colonialistic exploitation of the region.

La Pastorale de Fos was created after four months of investigation and interviews with natives of the Fos region, an area with strong cultural traditions that was severely affected by the installation, between 1970 and 1973, of a port complex and heavy steel industry.[35] The play was commissioned by the local government of Martigues, which had been impressed with a previous Carriera creation on the problems of the Cévennes mining area. Until 1975, when la Carriera received its first subsidy from Martigues, the troupe had been scrambling to make a living. At first, the company members worked as agricultural laborers during the day and performed their impromptu plays at night. They lived together in a small village near Montpellier and shared everything they earned. But communal life proved draining, and in 1972 most of the actors left. Claude Alranq and Catherine Bonafé decided to continue la Carriera as a professional troupe. They engaged new actors and started performing their original creations throughout France. This produced *La Guerre du vin* ("The Wine War") in 1973 and *Tabò ou la dernière Ste. Barbe* ("Tabò or the Last Saint Barbara"; a play about the Cévennes region) in 1974.

Lo Teatre de la Carriera tries to incorporate the fertile Occitanian cultural material that has been abandoned. The culmination of these efforts came in *La Pastorale de Fos,* in which la Carriera used the traditional form of the Provençal pastoral play. This form had been shelved as "folklore" like most of the Occitanian culture but is still extremely popular in the villages and towns of the region. The villagers that produce these Christmas plays pretend to tell the story of the Nativity while actually commenting on contemporary life. For that reason the pastoral had been banned by church and state authorities during several centuries. Likewise, la Carriera used the popular imagery of the pastoral to talk about the history of Fos's industrialization.

La Carriera's adoption of the old dramatic pastoral form serves both as a reconquest of the Occitanian patrimony and as an appropriate aesthetic structure for the adventures of a local girl with a despised foreign worker called the *Boumian,* or gypsy bogeyman. Catherine Bonafé explains:

> We tried to treat the problem of the arrival of the immigrant worker. In the Provençal patrimony there has always been a foreigner. He is the bogeyman, the gypsy who is accused of everything bad. So we said, "Today's bogeyman is the guy who comes from North Africa, the Moroccan, the Algerian." And at the end of *La Pastorale,* when the most Provençal of all traditions is reenacted [i.e., when the oldest inhabitant of the village passes on the new year to the youngest inhabitant], it happens that the patriarch prefers to perform that tradition, that passing on of the past to the new time, with the bogeyman rather than with the youngest of the Provençals. Boy, did that cause a scandal![36]

The play is set in Pamparigouste, which, according to oral Provençal tradition, is an imaginary country in the neighborhood of Fos. In the first tableau, the young Chichois is elected mayor after a speech in which he defends regionalism and the construction of a new port and an industrial complex.[37] This modernization project is symbolically called *la Tarasque,* the name of an amphibious monster that used to terrorize the banks of the Rhône river before Christianity. During the festivities surrounding Chichois's election victory, the new mayor's girlfriend Mireille falls in love with a newly arrived Boumian.

In the second tableau, Chichois is lured into adopting the values of the regional political elite, and he consequently ends up authorizing the expropriation of fishing waters and shepherd lands for an urbanization project, a superhighway, and a polluting pipeline. He pacifies the fishermen and the shepherds with bribes but is unable to obtain the cooperation of Nostradamus, a wise old man whose character is based on a sixteenth-century Provençal scholar by the same name.

The third tableau dramatizes the plight of the exploited immigrant workers—their layoffs and their numerous accidents on the construction sites. This scene features a pantomime between clownesque types representing black and white workers and peasants and fishermen to underline the fact that the corrupting forces of industrialization can only be overcome in proletarian solidarity. *La Pastorale de Fos*, then, urges unity with the immigrant workers, for both Provençal natives and foreigners fight a common enemy: "On the job we're all bogeymen, good for squeezing and for dumping, as long as we were divided. . . . Black workers . . . and white workers . . . and those of the land . . . and those of the sea. . . . The Pierrots and the Augusts, and the Herculeses . . . and those from Pamparigouste. . . . And the bogeymen. All together . . . we shall overcome."[38]

The Nativity motif finds expression in the fourth tableau, where Mireille and the Boumian roam around to find a job and shelter for the birth of their child. After being chased away in many places, they finally find employment in an electronic Nativity scene sponsored by *la Tarasque*. Mireille plays the role of Mary while the Boumian is hired as the donkey. The scene develops into a hilarious parody of modern domestic life dominated by electronic entertainment. Modernization is thus shown infiltrating into traditional Provençal households and killing regional culture. The supreme symbol of this psychological control over the masses is the television set, the indoctrinary power of which is satirically analyzed.

Television is revealed as a reinforcer of racist prejudices against immigrant workers, and as a propagator of French as the dominant language of the region, effectively suppressing local patois. Likewise we are shown that television creates false desires (through commercials) and surrogate satisfactions. Worst of all, however, television is shown to be a mouthpiece of the central government, which, behind the attractive camouflage of gameshows and music programs, manipulates the audience into accepting absurd austerity measures and numbs the regional population's rebellious instincts through song and dance:

> Tonight we're going to play, with the entire family, a little economics game. Close all your holes. Except your ears of course. Close them well. Very good. Now I'm going to lower the heat. I'm going to raise the prices. . . . And if you're not happy, darn it, it's the strikers' fault! And if you're not happy, darn it, it's the fault of the bogeymen! One hit, two hits! Beat the strikers! One hit, two hits! Beat the bogeymen! [pp. 105–6][39]

As an alternative to the "Nativity of the future," Nostradamus organizes the traditional *Cacha-Fuóc* celebration in an old house which, for the occasion, has

been turned into a museum of Provençal cultural remnants. *Cacha-Fuóc,* cele-
brated on 21 December, is related to the prehistoric fires with which people used
to celebrate the return of the sun on the longest night of the year. In Provence, on
that date, the oldest and the youngest member of the family together carry a log
of a fruit tree to the fire place, thus symbolizing that the old and the young should
work together for a sparkling future. In the fifth and final scene of the play,
Chichois insists that he be allowed to carry the log to the fire with Nostradamus,
but the latter refuses, preferring instead the assistance of the Boumian. *La
Pastorale de Fos* emphasizes, then, that Occitania will be better off allying itself
with the sincerely committed strangers than with corrupt local politicians.

According to *La Pastorale de Fos,* the worst betrayal is that of local Occitanian politicians and businessmen who collaborate with the Parisian government.
These Occitanian opportunists renounce their own cultural heritage in exchange
for political and material favors, and they are, therefore, deserving of the
severest ridicule. For example, Chichois's moral degeneration through his betrayal of the regionalist cause is expressed visually in his progressive disfigure-
ment: the stage directions inform us that he is "always a little more deformed and
his nose gets longer" (p. 109).[40]

Satirization of Occitanian political milieu is prominent in *Mort et résurrection
de M. Occitania,* a 1976 revision of the play with which lo Teatre de la Carriera
had started its first regional tour in 1970. This work, performed more than three
hundred times, deals with M. Occitania's investigation into the causes of his own
death. He is resurrected by a sorceress and discovers that the symptoms of his
fatal illness were caused by capitalist exploitation: his head is inflated out of
proportion because of the empty promises of corrupt politicians and bankers; he
discharges red urine because when your native land is sick, "you are sick as well.
You are afflicted with the same disease. You pee red because of the murdered
viticulture."[41]

As well as a striking similarity in the title, *Mort et résurrection de M.
Occitania* shares a common allegorically satiric method with TPL's *Splendeur et
misère de Minette, la bonne Lorraine.* Just as Minette symbolized Lorraine's
working population and natural richness, M. Occitania represents the population
of Occitania, its economic potential and its cultural traditions. The names of
other characters are also allegorically significant. The loud-mouthed but in-
effectual Occitanian parliamentary deputy Candordino ("Candeur-dit-non") does
anything but speak candidly; the government envoy Métaneuf ("Mettre-à-neuf,"
"to make new") is responsible for modernizing Occitania; and the greedy banker
Manjatot ("Mange-tout," "he who eats everything") stops at nothing to make a
profit. These three are the chief villains of the play and are most severely
satirized. Candordino exposes his insincere loyalty to the region in the following
failed attempt to compliment himself:

> It's hard to be in the opposition. I am in it for you. But not too much, in order not
> to attract the effects of the government's wrath on the South. With slow delibera-

tion, in order to blackmail them into allotting subsidies, but enough to change life. My art is in subtle measuring. My studies as a pharmacist have prepared me better than any other profession for my political career. Yet I remain a winegrower through my parents. Thus I am in you as you are in me . . . and to defend you is to defend myself. [pp. 10–11][42]

Métaneuf is satirized through his own words as well and through those of his supporters when a publicity campaign designed to increase his popularity backfires. Thus, the regional director of the unemployment agency attests to Métaneuf's impeccable moral stature and selfless generosity in the following terms:

Mr. Métaneuf, words are not strong enough to express the good that you have done and still do. Thanks to you we now have gorgeous unemployment offices. They have soft and comfortable easy chairs, intimate carpets, and charming hostesses . . . the numerous unemployed can go there whenever they want. They will always be well received. [p. 60][43]

Métaneuf's close associate, Manjatot, is ridiculed when, in scene 9, he enters disguised as a colonialist, his attire clearly revealing the true intentions of his dealings with Occitania. He is Occitania's most blatant exploiter: he lends him money to buy a useless all-purpose viticulture machine, he buys Occitania's wine only to sell it back for three times the amount, and he takes the initiative to completely wipe out the Occitanian wine industry only to change the barren vineyards into the *bronze-cul européen*, "European ass-tan centers."

The chief satiric method of *Mort et résurrection de M. Occitania* consists, then, of satiric irony with which the satiric victims are made to expose themselves. Occasionally, however, la Carriera also employs the visual grotesque as a satirical instrument. In scene 8, for example, Candordino disguises himself as a prostitute to attract new industries to Occitania in order to alleviate its severe unemployment. La Carriera does not hesitate either to satirize its naive and passive fellow Occitanians. Thus they ridicule the resignation with which the unemployed agree to pay local taxes to subsidize potential investors, a fact which is visually expressed by four unemployed workers who are forced to strip naked and hand their clothes to Manjatot.

La Fille d'Occitania (1978) continues the mockery of the apathetic local population. The play attacks the Provençal natives who are content in their petty bourgeois materialism and no longer feel part of Occitanian tradition. Nine, Mr. Occitania's daughter, represents all young Occitanians who have left the region for jobs and opportunities in Paris. The play demonstrates that it is impossible to make Occitania survive if its children abandon it and refuse to speak its language. In the play, Nine returns from Paris to rediscover authentic Occitanian values and to deter others from going to the capital as she had done. From her own experiences she knows that Paris is not the paradise it is reputed to be:

"Farewell, Paris! Four years down the drain! Pills to get up early, pills to go to sleep, uppers to keep going . . . high heels to fart high! Aerodynamic bras! And supersmall panties! . . . Makeup to forget who you are and magazines for dreaming! Paris, up yours!"[44]

The action of the play involves the quest of Nine, her childhood boyfriend Totí-Motí, and the legendary deaf musician Lo Palhon, for true Occitanian values in order to make the Tamarou dance again. The Tamarou is a mythical Occitanian animal that symbolizes the region's vigor. Their search is opposed by local politicians and the complacency of Occitanian workers. The municipal council members are most severely criticized, however, by means of the low burlesque satirical method: their meeting is opened with a ceremonious lowering of their pants and their debates are punctuated by salvos of farts alternated with the insistent noises of defecating and urinating. Thus la Carriera leaves little doubt as to what value it attaches to the opinions and actions of those regional politicians who collaborate with the Parisian government: their statements are literally deflated by their farts. The satirized politicians are shown to feel no solidarity for their native region, and therefore their concluding speeches are put into their proper perspective by an instantly following "Marseillaise of farts" (p. 48).

Like the other plays discussed here, *La Fille d'Occitania* ends in a tone of militant exhortation to rise up against the Parisian oppressor. At the end, the heroes of the play are shown chasing Manjatot and his Occitanian cronies off the stage, implying to the audience that they do the same in real life. A final call for Occitanian unity follows as Nine and Totí-Motí manage to make the Tamarou dance, an undeniable symbol of hope.

La Fille d'Occitania was Claude Alranq's final creation for lo Teatre de la Carriera. Until 1978 he had been the troupe's chief text writer and artistic director, but after his departure these tasks were taken over by Hélène and Catherine Bonafé. The latter recalls the circumstances involving Claude Alranq's departure:

> He left early '78. Until then, he had been the only one who wrote. Everybody had his or her important part to do, and everything worked well that way. When he left, it turned out that, since '79 or so, mostly women started doing the writing. It was a little odd that this hadn't happened before. . . . For a long time we had already played an important role in the troupe; in propositions, in activities, in all kinds of projects, the women had often been the most constructive, the most realistic and had thus assured the group's continuity. That's why it's so surprising that now they suddenly brand us as being too feminist. . . . Many other regional troupes in Languedoc and Provence went through similar developments in the period between '78 and '80. A new wind started to blow, mainly inspired by women. It was scary, in that period. All those guys who had been leaders and founders of theatre companies collapsed in their professional and private lives. They no longer knew what to do, and they felt stifled in their troupes. They felt like moving on to other things.[45]

Since 1979, la Carriera has noticeably diversified its activities, alternating performances between official theatres and found theatre spaces. Like so many other radical troupes that survived the seventies, la Carriera finds itself caught in the contradiction that, if it wants to survive and continue its politically committed cultural activities, it must present itself as a legitimate theatre company. As a result, la Carriera resolved to start operating on two different levels. With a pragmatic attitude that is similar to the San Francisco Mime Troupe's, lo Teatre de la Carriera still plays predominantly for nontheatre audiences in spaces not designed for theatre productions. But in order to be subsidized it needs national exposure in Paris and at the major festivals. With *Miracle! Miracle!* la Carriera achieved this double objective.

Miracle! Miracle!, a dynamic collage of medieval fabliaux, songs, and legends taken from miracle and mystery plays, was la Carriera's official entry to the 1983 Arts Festival of Villeneuve-les-Avignon. Catherine Bonafé and Michelle Rochin, the two actresses who also created the play, subsequently took it on tour through most of Occitania. The tales selected for *Miracle! Miracle!* have only female characters and contain strong Occitanian elements. La Carriera highlights the female elements of these tales because it strongly feels that the male half of humanity has misrepresented woman's contributions to history for too long now. Through their research, Rochin and Bonafé discovered that the female stereotypes in the religious tales as we know them are, in fact, later impositions on originally much more complex characterizations. Their scrutiny revealed that the personalities of women in medieval literature were just as mulifaceted as those of women today: Eve turned out to be the accomplice of an equally guilty Adam, and the Holy Virgin was presented as a jealous wench and coquette, desperate at times. By brushing away the dust of ages of misogynous interpretation and mystification, la Carriera discovered some marvelous stories worth retelling in today's words and images for the benefit of all. With quick-paced changes of characters through one-touch alterations of their ingeniously designed costumes, the two actresses present a seemingly endless spectrum of female characters on stage. Transitions between scenes are provided by traditional Occitanian songs and dances with female themes, to which the performers accompany themselves with authentic percussion and simple string instruments.

Troupes like lo Teatre de la Carriera and TPL have been trying to create radical popular theatre for over a decade now with minimal financial means. They started out with some form of agitprop theatre and on that formal basis developed their own, identifiable aesthetic styles with which they tried to express the socioeconomic issues and cultural traditions of their regional target audiences. Popular theatre companies located in the vicinity of Paris started gaining attention from the national press (located in the capital) and the Ministry of Culture, whereas troupes that were geographically and culturally further removed from the capital had a much harder time getting recognition and financial support for their efforts.[46]

Catherine Bonafé, as a medieval Occitanian woman in *Miracle! Miracle!* (1983), tells an erotic tale about buying hundreds of cucumbers in a dream. Photo by Jean Clamour.

Catherine Bonafé and Michelle Rochin in one of the medieval songs that provide the transitions between the scenes of *Miracle! Miracle!* (1983).

Lo Teatre de la Carriera. *L'Enclave des Papes* was produced in the yard of a large provencal estate near Arles. In this photo the "leader of the Occitanian troupe" (r.), which has been invited to do an Occitanian version of *The Tempest* for the "ambassador," shares a joke with the "Parisian theatre critic."

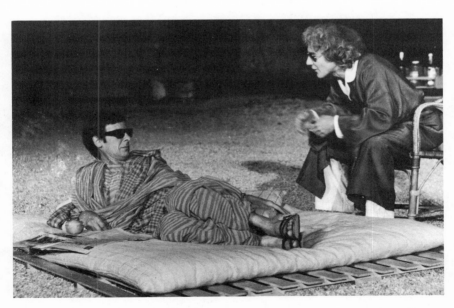

Lo Teatre de la Carriera. The wealthy Parisian publisher (r.) entertains his friend the ambassador in the garden of his Occitanian country estate in *L'Enclave des Papes* (1984).

When the Socialists won the French elections in 1981 and Jack Lang, a former sixties radical and popular theatre activist, was appointed minister of culture, the hope was raised that things would change for the better.[47] But frustrations continue, and in order to obtain recognition and the accompanying reward in the form of subsidies, radical regional troupes are forced out of the fringe into the mainstream. Tired of years of struggling in the margin, TPL has readopted a bourgeois repertoire and collaborated with the noted Théâtre de l'Est Parisien on the production of Charles Tordjman's play *Le Chantier* in 1981.[48] Lo Teatre de la Carriera is less willing to compromise and continues to tour its radical bilingual creations through southern France. In 1983 it did *Miracle! Miracle!* and a spectacular carnival show with a group of Occitanian musicians. But in 1984 it emerged from the margin by accepting an offer to collaborate with the Théâtre du Campagnol on a collective creation called *L'Enclave des Papes,* a play about Parisian cultural imperialism in Occitania. Finally, in the 1985–86 season, lo Teatre de la Carriera did a larger, thoroughly researched production called *Les Folies de Marseilles,* a popular theatre retrospective of the once thriving Marseilles vaudeville, which was modeled after the famous Parisian *Folies Bergères.*

CHAPTER 6

REGIONAL THEATRE IN GREAT BRITAIN

The 7:84 Theatre Company

Although May 1968 undoubtedly was considerably hotter in Paris than in London, the British capital also rocked with large contingents of youngsters protesting against the same issues that had provoked the outrage of their peers east across the Channel and west across the Atlantic Ocean. England had its own huge Vietnam demonstrations and occupied university buildings. As in France and elsewhere in the West, 1968 was the year that a young, radical left-wing movement came into its own in Great Britain. This development was also sparked by a growing discontent with Western consumerism at the cost of oppression in the Third World and environmental pollution. It was, therefore, not long before a rejuvenated radical popular theatre started addressing these issues in the British Isles as well.

In the wake of 1968 a great number of socialist theatres and playwrights developed.[1] The story of John McGrath and the 7:84 Theatre Company is, arguably, the most compatible with those of the previously mentioned troupes in France and the United States. In terms of sheer quantity and political sophistication, the work of both 7:84 companies (England and Scotland) is superior to that of most other socialist theatre groups in Britain. Furthermore, in a series of lectures delivered at Cambridge University that were later reprinted under the title *A Good Night Out*, McGrath established himself as an astute theoretician of the radical popular theatre.[2] Under his guidance and based on a firm political consciousness, a solid knowledge of popular cultural tradition and a predominantly satirical temperament, 7:84 has established itself, in many ways, as Britain's chief alternative theatre group.

As in the case of so many other popular theatre groups, 7:84 is more or less collectively organized, but its very existence, perpetuation, and artistic style depend on the initiative and creativity of a single person. John McGrath started writing plays when reading English literature at Oxford in the late fifties. Although his early writings were hardly radically popular in objective, they were, nevertheless, clearly concerned with social justice and revealed an obvious leftist leaning. McGrath was introduced to the bourgeois theatrical establishment while working as a playscript reader at George Devine's Royal Court. He met John Arden there and even had some of his own plays produced. In the mid-sixties, he became involved in television and created the highly successful *Z-Cars* police series. But when the program abandoned its sympathetic focus on lower-class social problems in favor of a hero-oriented, action-filled crime drama, John McGrath left the BBC for the movies. Being involved in television, film, and theatre gave McGrath an interesting perspective on mass communication and also a great deal of mobility. Working for Ken Russell and Carl Foreman in the period between 1967 and 1971, John McGrath often traveled to the United States and France; he met people like Herbert Blau and befriended several members of the Living Theatre. Through Blau, John McGrath found out about the San Francisco Mime Troupe and some of the other alternative theatre groups in America. But he feels that most of the groups that emerged from the '68 revolt started their activities more or less independently of each other:

> Although there was a terrific chain reaction around the world, there was an enormous mobility of ideas around the sixties. In Europe, the ideas were moving between the street protests in Germany in 1967, and Italy and France in '68. Also, in London we had massive anti-Vietnam demonstrations from '66 to '68. The style in which things were communicated was characterized by great excitement among young people. And at that same time you had the Chicago convention and the American peace movement.[3]

In May 1968 McGrath went to Paris as a representative of British writers and artists to express solidarity with the occupants of the Ecole des Beaux-Arts. Together with his friend Jean-Jacques Lebel, McGrath became involved in a revolutionary arts committee constituted by anarchists, Trotskyists, and Maoists.

According to McGrath, the changing attitude of the mass media was most instrumental in putting down the May uprising and, indirectly, gave the essential impulse for the birth of radical popular theatre:

> In England it was striking to see that anti-Vietnam demonstrations were getting bigger and bigger because everytime there was one there was this massive media coverage. And next time there would be even more people. Then, suddenly, there

was this huge demonstration and nothing on television. It was scarcely mentioned that there had been a demonstration. This happened in America as well and it helped De Gaulle win the vote in the autumn of '68. Suddenly things calmed down. No longer contestation, no longer dramatic tensions in society. The access to mass media was stone dead. I worked in television before that and I knew how it was working. That is why there came to be such an emphasis on theatre opposed to the mass media information channels. The connection between the way the excitement of '68 was suppressed and what happened afterwards is as important as the connection between the ideas of '68 and what happened in the theatre later.[4]

McGrath's experiences during the turbulent late sixties proved a turning point in his career. He admits that *Random Happenings in the Hebrides,* a play which he was writing in 1968, underwent a radical change under the influence of what he experienced in Paris: "Apparently it had nothing to do with Paris and people throwing paving stones, but that experience went into it."[5]

McGrath's plays up until 1971 were rather realistic, albeit socially committed, works. With *Trees in the Wind,* McGrath took the first step toward a more truly popular political theatre. The play was first presented at the Edinburgh Fringe Festival with a randomly selected group of actors. This improvised company took the play on tour and was initially funded by money that McGrath had saved from his screenwriting. Thus the 7:84 Theatre Company was born:

> 7:84 was chosen as the name of the group to draw attention to a statistic published in "The Economist" in 1966 which asserted that 7% of the population of Great Britain owned 84% of the capital wealth. Although this proportion may have fluctuated marginally over the years, we continue to use it because it points to the basic economic structure of the society we live in, from which all the political, social and cultural structures grow. The company opposes this set-up, and tries to indicate socialist alternatives to the capitalist system that dominates all our lives today.[6]

But the artistic way in which 7:84 presented its socialist alternatives on stage changed considerably during the first decade of its existence.

Trees in the Wind was the first play produced under the 7:84 label. It was still predominantly realistic, with hardly any popular theatre features other than slang and humor. Yet, the play constituted a necessary phase in the troupe's development. It was very much an expression of the revolutionary late sixties and the student movement. It dealt with women's issues and sexual liberation as well as the effect of a radical commitment on one's private life. *Trees in the Wind* contains two powerful characters in Carlyle, the liberated student activist, and Joe, the fanatical Marxist gone capitalist. Joe in particular is a comic figure. Nevertheless, he is disturbing in his pseudosensible criticism of the Marxist analysis of society's power structure. He abandons the working class because financially he cannot afford to be part of it; the temptations of capitalist success are too strong: ". . . I know the way it all works. Four years of rigorous Marxist training, and you should be able to play the Stock Exchange like Ludo with loaded dice."[7] His basic argument is that revolutionary fervor does not put any bread on the table and that leftist insurgents have to fight against the invincible forces of capitalist-controlled mass media. For Joe, the class struggle has, then, become a meaningless, romantic, and self-defeating battle. Thus, Joe becomes the epitome of all those other workers who have been "lead by the nose. Blinkered. Deafened. Rolled in butter and fried . . . given promises, promises, wooed, and won, and seduced, and garrotted . . . atomised . . . and refrigerated, pressure-cooked, automobilised . . . tellified and radioed and technicoloured, and . . . taught to love trinkets more than freedom" (p. 2.29).

Trees in the Wind is a strongly text-based play; its discussion dominates its action. It intends to make an ideological point rather than analyze a sociohistorical situation, as the later 7:84 creations are prone to do. The play is a dramatic footnote to a quote by Chairman Mao, who said that "wind will not cease, even though trees want to rest." Joe is supposed to be one of the tired trees and represents the conceited individuals who have grown weary of the class struggle. They were the ones who committed themselves to the imminent revolution with infinite confidence in their alleged superior individual abilities, thinking that their contribution would make all the difference. Not surprisingly, people like Joe are also the first to abandon the struggle when things do not quite work out the way they had planned. Carlyle correctly points out that people like Joe "are often blind to the strength of the collective—they see only that of the individual. The history of social development is not the history of the big men, but of the labouring masses" (p. 2.32).

Stylistically, *Trees in the Wind* is still close to the type of post-Osborne plays that McGrath was later to reject vehemently in his *Good Night Out*. The play is set in the three-room apartment of three girls whose occupations and perspectives are sufficiently different to make their interactions dramatically interesting. Joe intrudes into this domestic setup to challenge the three roommates sexually and ideologically. Fortunately, the talk is good, but, in general, the play is too static to make successful popular theatre.

Alternating with 7:84 tours in Scotland and England, John McGrath did some interesting work for the Everyman Theatre, a community playhouse in a working-class district of Liverpool. It was the professed aim of the Everyman to reach out to a proletarian audience by means of low ticket prices, an informal entourage, and the sale of beer during performances. McGrath's *Soft or a Girl* helped to establish the Everyman as a place where "the working-class blokes came with their wives for a night out."[8]

Soft or a Girl uses the framework of a rock concert, a form of entertainment that is extremely popular among young workers. The songs composed and performed by a Liverpool band form the play's structural backbone. Everything else in the play is also distinctly Liverpudlian: the accent, the setting, and the characters. But the show is not only geared to the young; the narrative framework is provided by two middle-aged fathers, one a radical worker, the other a bourgeois dentist, who, while on civic guard looking out for German bombers in 1940, used to delight in singing music-hall songs together. Thus, *Soft or a Girl* draws on two major elements of popular culture: vaudeville and rock music.

John McGrath is an extremely pragmatic cultural agitator. He quickly discovered that in order to communicate with the working class he would have to address the workers in their own idiom and draw on their cultural experiences. He also knew that the traditional theatrical conventions were meaningless to a working-class audience brought up with television and cinema. Here, McGrath's experience as a screenwriter proved of capital importance:

> I think that I personally learned more about writing for a popular audience from having my screenplays butchered time and again by Harry Saltzman—one of the producers of the Bond films—or, on a different level, by Fred Zinnemann—producer and director of *A Man For All Seasons, Julia,* and, above all, *High Noon.* These two, and some of the other producers and directors of crude, vulgar commercial movies know more about pace and movement than almost any author since Homer. . . . The level of plot invention per line, per page, per scene, is immensely high, much higher than most post-Osborne playwrights would think at all necessary.[9]

Soft or a Girl is extremely fast-paced with quick scene changes between the central story "involving a Liverpool girl who goes to university and feels she is leaving her class behind, and the working-class boyfriend who couldn't make it to university, but gets off with a cute middle-class girl he meets while driving his delivery van."[10] This love story is presented as a future vision of the two fathers who comment on the action one night in 1940 with epic distance. The swift shifts in historical periods, the self-conscious acting on the part of the two dads who constantly remind each other to get "on," and the narrative songs performed by the rock band all contribute to an overriding sense of theatrical playfulness and informality. According to John McGrath, working-class audiences have absolutely no problems with such looseness of form, and it is not because they are "unused to the theatre, and therefore naively accepting—on the contrary, it is the sophistication of the audience of the folk tale, able to shift ground with ease if given secure guidance."[11]

The title of *Soft or a Girl* refers to Mick Hurley's naive and unassertive behavior. Through him, the play mildly satirizes the political apathy and the social conservatism of young working-class "blokes" like Mick. The younger generation is a living disclaimer to Hurley senior's wartime optimism. During the forties Mr. Hurley, a sharp-witted, radical deckhand on a ferryboat, had expressed confidence that after the war the proletariat, so divided by religious fanaticism, would join hands in the common fight against the bosses and landlords. But his look into the future reveals that nothing of the kind actually occurs. In 1971, Mr. Hurley has become a burnt-out radical, ashamed of his son's lack of politization and pride. Mick, an incorrigible romantic, is the typical product of the present-day consumer society. Indoctrinated by the bourgeois values diffused by the mass media, he dumps his energetic, revolutionary working-class girlfriend in order to follow Ella, an animated caricature of the feminine woman portrayed by cosmetics commercials.

Ella is the daughter of Mr. Martin, who was Mr. Hurley's wartime buddy. While on guard, Martin and Hurley are the best of friends: they sing vaudeville songs together and even speculate on a future, classless society. But the dramatized vision of the future, although clearly theatrical and nonnaturalistic, leaves them little room for optimism; at the play's conclusion, the two war cronies meet again after a thirty-year interval as Mr. Martin pays a courtesy visit with his daughter to the humble residence of the Hurleys. Politically, this is the play's most significant scene since it dramatizes a class conflict of sorts. During the confrontation, Mr. Hurley is brought to the realization that he himself has been "soft or a girl," and not his son. He had expected a joyful reunion with his old comrade-in-arms, but he soon discovers that Mr. Martin no longer remembers the old Flanagan and Allen songs and has lost his taste for beer. The well-to-do dentist now listens to opera and consumes more sophisticated alcoholic beverages. Jenny, Mick's ex-girlfriend, makes Mr. Hurley realize that he and Martin are "different men now [because] there's a system, you see, has driven a wedge between us. I want to smash it, but he wants to keep it, he perpetuates it. And we all play our parts in that system" (pp. 2.48–9). A violent and more physical attack on the representative of the bourgeoisie is cut short, however, by the fictional boundaries of the show, and Mr. Hurley concludes, "tonight, Mr. Martin, it's comedy night" (p. 2.50), as he joins his ex-partner in a merry finale to remind the audience that the real class struggle must be waged outside the theatre.

Soft or a Girl, although playing on two different temporal and fictional levels, still lacks the historical perspective of subsequent 7:84 plays. Nevertheless, theatrically speaking it is an extremely effective show that manages to question its audience's fixed social patterns and materialism. The play does not fall prey to pure antibourgeois invective either, partly because the younger Mr. Martin is such a likeable fellow who defends Mr. Hurley and harshly criticizes his older self and his silly daughter.

After *Soft or a Girl,* John McGrath continued to work with both the 7:84 Theatre Company and the Everyman Theatre. In 1972, 7:84 performed at the Everyman with four different plays, including *Trees in the Wind.* McGrath's next play, *Fish in the Sea,* was also written with a specific Liverpool audience in mind. Again, the musical punctuation was provided by popular rock music, but in his preface the author explained that the play's political content was supposed to be more challenging than that of previous shows:

The main elements I wanted to set in some form of dialectical motion were—the need for militant organisation by the working class; the anarchistic, anti-organisational violence of the frustrated working-class individual in search of self-fulfillment here and now; the backwardness of some elements of working-class living: attitudes to women, to socialist theory, to sexual oppression, poetry, myth, etc.; the connections between this backwardness and Christianity; the shallow optimism of the demagogic left, self-appointed leaders of the working class; and the intimate realities of growing up and living in a working-class home on Merseyside.[12]

McGrath's intentions with *Fish in the Sea* were, then, to point to the weaknesses of the revolutionary class. The title of the play significantly refers to Mao's comparison of the party to a fish and the masses to the sea in which the fish swims. Analogously, the play seems to argue that the fish is somewhat diseased and the water polluted and that both are in sore need of cleaning up.

With *Fish in the Sea,* 7:84 continued its motto of "a good night out." The play is full of funny moments, and, while the author warns against both epic and naturalistic acting, he stresses the effort to create a "level of contact and communication with the audience over and above the realities of any one character, or group of characters" (preface). The play focuses on the personal and political development of the members of the Maconochie family. But it is not unusual to see, for example, the father address the audience directly after his three daughters and his wife have asked him for more spending money:

Oh Christ! Here we go—anybody else care to strip me of my final quid? *(To woman in the audience):* What about you, Madam, I'm sure you've got as good a reason as any of this lot for taking away the last of my beer money, come on, don't be shy, it's only worth ten bob anyway, here you are my love. [pp. 11–12]

The humor, the catchy tunes of the music and the direct contact with the audience create a festive, informal atmosphere in which the more serious business, including attacks on the workers themselves, is accepted more easily. Joviality is a trademark of 7:84, and, whenever closing time restrictions allow the actors to stick around and chat with the audience about the performance, they will do so with pleasure.

As in the original work of most other contemporary radical popular theatre companies, there is more than just a touch of Brecht in 7:84's political theatre. First and foremost, there is the music. Like Bertolt Brecht, who had learned the effectiveness of narrative songs in the highly popular cultural medium of the political cabaret in the early part of this century, McGrath also employs songs for functional reasons. They are used to advance plot, to form a link between one scene and the next, or, most importantly, to comment on a character's behavior and to draw the specific actions of one individual or a family into a more general political perspective. Not surprisingly, John McGrath mentions the cooperation between Brecht and Kurt Weill as one of the most successful initiatives ever of combining popular music with political theatre.[13] He also recognizes Brecht's invaluable contributions to the development of the style and language of modern political theatre. But McGrath objects to the patronizing, pedagogical attitude he detects in Brecht's epic theatre, which creates not only an aesthetic distance between stage and audience, but also an intellectual one. The contemporary popular political theatre wants to narrow the gap between stage and audience by means of a jolly, generous, community atmosphere while avoiding the pitfalls of naturalistic theatrical illusions. The contemporary radical popular theatre practices theatrical distancing playfully and not as a polished, aesthetic tool. There is, therefore, marked difference between the epic acting style as it is perpetuated by the Berliner Ensemble and the theatricality of the radical popular theatre.

Unlike Brecht, McGrath sees no use for distant, exotic locations. His plays are set in recognizable and identifiable places. In a play like *Fish in the Sea,* for example, he is very conscious of writing for a Liverpool public and introduces characters that speak with a strong Merseyside accent. Much of the usual 7:84 humor is based on funny, typical behavior of domestic working-class life and the colorfulness of its slang. *Fish in the Sea* contains an amusing scene in which two of Maconochie's daughters fight over a pair of nylon stockings to wear for a dance. As one of them threatens to pull her sister's hair, the other one quips: "You touch my hair, you jealous cow—just you touch it and I'll give you such a swipe across the earhole you won't be able to stop the ringing for a fortnight!" (pp. 9–10).

Considering the dynamic, ever-changing nature of the contemporary radical popular theatre, a discussion based on its script alone is necessarily incomplete. Nevertheless, reading *Fish in the Sea* one gets the impression that its author has been somewhat too ambitious with this play. Showing all the elements of working-class life that he mentioned in his preface through the thoughts and actions of one family is an impossible task. Consequently, the play creates the impression of being too contrived; it is more a collage of sketches dramatizing the various phenomena that McGrath wanted to highlight than an organic whole. Fortunately the scenes are fast-paced, the characters interesting, the songs entertaining, and the speeches powerful.

The need for a militant organization of the working class is expressed in several scenes that dramatize the occupation of the steel factory in which Mr. Maconochie and his son-in-law Willy are employed. Significantly, under the influence of his friend Yorry, Willy exchanges his obsession with soccer and beer for a militant political consciousness. Yorry, who had to struggle free from under the oppressive Baptist yoke of his father and the intellectual constraints of theoretical radicalism, also undergoes a profound change: from overprotected sissie afraid of girls he turns into an effective, militant organizer of the working class. Even Mr. Maconochie, disillusioned after having lived through five

Labour governments that changed nothing, rediscovers some hope and excitement with the factory occupation:

> Then bugger me: *this* happened. Action. Determination. At last. Young Willy—a new generation—getting stuck in there like a good 'un. Even Yorry, for all he's a bit damp behind the ears—everybody was alive, and having a go. It's "got" to work. I think—I think, if it doesn't, come the eighties, I'll be on the way out. But it "will." It must. Don't you think? [p. 76]

The final question, posed directly to the working-class audience, is charged with ambiguity: "Aren't you thinking?" and "Don't you agree?"

The backwardness of the working class, and particularly its narrow-minded attitude toward women, minorities, and socialist theory, forms one of the main issues of *Fish in the Sea*. The play is injected with a healthy dose of satire to expose these biased reactions. Sandra Maconochie, for example, is mocked for her exaggerated reliance on the "wisdom" and questionable values of teenage magazines and other such publications that manipulate the consumer mentality of the masses. As a result, when she gets married she insists on having a flashy church wedding with limousines and a fancy reception, even though her father and her husband-to-be are out of work. Mrs. Maconochie quite rightly puts her daughter straight by telling her that when she got married "it was a toss-up between a fish-supper for all or ham sandwiches" (p. 49).

Fish in the Sea not only criticizes the soap opera mentality of working-class girls but also the macho mentality of the men. For this purpose, Mary Maconochie serves as a deflating satiric agent:

> Men. Think all they've got to do is put their arm around you, breathe their stinking breath up your nose, whisper a few corny phrases, fumble for your tits, and bingo, you'll satisfy their every whim. Once that's all over, and you're lumbered with them for life, all you've got is cooking and washing and ironing—you're supposed to be a lovely, warm, kind person that everybody loves—mum. Mum's the word. [p. 40]

Likewise, the typical working-class prejudice against homosexuals is ridiculed as the striking factory occupants receive a letter from the Gay Liberation Front—"Fucking Fairies Union"—which turns out to contain a sizeable contribution for the Strike Fund, thus teaching the workers that sexual oppression and economic exploitation are related.

Fish in the Sea also exposes the relation between the workers' predicament and the activities of two institutions that traditionally enjoy the respect of the proletariat: the Church and the Labour party. The religious control over the working class is represented through the figure of the ridiculous, authoritarian reverend Teifian Griffiths of the Tuebrook Ebenezer Baptist Chapel who "conned all the lads of the neighbourhood into playing ping-pong for God" (p. 2). The Labour party is satirized through the cabaretesque song "Three Labour MPs" in which three Labour politicians who pretend to have come to the rescue of the factory occupiers expose themselves as defenders of the political status quo. They reveal that they are more interested in getting proletarian votes than looking after proletarian interests:

> THREE MPs: We will give you pie in the sky
> And you can catch it flying by—
> If you'll votey, votey, votey, votey
> If you'll vote for us. . . .
> BAND: Three Labour MPs,
> Oh what a disease—
> If ever the bosses are shaking with fright,
> Get three Labour MPs.
> THREE MPs: Don't rock the boat, be good now, boys,
> Go back to work and shut your noise,
> And we'll see Wedgey, Wedgey, Wedgey,
> We'll see Wedgewood Benn. . . .
> Oh we will lead you in your fight,
> Then we'll drop you right in the shite,
> If you'll votey, votey, votey,
> If you'll vote for us. [p. 67]

Finally, the "anarchistic, antiorganisational violence of the frustrated working-class individual in search of self-fulfillment here and now" finds expression in the none-too-positive character of Andy. He is the seventies version of the angry young man: the punk constantly looking for a fight in which he can express his rage against society. He indulges his anger rather than try to understand its socioeconomic causes. He is in constant need of quick excitement and finds it doing a few freelance jobs for the IRA. Andy explains his actions: "So you take a few risks—shoot a few soldiers, blow up a few pubs—but you get used to taking those risks. Your whole life's a bloody risk. But at least you're out of dying alive through sheer bloody slavery" (p. 74). 7:84 is sympathetic to the plight of working men and women and all the oppressed people all over the world, but it does not condone senseless violence like Andy's, or what it regards as the misdirected war of Protestants fighting Papists in Northern Ireland. In their eyes, these religious adversaries should unite to kick out the British imperialist.

It is 7:84's professed objective to put its shows in the service of the political struggle for an equitable, socialist society. But often its plays are also inspired by a certain frustration over the failure of the working class to vote for its own interest. The theatre company has also had to struggle against opposition from the government. After a successful national tour of *Fish in the Sea,* 7:84 had planned to produce John Arden's and Margaret D'Arcy's *Ballygombeen Bequest* and *Sergeant Musgrave Dances On,* McGrath's adaptation of Arden's modern classic *Serjeant Musgrave's Dance.* At the end of 1972, however, this project was canceled because of libel charges filed by the British government against the authors and the company. Both plays deal with the explosive situation in Northern Ireland and attack the activities of both the Provisional IRA and the British military. Consequently, 7:84 was denied a lucrative grant from the Arts Council and was forced to stop its operations indefinitely. The troupe split up: Gavin Richards, a talented actor-director, settled in London and started the Belt and Braces Theatre Company; other company members also returned to the capital to do freelance work; and John McGrath, his wife, Elisabeth MacLennan, David MacLennan, and Ferelith Lean went to the north to start the Scottish branch of the 7:84 Theatre Company.

With the Liverpool plays, John McGrath had already expressed his belief in the importance of radical regional theatre that speaks to the concerns of a regional audience in its own terms. With the formation of the Scottish 7:84, McGrath's radical regional commitment became even more evident. The first creative product to emerge from this new theatrical venture was *The Cheviot, the Stag and the Black, Black Oil,* a play about the exploitation of the Scottish Highlanders by mostly English landowners and industrialists and their Scottish associates. Covering three centuries of capitalist oppression—each symbolized by one of the three elements of the play's title—the play intends to set the effects of capital on traditional Highland living into a historical perspective. John McGrath consciously chose the *Ceilidh,* a traditional form of entertainment of the Highlands, as the basic formal structure of the show and added new lyrics to popular folk tunes and more than a touch of his characteristic humor.[14] After its initial performance in Edinburgh, *The Cheviot* was taken on tour to the remotest of villages in Northern Scotland and the Hebrides Islands. After some hundred performances the play was taken to Ireland, where the Gaelic audiences also positively related to the traditional formal elements and recognized the historical analysis of the Scottish situation as their own. Traveling in an old van and doubling as musicians, technicians, and public-relations managers, the actors of 7:84 established their company as a true radical popular theatre.

The Cheviot, the Stag and the Black, Black Oil is, in many ways, a paradigmatic radical popular play. It explicitly addresses the regional political struggle against economic exploitation of the Scots in general and the Highlanders in particular. The 7:84 Theatre Company took the play to the remotest areas of the Scottish Highlands in order to entertain and inform the rural target audience. Although the actual text was created by John McGrath, most of the character conceptions and historical documentation came from the improvisation and extensive source study of the actors and actresses. For this purpose, each company member was given a special area which he or she had to investigate in libraries and museums. The memories told by old Highlanders also went into the play. A preliminary version of *The Cheviot* was presented at a conference on the future of Scotland, and many valuable suggestions were incorporated in subsequent versions of the play. Furthermore, songs and lyrics were often adapted to local circumstances and the musical tastes of the audience. The play also contains a good deal of humor in the form of puns, mimicry, theatrical playfulness, and sharp satire. Finally, the performances of *The Cheviot* were always preceded by catchy fiddling and the singing of folk songs, and afterwards the company (featuring John McGrath on drums) doubled as a rock band and folk musicians that kept the audience dancing until deep in the night. The traditional *Ceilidh* structure is flexible enough to accommodate such varied application:

> This is usually a gathering at which all, or most of those present, with or without the aid of whiskey, sing a song, tell a story, play an instrument, have a good blether, and occasionally end up dancing until the next morning. In the past, these gatherings had also had their political side, particularly at the time of the Land Leagues, and stories of Highland history and oppression had been passed on.[15]

Throughout the play an atmosphere of joyful public celebration pervades. The "good night out" begins with animation by a fiddler and actors and actresses preparing their props and costumes while chatting with the audience. A master of ceremonies comes on to warm up the audience with some traditional folk songs and establishes the format for the evening: "Later on we're going to have a few more songs like that one—if you know the words, join in—and then we're going to have a dance, and in between we'll be telling a story. It's a story that has a beginning, a middle, but, as yet, no end—" (p. 2). The story itself is presented in a Brechtian alternation of showing and telling: dramatized illustrations of the Highland expulsions interchange with documentary-style presentations of facts. Gaelic songs add a bilingual aspect to the show, and, throughout, the cast of eight jumps in and out of character to portray the large collection of historical and fictional figures that animate the play.

The play is so full of information, analyses, satire, characters, and songs that only a relatively loose cabaret-revue structure can keep its components together. In this way, *The Cheviot, the Stag and the Black, Black Oil* manages to convey that the cruelty of the Clearances is not an isolated incident imposed by some sadistic individuals but an inherent consequence of the capitalist system expanding over the entire globe. To emphasize this point, an old man from the eighteenth century and just evicted from his Highlands home steps forward to address the audience:

> Huge profits were being made already as a result of the Industrial Revolution, and improved methods of agriculture. This accumulated wealth had to be used, to make more profit—because this is the law of capitalism. It expanded all over the globe. And just as it saw in Africa, the West Indies, Canada, the Middle East and

China ways of increasing itself, so in the Highlands of Scotland it saw the same opportunity. The technological innovation was there: the Cheviot, a breed of sheep that would survive the Highland winter and produce fine wool. The money was there. Unfortunately, the people were there too. But the law of capitalism had to be obeyed. [p. 15]

The old man makes a clear connection between the Scottish peasants being kicked off their land in the eighteenth century and the plight of the oppressed people elsewhere in the world. This relation is dramatically illustrated by a scene in which deported Highlanders are forced to settle Indian territories of Upper Canada. This episode is somewhat enlivened by comic horseplay in which the audience participates as they are supposed to warn the "Sturdy Highlander" when they spot a Red Indian. This develops into a "They see me/they don't see me" routine but the message remains clear: "Red Indians were reduced to the same state as [the Scottish] fathers after Culloden—defeated, hunted, treated like the scum of the earth, their culture polluted and torn out with slow deliberation and their land no longer their own" (p. 29).

For the radical popular theatre there is no question that oppression and exploitation go hand in hand with the suppression of indigenous culture. In a documentary interlude, *The Cheviot* indicates that, in the eighteenth century, speaking Gaelic was made illegal and that delegitimization of Gaelic culture continues even to this day. With its play, 7:84 wants to show how Church, state, and educational institutions united to destroy the native culture of Scotland. It also indicates possible ways in which Gaelic culture could be revived and, moreover, how such a revival is indispensable to prevent the third phase of economic expropriation from taking place.

The title of the play refers to the three elements that made Scottish real estate profitable for capitalist investment during three distinctive historical periods. The cheviot arrived on the scene in the early 1800s and forced the Highlanders out of their homes. The stag and the tourist industry started in the Victorian era and developed Scotland as a sporting ground for the idle rich with no regard for the native inhabitants. Finally, the black, black oil refers to the discovery of petroleum off the Scottish coast in the early 1970s bringing huge profits to foreign investors and only social and economic disaster to the Scottish work force.

The subject matter of *The Cheviot* almost demands to be cast in historical tragedy, but, along with the rest of the international radical popular theatre movement, 7:84 believes that tears do not purge and only blur a clear analysis. The contemporary radical popular theatre avoids melodrama; it has a satirical temperament and feels a commitment to provide comic and musical entertainment. Also it seems to dance cheerfully through the most atrocious historical facts. But the play drives its points home while also remaining faithful to its objective of providing the audience with a good night out.

The satire of *The Cheviot* is similar to that of other radical popular plays discussed in earlier chapters. The satirical victims are often regional politicians selling out to the central government and to ruthless capitalists; the most frequently used satirical technique is deflating "self-exposure." The play is full of satire that deconstructs the power structure: representatives of official institutions that help perpetuate the status quo at the expense of the common man are severely mocked. Thus, the Church is satirized for attempting to subdue the revolutionary anger of the Highlanders who were deported from their own lands to the coast or even to Canada. Instead of explaining this eviction as profit oriented, the Church justified it as "a judgment from God, and a warning of the final judgment to come" (p. 13).

After the Clearances had effectively depopulated the Highlands and the Hebrides, the new wilderness was turned into a hunter's paradise for the leisure class from south of the border. But in the course of the twentieth century, tourism developed as an industry and bought the aristocracy out of the area. Andy McChuckemup of Crammem Inn Investments Ltd., a caricature of the greedy real-estate developer, describes his plans for modernizing the Highlands:

> The motel—as I see it—is the thing of the future. That's how we see it, myself and the Board of Directors and one or two of your local councillors—come on now, these are the best men money can buy. So—picture it, if yous will, right there at the top of the glen, beautiful vista—the Crammem Inn, High Rise Motorcroft—all finished in natural, washable, plastic granitette. Right next door, the 'Frying Scotsman' All Night Chipperama—with a wee ethnic bit, Fingal's Caff—serving seaweed-suppers-in-the-basket, and draught Drambuie. And to cater for the younger set, yous've got your Grouse-a-go-go. [pp. 48–49]

The list of satirized capitalist exploiters is further extended with Texas Jim, an abrasive "free-booting-oil-man" who enters wearing a ten-gallon hat and, like his aristocratic and bourgeois predecessors, claims, "These are *my* mountains," in a bluegrass country music voice. He is assisted in his cabaret routine by Mr. Whitehall, who obviously symbolizes the involvement of the British government with the American oil tycoons. Texas Jim apparently finds Whitehall much more cooperative than the fellows he had to work with in Norway, Algeria, and Libya, who charged him an arm and a leg in taxes. Whitehall did not want to discourage American oil companies and masked its leniency by publicly promising Scotland an industrial boom. But the Texas oil magnate blatantly reveals his true interests through an attractive little song:

> There's many a barrel of oil in the sea
> All waiting for drilling and piping to me
> I'll refine it in Texas, you'll get it, you'll see
> At four times the price that you sold it to me. [p. 63][16]

Significantly, the actors who play Texas Jim and Whitehall are the same people that played the aristocratic hunters of the nineteenth century and the eviction supervisors of the Clearances.

The Cheviot sets up convincing historical parallels to reveal the capitalist intentions behind the present oil boom. Through songs, documentary drama, and dramatized historical particulars, the play attempts to explain that the development of the Scottish oil industry is not an isolated case. It is just another chapter in a long string of economic exploitation initiated by outside capitalists and condoned by the local ruling class:

> Then it was the Great Sheep.
> Now it is the Black, Black Oil.
> Then it was done by outside capital, with the connivance of the local ruling class and central government—And the local people had no control over what was happening to them. Now it is being done by outside capital, with the connivance of the local ruling class and central government. Have we learnt anything from the Clearances?
> When the Cheviot came, only the landlords benefited.
> When the Stag came, only the upper-class sportsmen benefited.
> Now the Black, Black Oil is coming. And must come. It could benefit everybody. But if it is developed in the capitalist way, only the multi-national corporations and local speculators will benefit. [p. 73]

And after this recapitulation, the play ends with a call for organized opposition through a Gaelic song from the 1890s.

With *The Cheviot, the Stag and the Black, Black Oil,* the Scottish 7:84 Theatre Company established a strong reputation for itself in the British Isles and beyond. The show toured for many months and was subsequently broadcast on television throughout most of the British Commonwealth. 7:84–Scotland consolidated its working-class support with a number of plays dealing with the historical development of the labor movement in the Scottish urban centers. These plays—among which *The Game's a Bogey* (1974), *Little Red Hen* (1975), and *Yobbo Nowt* (1976) stand out—are all structured on the same aesthetic principles as the previous creations, although their story lines are considerably more focused than the rather disparate *Cheviot.* All three later plays present their historical analyses through the particularized stories of specific individuals. In other words, they present a human context with which the working-class spectator can identify. As before, music, song, and humor play an essential part in these plays that were performed throughout Scotland in community centers, school halls, trade council clubs, and regular theatres.

Meanwhile, the English 7:84 was revived in 1975 with a new production of McGrath's *Fish in the Sea.* It has remained active since, supported by an annual

ARC Theatre Company. One of the many songs in *The Game's a Bogey* (1984),
a musical play by John McGrath about John McLean, a Scottish socialist worker
and activist.

grant from the British Arts Council. John McGrath is artistic director of both the
Scottish and the English companies and in that capacity supervises the stylistic
continuity of all 7:84 productions. The great majority of the plays produced by
7:84 (England and Scotland) are from the hand of John McGrath himself, but in
recent years other playwrights have also been commissioned to write plays.
According to Bob Rae, 7:84–England's friendly publicity manager, the works of
the other authors differ considerably from the typical John McGrath play:

> Throughout McGrath's work there runs a very recognizable line of sympathy for
> working-class people, and a desire to get them to recognize their own history, their
> own culture, and by recognizing that, to change the situation. This lies behind
> most of McGrath's writing. Now we also do other shows like *One Big Blow* which
> do not contain one coherent line, or one direct statement saying how the workers
> historically got into this situation and how changes could be obtained. It doesn't
> say that. It presents an entertaining picture of news items differently from what
> people would read in the newspapers. It presents the humor of their lives, some of
> the warmth of working-class lives. It makes no great ideological points. And it is
> very theatrical, which is considerably different from what McGrath does.[17]

One of the latest 7:84–England productions was *Ticker Tape and V-signs/Jimmy Riddle* (1983), a double bill written by Peter Cox. *Ticker Tape and V-signs* features the story of a young black soldier who returns to a triumphant welcome after fighting in the Falklands war. His heroic reception is placed in contrast to the racist treatment his mother received when she arrived in Britain several decades ago. *Jimmy Riddle* is a one-man, one-act play about the emotional sufferings of a shop steward at the closed-down British Leyland No. 2 Plant in Speke, Liverpool. In the play, Jimmy returns to the vacant apartment from which he had been evicted after his wife and children left him. In a long, lively monologue with imagined appearances of his wife and two children, several flashbacks, and an imaginary soccer match in which he scores a hat trick, Jimmy tells about the experiences he has had since he was sacked. "He is washing out at the unions," explains Bob Rae,

> at the newspapers, at British Leyland, the largest nationalised car factory. Which has been the butt of rightwing attacks ever since it was nationalised. Basically what they wanted to do was to chop it all down. Jimmy Riddle got sacked by the management. Jimmy, with his typical big mouth, lashes out at them. Now, a McGrath play would have sought to explain what happened to people and put it in a historical context. Whereas the play that Pete wrote wanted to present an alternative view of the situation, and give an expression of the situation in working-class language, in terms of working-class experience, the limited working-class experience of a rather narrow-minded shop steward who is very sexist, who is a fairly ordinary sort of bloke—I don't mean that in a patronizing way— who is, in any event, not a great political thinker. But he has something to say, a typical man in that sort of situation. It is more than one can read in the newspapers. Here we see a man who is worried about the relationship with his wife, he is wondering why his friends are deserting him. There is no explicit ideological message.[18]

Like the Scottish 7:84 Theatre Company, the English 7:84 goes to working-class audiences and performs predominantly at labor clubs, community centers and other places frequented by workers and their class allies. The English 7:84 firmly adheres to the ingredients that have guaranteed the success of the Scottish company and the international radical popular theatre at large. In its shows, 7:84 highlights particularly: 1) a high political content without underestimating the awareness of the audience; 2) the element of song; 3) strong theatrical elements that make the performance visually exciting; 4) a great deal of humor, for 7:84 is not just agitprop, not merely dramatized political messages—it wants people to enjoy themselves.

7:84 has very high production standards. Most of its venues are at nontheatre situations that are technically limited. Yet, Bob Rae says, "We go to labor clubs and tell them that we'd like to present them with a piece of theatre that is as good,

The 7:84 Theatre Company-England. Poster for *V-Signs* (1983).

quality wise, as any show on the West End. We own all the equipment ourselves and wherever we go we take a rig with us, because most of the places that we perform at are very poorly equipped to receive a theatre company."[19]

Both 7:84 companies regard themselves as radical popular theatre enterprises. John McGrath oversees the activities of both branches from his Edinburgh office. The English troupe consists of three full-time actors, plus a person who covers the administration, one technical manager, and Bob Rae as publicity manager. Throughout the year, both companies commission directors, costume makers, and writers, as well as actors. Many people return after a commission, which is important for the perpetuation of stylistic continuity. All the guest directors are socialists. Although actors and directors are not directly involved in the company's policy-making process, they participate in the play's creation from beginning to end. They often conduct interviews with prospective target audience members, and the writer incorporates the results of improvisational ensemble rehearsals in continuously updated versions of the play. Such a time-consuming, intensive contact between writer and performers is necessary to create a close-knit group that is committed to the show. "Just imagine, six, seven, eight weeks of one-night stands, working together, requires a high level of commitment, otherwise you wouldn't do it," explains Bob Rae, "if an actor is ready to do that, he doesn't just do it for the money."[20]

7:84 defines itself as being in opposition to the dominant culture; yet, over the years, it has managed to gain high respect for its productions, both from working-class and bourgeois circles. Today, its main objective remains to give cultural confidence to the workers by means of top-quality theatrical products. 7:84 sees itself not only fighting the cultural establishment, it also combats the potent forces that manipulate public opinion. According to Bob Rae, however, 7:84 does not glorify the proletariat:

> Jimmy Riddle, for instance, is no hero. But he's somebody to be respected, to be understood, not to be ridiculed. And I suppose it affected people that saw the play in such a way. And next time there'll be a lot of attacks against shop stewards, they will perhaps say, "Well, it's the same bloke, not just some political figure but a natural person. He actually has far more in common with me than the picture presented of him by the newspapers."[21]

The use of proletarian cultural traditions is an obvious and indispensable factor in promoting the cultural and social confidence of the working class. 7:84 draws its inspiration from the Unity Theatre of working-class writers and the music hall. Proletarian culture in England goes back a long way, and 7:84 uses whatever forms it finds useful. In a show called *Trafford Tanzi* written by Claire Luckham (1982), for example, the English 7:84 used the format of freestyle wrestling. And many of John McGrath's plays are strongly influenced by the music-hall show structure: bits of plays, stand-up comedy routines and songs held together by an MC.

The 7:84 Theatre Company-Scotland. The Citizen's Theatre in Glasgow, venue for 7:84-Scotland's production of *The Ragged Trousered Philanthropists* (1984).

In 1984, the Scottish 7:84 toured with a theatre adaptation of Robert Tressell's classic proletarian novel *The Ragged Trousered Philanthropists,* thus holding true to its often proclaimed objective to present "the realities of working-class life and history directly to working-class audiences without translating it into the language of middle class 'theatre' that has dominated our stages since the nineteenth century."[22] The play is set in the west of Scotland in 1908, where a group of housepainters is working on the new home of the provost of Mugsburgh. The play feelingly depicts their fears of being fired, their rivalries and intrigues, and their humoristic solidarity that is often expressed in song. The play is written in an urban Scottish dialect and contains a goodly amount of verbal humor attuned to the regional taste. It is a visually very sophisticated show that gently mocks the lack of political consciousness on the part of the construction workers and viciously satirizes the ruthless capitalists and their boot-licking associates.

Appropriately, *The Ragged Trousered Philanthropists* opened at Mayfest, Glasgow's annual festival of popular theatre. The atmosphere of the performance that I witnessed at the Citizens' Theatre could be likened to that in the stands of the Glasgow Rangers soccer stadium: the spectators wore 7:84 T-shirts, buttons, and caps; they talked about the actors as about famous soccer stars, and they surrounded tall, white-haired John McGrath as a popular hero. They chanted along whenever the highly competent actors would tune up one of the many popular working-class ballads that punctuated the play.

The English 7:84 was also represented at Mayfest '84 with a new play called *School for Emigrants,* a collective creation directed by Canadian Paul Thompson. The play is set in Rotherham, a steelworkers community in the Midlands that sports an unemployment rate of 65 percent. The actors of 7:84 talked and worked closely with Rotherham residents in the local community center, and, based on their stories, they created *School for Emigrants,* a play about a Canadian labor recruiter who comes to Rotherham to find and train suitable workers for a company in the New World. With promises of big bucks he succeeds in getting a group of people interested in emigrating and educates them to the American way of life. At the end, however, the few potential emigrants who remain find themselves at Heathrow airport with a one-way ticket in their hands. They decide that escaping from Rotherham is not a constructive way of dealing with the problem, and one by one they return home, stripped of an illusion but considerably richer in solidarity.

School for Emigrants serves the important purpose of giving courage to the increasing numbers of unemployed workers in the British Isles. 7:84–Scotland also decided to provide cultural support for the 1984–85 miners' strike with an adaptation of Joe Corrie's 1926 play *In Time of Strife.* Britain's radical left interpreted the miners' strike as a potentially powerful destabilizing force that could undermine both Thatcher's reactionary government and Labour's traditional hold on the working-class vote so that a new leftist movement could emerge. *In Time of Strife* was revived because it was an important but unrecognized contribution to Scottish culture and because it dramatizes the sufferings of a Fife community shortly after the six-month strike of 1926. The play particularly highlights the perseverance of women to keep the strike going.

Throughout its career, 7:84 has made a concerted effort to emphasize the importance of women in the class struggle. In plays like *Little Red Hen* (1975), *Blood Red Roses* (1981), *Men Should Weep* (1982), *Women in Power* (1983), and the recent *Baby and the Bathwater* (1984–85), powerful women are featured who persevere in the political fight when men are ready to give up. Usually McGrath's wife, Elisabeth MacLennan, plays the female leads, as she did to high c   ical acclaim in the one-woman show *The Baby and the Bathwater.* In this political cabaret that is filled with songs and music from Chilean composer Carlos Arredondo, Elisabeth MacLennan plays a variety of roles ranging from George Orwell's "Imperial Policeman" and Julie from Pilton, who is terrified of Communism after reading *1984,* to Rigoberta Menchu, the 25-year-old Quiché Indian representative of the Guatemalan *Unidad Campesina* ("United Peasants"). The title of the show constitutes really a question to Orwell. Did he, 7:84 asks, throw the baby away with the bathwater when he rejected Communism following the Spanish Civil War and the Stalinist purges in the USSR? In passages like

Rigoberta Menchu's account of her mother's sadistic torture at the hands of Guatemalan soldiers, the show leaves little doubt that he did.

Meanwhile, 7:84–Scotland's future plans include a continuation of tours to the Highlands, the Hebrides, and the Shetland Islands with shows that speak to the concerns of the regional Scottish population. In a preface to *The Albannach*, a play based on the novel of the same title by Fionn MacColla, John McGrath expressed the company's intention to present "a series of plays based more on stories than on argument, more narrative than polemical. And to go with them, bigger casts and more theatrically ambitious productions." One of the first of these new enterprises was a large-scale project with an Edinburgh community center in the spring of 1986.

7:84–Scotland's "expand-or-perish" strategy seems to be typical of a general trend in the radical popular theatre of Great Britain. On the one hand, the once-militant theatre artists want to pursue their artistic ambitions. On the other hand, decreasing government spending has made it increasingly difficult to obtain theatre subsidies. 7:84–Scotland has been relatively free from such worries since it continues to be supported by the progressive Scottish Arts Council. But despite vigorously fought publicity campaigns, 7:84–England has lost all its British Arts Council funds and has been forced to indefinitely halt its activities as of August 1985. Other leftist fringe companies have suffered similar fates. The Arts Council of Great Britain has even threatened to withdraw the subsidy of the Royal Court Theatre, the institution that was single-handedly responsible for the emergence of the powerful British drama of the sixties and seventies. Margaret Thatcher's subsidy policy has effectively eliminated most progressive forums for young playwrights. Even dynamic regional companies like 7:84–Scotland have decided to take fewer risks in their programming. There is material enough for political theatre in Thatcher's Britain, but the revolutionary fervor that animated so many moneyless troupes in the late sixties and early seventies seems lacking now and may well result in the untimely death of Britain's radical popular theatre movement.

CHAPTER 7

EMANCIPATORY DRAMA FOR CHILDREN AND YOUTH IN WEST GERMANY
Radical Popular Theatre for the Next Generation

The development of radical popular theatre in West Germany is harder to trace than in any other country discussed so far. Many groups came and went without leaving any documentation and scripts at all. Today, there is a bustling activity of *freie Gruppen* ("Free Groups"), who call themselves free because they are unsubsidized groups that create emancipatory theatre for the masses. Only a few of these troupes, however, have roots all the way back in the late sixties.[1] Once successful popular troupes like Berlin's Hoffmann Comic Theater and Munich's Rote Rübe have been defunct for years now. In West Germany, the most consistent effort to make radical popular theatre has been made by a number of youth and children's theatre groups, among which particularly the Grips Theater from Berlin stands out.

The only way to get an idea of how the contemporary West German popular theatre movement developed from the student revolts of the late sixties is to talk directly to those artists who witnessed and participated directly in its activities. From all accounts it can now be established that most of the theatrical reactions to the authoritarian repression of the late sixties took the form of agitprop street theatre. Highly documentary in nature, street theatre pieces quickly digressed into boring, stilted calls for revolution and soon made way for the understanding that successful popular theatre should convey political meaning not through the undramatic presentation of dry facts but through fun and entertainment. Wolfgang Anrath, now artistic director of Munich's Theater K (K stands for *Kollektiv*), recalls:

> I started with street theatre in January '68. The main activities of the street theatre in those days were directed against the declared state of emergency. What we did back then was with original texts taken from the fascist period and texts from the state of emergency. We made a scene collage with these texts and added commentary to it, and thus we simply transformed documentary texts into action. We traveled around in the streetcar and the bus and played everywhere. Whenever the new situation called for it, we made changes, until May '68.[2]

Pure agitprop proved unsatisfactory, and already in the fall of 1968 Anrath started experimenting with other theatrical forms. He used Bavarian peasant farces and music in what developed into highly successful political revues that were performed in neighborhood bars and on construction sites. In 1970 Anrath decided to start a long-term theatre project with professional actors; this became the Theater K, which today is considered one of the more important youth theatre companies in southern West Germany.

Theater K is, however, but a minor enterprise compared to the quality and professionalism of West Berlin's Grips Theater. Although primarily catering to an audience of grade school and high school pupils, Grips's plays come closer than any other contemporary West German drama to the style of the international radical popular theatre movement. Volker Ludwig, director and chief playwright of Grips, himself admits to feeling a close affinity with foreign radical popular theatre groups that cater to adult target audiences:

> We don't really think of ourselves as a theatre for a specific age group but rather as a certain type of political theatre. The theatrical form that we create for children and youths could be continued just the same as theatre for adults, and maybe we will do that too. We have tried it in one play, *Eine Linke Geschichte* ["A Story of the Left"]; this is a play about ourselves, a big success. It's the story of two students who met during an anti-Vietnam demonstration in 1966, and we follow their political development. We see a clear link, then, between radical children's theatre and radical people's theatre for grown-ups. And our theatre is also understood that way. That means that the evening performances of our youth plays are always sold out. They also attract a normal theatre audience for lack of any other theatre that is critical of the times.[3]

Grips's plays for children and youths are, then, legitimate forms of radical popular theatre that recruits its target audience among the next generation.

Like so many other radical troupes, Grips's origins lie in the student movement of the sixties. Its original founders were leading members of the Berlin Reichskabarett, a student group that created programs of satirical sketches interspersed with topical songs. German *Kabarett* is a highly entertaining, fast-paced form of satire in performance that, with its strong musical element, is closely related to the popular theatre that emerged in the United States and Western Europe after 1968.

One of the characteristic features of *Kabarett* is its satirical response to current political events. The Reichskabarett was no exception and often stood at the center of great controversies. Ludwig explains:

> In 1967 we made our first Vietnam show. People simply didn't believe the facts. That's because Berlin is an extremely pro-American city because of the airlifts during the blockade. That's why polarization was so strong in Berlin. But after a while our theatre became an enormous success; it became fashionable to be leftist. We even got good reviews from the [reactionary] *Bildzeitung*, although our shows became more and more aggressive. So after a while we no longer saw the point in doing *Kabarett* for such an audience.[4]

The people of the Reichskabarett decided to pursue different theatrical avenues, which fairly soon resulted in the resolution to perform children's theatre. According to Volker Ludwig, this decision was partly prompted by the fact that theatre in West Germany was and is a very bourgeois affair: only 5 percent of the population attends the theatre on a regular basis. The Reichskabarett people, however, wanted to reach a different audience:

> *Kabarett* was much more intellectual; it was for students; it had a function all its own. We wanted to reach the entire population, and that was only possible through youth and children's theatre. Children's theatre reaches school classes, and these classes had been been made politically aware by school teachers who had been politicized at the same time as we.[5]

The Reichskabarett founded its Theatre for Children not because it absolutely wanted to work exclusively with children but because it wanted to create political theatre for a target group that was in dire need of solidarity. Children constitute, of course, just as legitimate an audience for radical popular theatre as oppressed adults. Furthermore, in the late sixties, West German children's theatre consisted predominantly of Christmastime fairy tale dramatizations. Just as children's literature in general is rarely taken seriously as an art form, children's theatre was derided by professional performers. The sustained creative efforts of Grips over a period of fifteen years, however, have by now gained a worldwide reputation. The troupe has performed throughout Europe, and its plays have been produced professionally more than five hundred times in twenty-six different languages. Amateur productions are countless.

Although the Reichskabarett started doing children's plays in 1966, it did not become a full-time children's theatre until 1969, when a quarrel split the *Kabarett* in two. The faction that later started calling itself Grips (after a German expression meaning "the ability to get a quick grasp on a situation") conceived of children's theatre as a means to effect social change, just like *Kabarett*. The ideological motivation to make emancipatory theatre for an underprivileged social group was, as for so many other radical troupes, inspired by ideas about antiauthoritarianism and the revolutionary function of culture. Aesthetically speaking, however, Grips disclaims any direct influence from groups such as el Teatro Campesino and Bread and Puppet who performed in Berlin in 1968. The awareness that its theatrical forms had a great affinity with those of other prominent foreign radical troupes came much later. Grips does, however, admit that a Brechtian type of distancing forms an essential aspect of its style. This distancing is particularly evident in the fact that adult actors play children. Nevertheless, *Kabarett* forms the most important source of formal inspiration for Grips's plays:

> The great advantage that we have is that we come from *Kabarett*. That is, in *Kabarett* you learn timing. One knows that the greatest sin is to bore people. If you can't entertain the people, you shouldn't take their money. Entertainment is the most important. That was also very clear with the San Francisco Mime Troupe, who played here a few years ago. Or with Molière, who said, "If you move someone to tears, the entire contents flow away; in order to laugh one must understand first." It should, therefore, not be laughter at someone else's expense but a laughter of recognition. In addition, in *Kabarett* one learns not to drag things on too long and to focus on a specific audience. And one learns also to translate these things into song. I am convinced that Grips would never have become a success without its *Kabarett* tradition.[6]

Grips's plays are marked, then, by the pace, the music, and the good humor of *Kabarett*. They do, however, contain linear plots instead of self-contained sketches, and developed personalities rather than caricatures or stereotypes. The German theatre critic Arno Paul has pointed out that the primary reason for adding these structural dramatic elements to the *Kabarett* frame was that children need a narrative line for guidance in discovering the connections and contradictions in a developing situation. Furthermore, a firm narrative structure also enables them to understand human behavior as a changeable process rather than as a fixed given.[7]

Grips's plays have developed considerably over the period between 1969 and 1984, although the basic style and creative process have remained more or less unchanged. As with so many other radical troupes, the creative process at Grips can best be described as collective. Although there is a main author—in most cases Volker Ludwig and an associate—there is strong input from the actors:

We insist that an author stay with us till the very last day. He must allow a lot of input from the actors. The actors have by now so much experience that they know what will work and what won't. So the thing works as follows: a subject is proposed at a general meeting. It is accepted or rejected. Anyone can speak up if he or she has problems with it. Then the authors are asked to write a play on the subject. As soon as a skeleton structure of the play is ready, a cast is selected and a production group is formed which consists of technicians, directors, actors, musicians, etc. This group researches the subject together with the authors. That is to say, we have division of labor just like any other theatre, but we work much more intensively together.[8]

The research part is taken very seriously. For the radical popular theatre, so intimately involved in political and social reality, a thorough investigation of its sources is indispensable. Emotional arguments have little or no place in its plays, and every action and speech must be substantiated with documented facts. In the preparatory stages of a new play, Grips stays in close contact with its target audience. Directors and authors visit schools to talk with teachers and pupils. Also, when the creators feel somewhat insecure about a play that is being rehearsed, they invite a teacher and a group of children to come and watch a few scene cuttings and invite their comments and criticisms. As far as the themes are concerned, Grips makes a concerted effort to move along with the changing preoccupations of its audience. Thus, for the recent play *Alles Plastik* ("Everything is Plastic"), the troupe asked 700 West Berlin high school students to write an essay with the title, "I am forty years old and look back on my life." This project resulted in the staggering discovery of a pervasive "no-future" mentality among adolescents. Over 20 percent of the students thought that they would live to see the end of the world. Even the most optimistic among them wanted to live the few years left them in unconcerned luxury.

Grips's intense contact with its target audience extends into the postproduction period. The troupe supplies inexpensive, printed texts of the plays, which also include the materials and conclusions of the preproduction source studies. These *Nachbereitungshefte,* or "follow-up guides," are full of facts, figures, and theoretical essays and can form the basis of fruitful classroom discussions. Subsequently, through reports from teachers and students, Grips receives the feedback that is so essential to any political theatre that hopes to make an effective contribution to social change.

Structurally and thematically speaking, the more recent Grips plays are substantially different from those of, say, a decade ago. The plays have become more complex and more realistic. The early plays were marked by a pervasive antiauthoritarian attitude and by a desire to let children establish themselves. Children on the Grips stage used to be little supermen who knew everything better than the adults; the grown-ups were often stereotyped. *Der Spinner* ("The Dreamer"), the children's play that Grips performed in the spring of 1984, is a rewritten version of a much older play that was first produced in 1973. A comparison of the two plays well illustrates the evolution in Grips's play structure over a ten-year period.

The original version of *Der Spinner* was entitled *Nashörner schiessen nicht* ("Rhinos Don't Shoot") and premiered at the opening of Grips's new permanent playhouse at West Berlin's Hansaplatz. With the improved facility, Grips was able to dramatically represent dream sequences and fantasies on stage, a practice which has become a hallmark of Grips performances ever since. On the whole, *Nashörner schiessen nicht* is much less focused on the psychological and social effects of the fantasy manipulation by commercials and advertisements than *Der Spinner*. More than anything, the original play emphasizes the protagonist's acquisition of class consciousness and the ultimate victory of the proletarian characters over the capitalist exploiter.

Both plays have the same basic plot, but the character construction and the resolution of the later version indicate a crucial change in thematic focus. Both plays tell the story of twelve-year-old Wolfgang Hannemann, an energetic grade school pupil blessed with an overly active imagination that causes him to dream about possessing big mansions, beautiful girls, and shiny sports cars in exotic settings. Wolfgang's lapses into a fantasy world of glamorous success form an obvious escape from the gloomy working-class conditions in which he has been brought up. In both plays, Wolfgang's imagination is fed by his real encounter with a millionaire environment through his upper-class friends Oliver and Pia Steinberg and through the opportunity that their father gives him to act in a television commercial.

Nashörner schiessen nicht analyzes the class structure of the contemporary society in a way that children are likely to understand. In the first scene, Wolfgang reveals himself to be blinded by the luxury and beauty of the rich, presented to him by travel brochures and advertisements. Concurrently, he is ashamed of his father's low social position. Mr. Hannemann makes a meager living as a billposter, a job marginally related to the advertisement industry. The first scene of the play ends with Wolfgang's clear rejection of his working-class background, for which he holds his father responsible instead of the economic system: "I will become something better! Something with which one can make loads of money and one can order others around. . . . And one can drive around in a big fat car and not on such a lousy bicycle as you do! And one lives in a white villa and not in such a dive as we!"[9]

Wolfgang's unrealistic worldview that has led him to an obsession with material possessions and social status is clearly inspired by the beautified images of advertisements. It is not surprising, therefore, that he indiscriminately accepts the well-groomed representatives of the upper middle class as attractive and, therefore, automatically benevolent. When Mrs. Steinberg enters in a fancy sports car, the stage directions inform us that Wolfgang stares at her as an appearance from his travel brochure (p. 14). And it is only a matter of time before he falls in love with her fashionably dressed, tennis-playing daughter, Pia, and drops his working-class love, Rita.

The main reason why Wolfgang is accepted by the obnoxiously spoiled upper-class brats is his creativity in acting out his outrageous fantasies. Wolfgang is simply great fun to be around despite his proletarian background. Oliver and Pia have been taught to despise working-class people, but Wolfgang takes no offense at their mocking his father's measly job. Instead, the young hero interprets his father's economic explanation of why it is so hard for the lower classes to become financially successful as a mean attempt to shatter his fantasies. But Mr. Hannemann gets the final word in scene 3 as he summarizes his point in a song:

> Really, there are people who tell you straight out
> That everybody has the same chances!
> When you are a shoeshine boy and work your butt off,
> Then, who knows, some day you'll be a millionaire.
> But of course! It has happened before!
> Only one in a million gets a chance like that!
> One guy has a lot of money, and only needs to go to the bank,
> The other one has to rely on the Sweepstakes his entire life.
> The children of the well-to-do almost always go to college,
> But the others don't even have their own room.
> Ha! Equal chances! They have never existed. . . . [p. 46][10]

He is fully aware of the dirty tricks that advertisement people play on their victims, who believe slogans without further thought. He has discovered that, despite what the ads say, Pepsi Cola does not make you young and beautiful and that gorgeous girls do not fall for the fancy cologne you are wearing. He also realizes that the longer his son continues to take advertisement images at face value, the more trouble he will have surviving in the real world. The sooner Wolfgang finds out about harsh economic reality, the better it will be.

The second part of *Nashörner schiessen nicht* shows Wolfgang's gradual awakening to the true nature of the capitalist world and the fake benevolence of the rich. The first flaw he discovers is the ruthlessly opportunistic Mr. Steinberg, who has no time for his children, does not love his wife, and is only concerned with making a fortune. Wolfgang gains a dawning awareness that it takes more than a luxurious house, a few expensive cars, a private tutor, and an endless supply of strawberry milkshakes to make a happy family. But before he reaches his ultimate moment of revelation, he first becomes Steinberg's victim in a blatant case of exploitation.

Steinberg sees a wonderful opportunity to capitalize on Wolfgang's uninhibited acting talents for a candy commercial. The young boy sees Steinberg's invitation as a perfect chance to become a movie star. During the preparations for the commercial, Wolfgang gradually starts seeing through the glamor of the

Steinbergs. First, when the candy company calls to request an additional girl in the commercial, Mr. Steinberg categorically refuses to use his own daughter. He does not want to embarass his family name in front of the entire world. Instead, he prefers to hire cheerful working-class children cheaply and ends up casting Wolfgang's ex-girlfriend, Rita. When Wolfgang tells Mr. Steinberg how to get to her house, Pia reacts with disgust: "Yech! Isn't that that stinking neighborhood where people live in rat holes? . . . *(To her mother)* You said so yourself! And also that they never wash themselves! And that they steal everything!" (p. 74).[11] Whereas Wolfgang had not taken offense at Oliver's denigrating his father's profession before, now his pride is visibly hurt by the social prejudice of the Steinbergs. He initially expresses this playfully by pretending he is a rat who steals little girls like Pia. This instance marks the first time in the play that Wolfgang's fantasy is inspired by reality and serves a social purpose: playing a rat, he proceeds to actually bite Pia to teach her that "when rats from Otto Street bite, it really hurts!" (p. 77).[12] From this point on, Wolfgang's class consciousness develops rapidly as he becomes aware that the Steinberg's friendliness is all fake; when Pia invites him to their house on the seaside, Mrs. Steinberg objects, implying that they do not want working-class people to go there; Wolfgang learns that he is going to get paid fifty Deutschmarks for his role in the commercial, whereas Mr. Steinberg will make fifty thousand; and when the boy learns that the Bahama setting of the commercial is not real but only a gigantic photograph in the studio, he finally understands the economic exploitation and the manipulation of illusion involved in the advertisements that had previously dominated his fantasies. Mr. Steinberg explains this to him in no uncertain terms:

> You have to eat a lot so that the children will buy a lot! Day after day! Buy, buy, buy! . . . That's why we're making the film! They have to want! And then they'll buy. Whether they want or not. Just imagine! That's the beauty of our profession: if we do a good job, we can incite millions of people to buy something they don't really want at all. [p. 86][13]

And from that moment on, the aesthetically attractive world of white villas and expensive sports cars starts crumbling. In the remainder of the play, Wolfgang learns to apply his fantasy and acting talents to expose the essential ugliness of the rich.

In the play's final dream sequence, Steinberg appears as a cutthroat gangster who is about to kill Wolfgang when Mr. Hannemann and Rita enter to save the hero. This dramatized fantasy serves the double function of expressing Wolfgang's profound change in perception and of announcing the play's finale, in which the children, aided by Hannemann, defeat Mr. and Mrs. Steinberg in a playful and satirical revenge. Interestingly, in this final scene Pia and Oliver act in solidarity with Wolfgang and Rita rather than with their own parents. The children's revenge consists in their making a parody of Steinberg's candy commercial. Wolfgang uses his superior imagination and actor's skills to exaggeratedly imitate Steinberg as the director of the film, effectively satirizing him in the process. And when Oliver suggests continuing the parody in one of the outrageous fantasy games involving yachts and shooting rhinos that Wolfgang used to play before, the latter expresses his newly gained political consciousness by stating: "Rhinos don't shoot! They do things that are totally different! Rhinos eat grass! . . . And they can run real fast! . . . But when someone hurts them or tries to mess with them, they become real angry! That's when they tear everything up with their big horn!" (p. 107).[14] He proceeds to play a mad rhino and attacks Steinberg, and in no time at all his father and friends follow his example.

Nashörner schiessen nicht emphasizes Wolfgang's development from an irresponsible dreamer who despises his social background to a lucid, class-conscious youngster who learns to use his fantasy pragmatically. Even though Wolfgang undergoes a similar change in *Der Spinner*, the focus in the later play is much less on economic and political elements than on social and psychological ones. Furthermore, the personalities of Mr. Hannemann, Mr. Steinberg, Oliver, and Pia are constructed differently.

Der Spinner differs most conspicuously from *Nashörner schiessen nicht* in its language, which is updated with the latest Berlin high school slang, and in additional social elements that fix the play firmly in 1984. Mr. Steinberg has divorced his first wife and is now married to Monika, a beautiful ex-model who drives a Porsche instead of an MG. Oliver is a frantic video game addict whose imagination has been incapacitated by watching too many horror movies. His father now makes commercials for video games instead of candy, and Mr. Hannemann, although still a billposter, is no longer the class-conscious proletarian crusader against capitalist exploitation but a laid-back, antimaterialistic individual who plays along with his son's fantasies rather than getting upset by them. Even Wolfgang's dreams have been updated: he fantasizes now about being the famous West German rock star Udo Lindenberg or the James Bond of *Moonraker,* and when he rejects his father's low social status he does so in favor of a specific alternative that he has seen in the television series *Dallas.*

More important than the play's updated taste, fashion, and diction, is the fact that the new version of *Nashörner schiessen nicht* has enlarged its focus to include Oliver and Pia in the learning process. In the original play, these two were rather mindless exponents of the upper class, but in *Der Spinner* they are presented as much more obvious victims of their father's paternal carelessness. They both crave human warmth, and, despite having an excessive supply of luxury toys, they are utterly unhappy at home. Oliver can only describe his dad with hatred: "He's not a real person at all. He only has money and deadlines on his mind, and worries that everything goes wrong, and thinks that everybody but him is an ass."[15] Mr. Steinberg is satirically presented as the stereotypical capitalist villain who has no time for his children and treats his wife as a slave and mere cosmetic element in his business entourage. While in *Nashörner*

Das Grips Theater. Wolfgang (r.) discovers an exotic island through his "telescope" in *Der Spinner* (1984).

schiessen nicht he found it too embarrassing to let his own children act in his television commercials, in *Der Spinner* he uses Wolfgang to play in a video game commercial while he literally beats Oliver away from the video game he is playing, shouting, "Damn it! Stop playing with that! . . . It drives people crazy!" (p. 28).[16]

Whereas Wolfgang's fantasy world is totally dominated by television, movies, and commercials, Pia's and Oliver's imaginations have become completely numbed by getting every material thing their heart desires. In the course of *Der Spinner,* Wolfgang's fantasy is redirected, and Pia's and Oliver's are reactivated by a simultaneous confrontation with harsh reality. As in *Nashörner schiessen nicht,* Mr. Hannemann serves as the gentle agent of this educational process. However, this time he does not teach his son to use his fantasy toward development of a proletarian class consciousness that would alienate him from the rich, but, instead, to employ it in solidarity with Pia and Oliver to fight against the ecological and industrial dangers that threaten the perpetuation of modern civilization.

The Mr. Hannemann of *Der Spinner* is content with his insignificant position in society, for it keeps him free from the enslavement of material desires and the corruption of power. He has traveled around the world as a ship's cook, and he knows that exotic foreign countries involve more than the white beaches, waving palm trees, and gorgeous women that James Bond movies show:

> Everywhere I have seen people starve to death and suffocate in shit, my dear! That's what your dream world looks like in reality. Don't you realize that you live in paradise here? When you're older you can go and have a look at the world. There are plenty of adventures there. But there's no place for dreamers. You have to learn something first! Be able to do something! Contribute something! Don't let yourself get fooled by all this television, cinema, and commercial shit! [p. 17][17]

But, while in *Nashörner schiessen nicht* Wolfgang was able to convert his apparent defeat into a class victory relatively painlessly, in *Der Spinner* he is unceremoniously kicked out of Steinberg's house when he refuses to cooperate on the video game commercial. Disillusioned and with his ego deeply hurt, Wolfgang flees from this hostile environment. His disenchantment is paralleled by Oliver's, who also escapes after his ruthless father insults him for being a worthless nitwit: "You are not worth anything! You're a loser! A nothing! What can you do anyway, eh? Stare at the tube! Drink coke! Eat cookies! That maybe. Gosh, you are like dead! . . . My God, why did I deserve this?—Get lost! *(Oliver hangs around)* Get lost I told you!! *(Oliver goes)*" (p. 29).[18]

In the final scene of *Der Spinner,* Oliver and Pia are treated much more prominently than in *Nashörner schiessen nicht.* Their problems are considered equally as important as Wolfgang's. Pia, genuinely worried about Wolfgang, discovers love and true human warmth while looking for him in his working-class neighborhood. And after initially being appalled by the stench and the delapidated buildings, she recognizes the friendliness of the people and the potential of the place. Significantly, she discovers Wolfgang while he kicks in a wall filled with advertisement posters and hides himself behind it. She follows him and consoles him with a tenderness of which she would have been incapable before. Thus she helps Wolfgang to overcome his depression, and together they plan adventures, not inspired by commercials and television, but by a desire to help humanity: "You know something: simply traveling around the world and looking at things is actually pretty boring. It only costs money. But if I have a skill that is useful to the Africans or the Indians, then they'll be pleased when I come" (p. 33).[19] They also include Oliver in their newly found solidarity. The latter has been so shocked by his father's rejection and is so obsessed with his futuristic video games that he only wants to die so he can avenge himself as a zombie on his father. Understanding his need for respect and human warmth, Pia, Wolfgang, Sonja, and Mr. Hannemann make Oliver the center of their final game; he becomes a tree that represents all nature threatened by environmental pollutors, and his friends become militant members of the Green Peace movement who set out to save him.

Although the themes and character constructions have changed considerably

Das Grips Theater. Oliver and his sister confront their stepmother in *Der Spinner* (1984).

between *Nashörner schiessen nicht* and *Der Spinner*, the basic style that identifies Grips as a popular theatre has remained unaltered. Even thematic changes are inherent to the concept of radical popular theatre. Being a political troupe, firmly implanted in a specific social environment, Grips forms a dynamic artistic collective that immediately responds to the changing concerns of its audience. Like other radical troupes, Grips accommodates changing tastes, an aspect that is particularly evident in the music and the diction, which incorporate the latest rock styles and slang. In order to stay close to its audience, the radical popular theatre must move with the times.

The entertainment value of Grips plays is extremely high and can be attributed to the successful collaboration between professional musicians, highly talented actors, and a large dose of humor. In *Der Spinner*, for example, much of the laughter originates in identification: the audience of children was elated to watch the brilliant actor who played Wolfgang reproduce their own speech patterns and intonations, and to see him take off into a fantasy play that very much related to theirs. But Grips plays also contain a fair amount of satirical humor. Although Wolfgang is, on the whole, an attractive character and enjoys the audience's sympathy, he is ridiculed for his lack of realism. Likewise, Oliver's video addiction is mocked through exaggerated presentation. In fact, most characters are treated with some measure of satire, but none is so severely mocked as Mr. Steinberg. His social status and arrogance are effectively deflated through his lack of genuine concern for other human beings; he treats his wife like a mere ornament and his children like little pests. To him, other people only serve as convenient objects of exploitation.

The plays that the Grips Theater created for youths and adults are essentially the same in spirit and style as the children's plays. Only the themes and characters are adjusted to match the concern of the older audiences. *Alles Plastik* ("Everything is Plastic"—1981), for example, is a play for people of fourteen years and over and deals with the apathy and the no-future mentality of that age group. *Alles Plastik* presents this pessimistic world view through four characters from distinct social backgrounds.

The first part of the play more or less realistically describes the different ways in which the existential apathy of the adolescents manifests itself in the lives of Micky, Goofy, Julia, and Antje: the first runs away, the second becomes a punk, the third stuffs herself with yoghurt and listens to her stereo all day long, and the fourth lives in a dream world of romance. The second part of *Alles Plastik* indicates some alternatives to the no-future mentality and is related to the struggle of the squatters who paralyzed Berlin in 1981. Julia and Goofy join the squatters in an occupied house, arguing that if there is no a priori future, one should create it for oneself. Antje and Micky arrive at the same conclusion after a somewhat lengthy detour of flirtations with right-wing ideologies, the former through a romantic involvement with an ultraconservative law student and the latter through a brief association with neo-Nazis. Thus, at the end of the play, the resignation of the theme song that considered all aspects of life—from material to ideological—to be plastic and false has been replaced by a musical call for action: "The whole world is rotting and suffocating/Because a bunch of assholes are pushing on the tubes/If you recognize that/and still continue snoring/Instead of fighting it/You live wrong!!!"[20]

The song still maintains that there is a great deal of evil in the world. But instead of purporting that nothing can be done about it, the song suggests that apathy is wrong and that the only positive attitude is to oppose the crooks who are destroying the world.

Like *Der Spinner* and *Nashörner schiessen nicht*, *Alles Plastik* has an episodic tableau structure and tries to win over its nontheatre audience with music and realistic humor. According to Volker Ludwig, awareness of the target audience's taste is even more important for youth plays than for children's plays:

> Children are still obliged [by law] to attend school and come to the theatre in groups. But in order to attract the youth, you really have to know for whom you're performing. We resolved to make theatre for the underprivileged who do not know the theatre at all. Only soccer and disco. Many of them also come to the theatre just to cause a riot, and when they are there they can't believe their eyes. We have

to get at them first by means with which they can identify: speech, attitude, slang expressions, everything has to be authentic. And as a result they are dumbfounded like little children. They also shout in agreement or disagreement, and when we ask them if they liked a particular play they can't really say. But they say, "I didn't like what that one guy said," or, "That guy was a real asshole." In the intermission they say, "This is much better than the movies," and "When does the movie continue?" 'cause that is the only thing they know. Our objective with these youth plays is to encourage them. That's why our theatre is called Theatre of Encouragement. That is, the youth are at the center of the play and achieve just a tiny bit more than in reality; little enough so that the youth can still identify itself with what goes on in the play, and yet enough so that they'll get a little more self-consciousness.[21]

In *Alles Plastik*, Grips reaches its audience most powerfully with the persuasive music of the popular Berlin rock band Alarm. Just as the four main characters of the play represent the entire social spectrum of the no-future generation, Alarm plays the entire range of current popular music types: disco, reggae, punk, and heavy metal. But just as the characters develop a little more courage and a sense of direction than the youths in the audience, the lyrics of the songs evolve from depression to hope. The trick is, obviously, to get the audience to accept all the elements of the play on the surface and then to sneak in a constructive political message underneath. For that reason, the exposition takes up half the play. Today's youth has a highly developed realistic imagination, accustomed as it is to television and cinema. The punk character must, therefore, be immaculately dressed according to the latest new wave fashion, he must speak in the most up-to-date slang, and he must be sure to support the right soccer team. Only when a character has been fully accepted by the extremely critical audience can changes and criticisms be implemented. Of course, the squatters are presented as more likeable than the fascist types or the right-wing law student. But the ultimate purpose of *Alles Plastik* is to show that the only possibility for a liveable future is to work in solidarity with others, disregarding their race, class, or political beliefs.

There can be no question that Grips enjoys an immense popularity in Berlin and beyond. After a decade-long struggle, the troupe has now even convinced the conservative municipal administration of its worth. Ever since Grips moved into its present permanent facility, it has more and more established itself as one of Berlin's prime cultural attractions. However, Gerd Hunger of Rote Grütze, another radical Berlin children's theater group, feels that this success has been obtained at a considerable cost:

They have a permanent theatre, a division of labor that we don't have: people selling tickets, stagehands, light technicians, actors, directors, dramaturges. . . . Grips also often goes on tour, but the real sensation comes when Die Rote Grütze is scheduled to perform: Grips simply delivers its piece, but we provide a theatre

party. Over the years, Grips has become very much an established theatre. Our
structure is much more open. We have different opinions about the plays, and
there is space to express and accommodate these different opinions. The Grips
actors are also no longer involved in the creative process of the play: there are one
or two writers and a director who make all the artistic decisions. . . . And that is
exactly the danger that I see in Grips: the actors are completely cut off from the
creative process. That was really obvious in *Eine linke Geschichte* ["A Story of the
Left"—1980]. I saw that play three times because it was also partly about me. In
the middle of the run they changed some actors. But to the smallest step, the tiniest
facial expression, they acted the same. With us, that would be totally impossible.
We also had some actor changes in the middle of a run: the idea of the play
remained more or less the same, but the character changed completely.[22]

Naturally, Volker Ludwig does not agree with Hunger's view of Grips's
creative rigidity. But he admits that the establishment in a permanent theatre
space has had some effect on the constitution of the audience, especially during
evening performances. The number of young workers that attend Grips performances is dwindling, and the number of bourgeois spectators is increasing.
Over the years, Grips has come to rely on the technical possibilities of its
playhouse and no longer feels the desire to go and play on makeshift stages in
community centers and the like. Besides, Grips argues, theatre is much more
effective if the audience has to make an effort to go to it and feels that it is
actually "going out."

Perhaps the greatest difficulty that most radical troupes in West Germany
encounter is the lack of good scripts. Grips has by now a solid financial
foundation for its enterprises, but every year it has to scramble to find an able
dramatist who is willing to work with the actors. Other groups have more severe
financial problems but also realize that good popular theatre is impossible
without good playwrights. In frustration, Volker Ludwig sighs: "Unfortunately
we don't have a Dario Fo in Germany!"[23] As a result, many free groups have
tried to imitate the Italian playwright's style or have produced translated versions
of his plays. However, it would seem that a truly meaningful popular theatre in
West Germany should concern itself with German issues and theatrical forms,
basing itself on the tastes and sensibilities of its target audience. Dario Fo only
works in Italy.

CHAPTER 8

FROM MILAN
FOR THE WORLD
Il Collettivo Teatrale
La Comune

Most of the elements of popular political theatre that have been discussed in the previous chapters converge in the theatre practice of Dario Fo, the most successful political playwright since Bertolt Brecht. Ten years ago, his popularity had hardly extended beyond Italy's borders, but since he started performing his one-man show *Mistero Buffo* in various European capitals his success has assumed astronomical proportions. By now, he and his work have effectively conquered stages all over Western Europe. German newspapers and magazines speak of an unstoppable Dario Fo wave, and respected Spanish publications like *Cambio 16* refer to his success as *la fiebre Dario Fo*, the Dario Fo fever. Its theatre critic Miguel Bayón concludes that "nowadays, Dario Fo is a very real ghost who roams throughout Europe."[1]

Even the conservative London daily *The Times* refers to him as "the greatest clown alive." Dario Fo is now also conquering the Americas: in May 1984 he toured Latin America, and after years of being refused a visa to the United States, he and his wife Franca Rame were finally allowed to go to New York to witness the opening of his play *Accidental Death of an Anarchist* on Broadway.[2]

Fo's plays are characterized by an energetic blend of farce, political satire, and radical, socialist viewpoints that, apparently, answers the need for innovative popular theatre that other playwrights and directors in the Western world are unable to create on a similar level. Although Dario Fo's recent flirtations with the commercial theatre are, to say the least, politically questionable, there can be little doubt that aesthetically speaking his work indicates the direction in which

124

the experimental political theatre should move in order to attract the crowds of proletarian spectators to which it wants to direct its messages.

After a brief stint as a student of architecture, Dario Fo began his theatrical career as a set designer and decorator in 1945. He became involved in writing and acting when he was asked to collaborate on a series of political cabaret-style revues. The most successful of these revues, *Il Ditto nell'Occhio* ("The Finger in the Eye"), was performed in Giorgio Strehler's Piccolo Teatro di Milano in 1953. Fo's period of commercial success started in 1959 when, together with his wife, the actress Franca Rame, he formed his own theatre company and performed a series of seven political comedies for a predominantly bourgeois audience. The popularity of Fo and Rame increased even more when they started doing a television series for the Italian state broadcasting system, RAI, in 1962. Dario Fo's success continued through 1968, when the events that affected public life in all of the Western world also caused great commotion in Italy. Fo joined the mass protests against the Vietnam War and became keenly interested in the ideas associated with the Cultural Revolution in China. As a result, Fo and his wife decided to leave the bourgeois theatre circuit in order to apply their talents to the struggle of the Italian proletariat. They organized their theatrical activities in a new company called Associazione Nuova Scena, which was subsidized by the PCI, the Italian Communist party. Nuova Scena proceeded to perform before large, working-class audiences in noncommerical venues throughout the country.

In 1970, Dario Fo terminated his collaboration with the cultural services of the PCI, accusing its leaders of using his troupe as a mere cultural signboard that was forced to reflect the party's political stance. At several occasions, Nuova Scena had been reprimanded for satirizing the PCI's bureaucracy and "revisionist" political line. This had resulted in a crackdown on Nuova Scena's cultural activities by the party headquarters. The clash was, however, indicative of a more complex ideological incompatibility between Dario Fo and the Italian Communists. In the party's opinion, culture stood above class structure and expressed the economic processes that determine history mechanically. Fo, on the other hand, attached much more importance to the developments of proletarian culture and saw art as a potentially powerful tool for the class struggle and the awakening of class consciousness. Like Gramsci, Fo refers to the example of the bourgeois revolution against the aristocracy: in the eighteenth century, the rising bourgeoisie developed its own culture—which was the expression of its own individuality and self-awareness—before it was able to successfully attack the feudal social structure. Thus, basing himself on Lenin's dual concept of culture—ruling-class culture suppressing the culture of the oppressed—Fo placed his artistic talents at the service of the cultural revolution of the workers. Fo firmly believes that economic exploitation under capitalism goes hand in hand with cultural expropriation. Therefore, to him the struggle to revive proletarian culture is as important as the daily political struggle in the factories and becomes a crucial element in the raising of class consciousness.

Following the conflict with the Italian Communist party, Dario Fo and Franca
Rame started a new radical popular theatre company that continues its activities
to this day: il Collettivo Teatrale La Comune. The foundation of la Comune was,
in many ways, similar to that of the groups discussed in previous chapters;
following a resolution to place their performing and writing talents at the disposal
of the proletariat, Fo and his associates based themselves in a working-class
neighborhood of Milan. They occupied an abandoned vegetable warehouse and,
with the help of enthusiastic local residents and after a long expropriation battle
with the city council, la Comune opened the Palazzina Liberty cultural center in
1974. There, the company premiered all its new plays and, despite sometimes
violent opposition from fascist groups and boycotts from the different Communist parties, managed to generate a popular following that is second to none in
the Western world. With the invaluable assistance of extraparliamentary left-
wing factions, la Comune set up an extensive publicity network in all major
Italian cities. The superb acting talents of Fo and his wife did the rest.

In 1986, il Collettivo Teatrale La Comune was no longer a full-fledged theatre
company; other than Dario Fo and Franca Rame there are no other actors
permanently on the payroll, and the Palazzina Liberty ceased to exist when the
city of Milan cut off its electricity supply at the end of 1982. Franca Rame
explains:

> At the start there were 40 of us—up to about 1973. Then we were 30. I don't
> remember the exact dates . . . but at any rate, we were a large company, and it was
> "us" who guaranteed everyone their wages, their meals, their travel expenses, etc.
> Whether or not the money was there, it was Dario and I who were answerable.
> And then, when people got involved as comrades in the collective, they got all
> carried away with the Red Flag, etc. . . . We had Mao Tse-Tung shoved up our
> back sides, Gramsci stuffed up our noses, Lenin coming out of our ears . . . but
> when the money began to run low and we had to talk about cutting pay levels,
> nobody wanted to know! And then you'd go out of the theatre, and there you'd see
> comrades from *Lotta Continua* doing political work, selling papers in the pouring
> rain. Our company, on the other hand, had some real "high and mighty" com-
> rades, with "guaranteed" wages, like trade union officials. Guaranteed by "us."
> And don't get me wrong . . . this was fine by us. Nobody was ever refused if they
> came asking for anything. No problem. No problem, because we had entered the
> struggle, and we said: "We are at the disposition of the class struggle. Therefore
> we shall put in everything we have." That was how we went ahead. And we sold
> everything. But at a certain point in our lives, we thought, "You must be joking.
> I'm perfectly happy to sell everything I have. But I'm not happy when I see people
> buying flats with the money that we were giving out." You see the point that I'm
> making? So we decided that we would be better off running an actor-managed
> company, taking all the responsibility on ourselves (which had always been the
> case anyway) and carrying on producing shows as we have done since then.[3]

Fo and Rame continue to play in culturally deprived zones in rural and urban
areas, at occupied factories and at rallies for political prisoners, and they often

donate the proceeds of their performances to radical causes. Without a doubt, Dario Fo is the most successful theatre artist to have emerged from the international artistic and political radicalization process of the sixties and seventies. No one else has been able to attract such overwhelmingly large popular audiences as he. He has filled entire soccer stadiums:

> We have attracted as many as 20,000 spectators for one performance. At the demonstration in Bologna we only played for one hour, but we performed for 70,000 people. On the average we get from one to one and a half million spectators per year. I think that no other theatre in Europe can match those figures. Right now, 10,000 spectators per evening have become something very normal for us.[4]

Fo's appeal now reaches beyond Europe into the Americas. His *Accidental Death of an Anarchist* has been produced from Bogotá to Buenos Aires, and from Sydney to Wellington. During a recent trip to India, I even saw a Bengali version of the play in Calcutta. A few years ago, the Black Tent Theatre from Tokyo and PETA from Manila did a coproduction of Fo's *Story of the Tiger*. No other Italian playwright, including Pirandello, has been produced so much abroad as Dario Fo, and his international reputation owes much to his unsurpassed comic talents as a performer and as a writer.

Like the advocates and practitioners of radical popular theatre in other countries, Dario Fo is fascinated by traditional forms of folk drama. He makes ample use of commedia dell'arte techniques, jokes from peasant farces, and the epic styles of street singers, traveling clowns, jugglers, and acrobats. He gathers these varied elements in a unique style of comedy that espouses the seriousness of the grim contemporary political reality with hilarious plot complications that rival the intricacies of the best eighteenth-century farces. Twenty years of continuous research have made Fo an authority on the Italian folk theatre from the twelfth century to the present.

Fo's interest in folk art stems from his conviction that in order to reach a large working-class audience one must, first of all, adopt its colorful idioms and idiosyncratic pronunciations. Secondly, he believes that one should build on the remnants of folk culture that still survive in the tall tales of fishermen and the narrative songs of street performers. Fo has traced the roots of proletarian culture all the way back to the twelfth century. He is particularly fascinated by the *giullare,* a wandering, multimedia performer who could dance, mime, sing, and do acrobatics. Fo is fond of recognizing a prototype of himself in the *giullare*. In his historical pursuit of folk culture, he has also discovered that proletarian art has been systematically suppressed or expropriated, first by the feudal ruling class and later by the bourgeoisie. Fo sees, therefore, the reappropriation and the development of this lost proletarian culture as a necessary preliminary step before any lasting political revolution can take place. According to him, it is the eminent task of the modern, progressive artist to help the oppressed classes rediscover their native art in a cultural emancipation process that will liberate them from their oppressors.

Fo holds that the history of culture as it is taught in our schools is a mystification of its true proletarian origins. For example, the septenary verse line is generally considered to be an invention of thirteenth-century courtly poets in the era when Italian poetry was supposedly at its height. But at a recent workshop at London's Riverside Theatre, Dario Fo pointed out how this type of verse line division already existed well before that period in the rowing songs of fishermen.[5] The same kind of historical falsification happened to commedia dell'arte. Cultural historians usually give prominence to the reactionary kind of commedia that was performed at the feudal courts:

> There was, however, quite another tradition of comic actors within the Commedia dell'Arte, also professionals, who didn't frequent the courts and nobility, but worked in taverns, worked in town squares, worked in far lowlier circumstances. And it is no accident that "their" work has never been collected and published. They've never been catalogued. They've never been studied.[6]

In his *Mistero Buffo* (1969), Dario Fo gathered a number of historically suppressed commedia texts and turned them into a very effective theatrical collage.

Mistero Buffo is the central piece in Fo's work. It is a theatrical proclamation of his credo; it marks the end of his bourgeois comedy episode and announces the sharp political satires that followed in the seventies. *Mistero Buffo* is a one-man show that requires the actor to jump in and out of different roles with dazzling speed. It is performed without props or set pieces and relies only on the actor's capacity to evoke different characters through slight changes in intonation, facial expression or gesture. *Mistero Buffo* is, therefore, mobile and "poor" (in the Grotowskian sense), as only the best radical popular theatre can be. It also reestablishes the modern popular theatre artist in direct lineage with the traveling players of the Middle Ages. Furthermore, the performer of *Mistero Buffo* behaves very much like a satirist who attacks received opinions and established institutions of state and church.

The title *Mistero Buffo* is obviously related to the popular medieval mystery plays and literally means "comic mystery play." Mysteries were originally intended to clarify complex concepts or obscure passages in the Old and New Testaments. Comic mysteries, however, did not originate in the Church but in the people's sense of the grotesque and their irreverence for bombastic church authorities. Comic mysteries were usually created by traveling buffoons but were later expropriated by artists who worked for feudal lords. As a result, literary historians list only aristocrats as authors of the comic mysteries. One of Dario Fo's chief objectives with his *Mistero Buffo* was, therefore, to rectify this form of cultural historical falsification and to honor the true creators of comic mysteries as superior artists who worked with and for the people.

Mistero Buffo tries to undo the attempts of society's rulers to uphold the status quo and justify their crimes with the aid of the Bible. In a lengthy introduction illustrated with slides of medieval prints and mosaics, Fo reveals how already back in the Middle Ages bishops defended the interests of the ruling class. He also shows how many comic mysteries used a religious fable to criticize the authorities and the social structure and that for that reason these theatrical forms were outlawed by the end of the fifteenth century. To underline this point, Fo introduces a medieval buffoon who asks his audience whether they really think that the Lord had arbitrarily divided the human race into haves and have-nots. Fo proceeds, then, to act a medieval clown who plays the part of God:

> Hey, you! Get over here! You have a beard; that's great! Take the crown: you'll be king! You there, come here! That your wife? You're a nice gal: you'll be queen! What kind of a crook's face is that?! All right: I'll make you emperor! And you there? You look like someone's just beaten the shit out of you. . . . OK, come here! I'll make you bishop. Come on, off you go! And I'll make you into a successful businessman! And you, yeah, come closer; look: all the land between here and the river will be yours! You're a nice guy! But take good care of it, will you! Don't you ever give any of it to someone else! Never! And work it well. . . . And you too! I'll give you this land over here. . . . Oh, I see, you two are related. Well, so much the better: that way it stays in the family! Let's see now. . . . You there, you get everything that lies on the coast. And you will get exclusive fishing rights. And you guys back there? Starvelings and miserables?! You there and you there and you there and you there and your wives, you'll work for that guy and that guy and that guy, till you drop, and whoever has the impertinence to complain will immediately go to hell, as I stand here as your sweet Lord, so help me God Almighty![7]

Needless to say the Vatican reacted as ungratefully to Fo's presentation of a capitalist God as the medieval church authorities did to the shows of the original buffoons. Consequently, they charged Fo with aggravated blasphemy and wanted *Mistero Buffo* banned from the stage.

The Catholic Church objected particularly to Fo's presentation of God the Father as the champion of ruling class interests. The Church also took exception to Fo's presentation of Jesus Christ as a revolutionary who tried to give pride and dignity back to the people. In the "Strage degli innocenti" ("Massacre of the Innocents"), for example, the *Mistero Buffo* narrator has one of the deprived mothers yell at God for having allowed the massacre:

> You ordered these murders, you commanded them . . . you wanted this sacrifice so that you could let your son come: One thousand of our children butchered for one of yours! A river of our blood for one cup of yours! You would have done better to keep your son with you, if we, poor Christians, were going to have to make so many sacrifices for him. . . .[p. 36][8]

However, in the next tale, this verbal abuse of the selfish, insensitive God is offset by the praises of a destitute blind man who is healed by Jesus and who, with regained self-respect, poetically describes the beauty of vision.

One of the hallmarks of the comic mystery is that it recounts the miracles of Jesus from a popular perspective. Mistero Buffo derives much of its humor from the dialects and slang expressions of the witnesses selected from among the popular masses. For example, the eyewitness account of a drunken guest to the Cana wedding comically opposes the elevated version of John the Evangelist:

> It was dead silent; it was almost as if we were in church during the Sanctus. Then this Jesus guy locked his fingers together and cracked them. He raised his one hand, but only three fingers; the other two he held pressed down to the palm of his hand. And then he made this weird sign over the water as only sons of God can. I was standing a little bit on the side because, as I told you before, water always depresses me so much, and I didn't look; I was sort of leaning against the wall absentmindedly, and suddenly I notice entering through my nostrils a smell of something like pressed grapes . . . no doubt about it: that was wine. [p. 64]⁹

Imagine the narrator slightly staggering and slurring, speaking with gusto in some colorful regional dialect!

Much of the humor in Mistero Buffo derives from the downtrodden's lack of respect for their superiors and from the laconical way in which the destitute regard their misery. In the "Moralit del ciego e dello storpio" ("Tale of the Blind Man and the Cripple"), for instance, the two invalids decide to join their functioning limbs and senses in order to get around: the blind man takes the cripple on his back so that they both can walk and see. The cripple pulls at the blind man's ears to indicate direction. But soon the blind man starts complaining about the cripple's weight, and when he discovers that his friend has not moved his bowels for six days, he exclaims, "I'm awfully sorry, but I want you to get down and do me the saintliest of favors by emptying out your illegal compartment!"¹⁰

Dario Fo's sense for grotesque detail is as strong as his sense for satire, and very often the two combine to deflate the arrogance of a notable or some bombastic upholder of the establishment. The drunkard in the "Wedding of Cana" scene is a prototype for Fo's later clownesque satirists, who get away with even the most blatant insults of the authorities. In this particular instance, the drunkard competes with an arrogant angel for the audience's attention and succeeds in humiliating this most elevated of all species by likening him to a grilled hen:

> Hey guys! You hear that? An angel who wants to get rid of me with a kick in the butt. . . . Me! An angel! *(He turns aggressively to the angel)* Why don't you come here, come here, my little angel. . . . Try and kick me out if you can! I'll pull

bunches of feathers out of you, like a frying chicken! I'll pull them all out, one by one, even those on your ass . . . on your behind. . . . Come here, my little chicken, come! [p. 62][11]

By focusing on the lowly, animalistic aspects of the angel's physique (feathers, ass) rather than on the pure and superhuman elements, the drunkard deflates the angel's self-importance and, by the same token, stresses the pride of the lower classes that he represents.

In the scene about Boniface VIII, a pope who reigned from 1294 to 1303, Fo attacks the highest church dignitary by literally undressing him in public. The joke of this particular tale is based on the anachronistic meeting of the elaborately adorned Holy Father and the shabbily dressed Jesus. In the first part of the scene, we see how the Pope is dressed by imaginary servants and how he complains about the weight of the garments and the incompetence of his attendants ("What a lousy profession, being Pope!"—p. 114).[12] When he has finally put on all his jewels, he starts singing a hymn and applauds himself on his beautiful voice. But he gets perturbed by Jesus's arrival who draws all the attention away from him. A farcical confrontation ensues:

Hello, Jesus, how's it going? What? You don't know who I am? Boniface, Boniface, the Pope. . . . What do you mean: what's a pope? Gimme a break! . . . The pastor, the shepherd, who was appointed by Saint Peter above that long line of super shepherds. . . . Don't you recognize me? Oh, yeah, maybe because of this funny hat. . . . That's only to protect me from the rain. . . . Maybe. . . . (*To one of his imaginary clerics*) Take everything off of me . . . the ring . . . he doesn't need to see the rings I'm wearing. . . .

Thus the Pope proceeds to take off all his glittering adornments, his fancy shoes, and his embroidered cloak and tops off his metamorphosis by putting dirt on his face to satisfy "that originality fanatic" (p. 116).[13]

"Bonifacio VIII" exposes the Pope as a hypocrite whose actions are all motivated by a desire to increase his popularity. When he first lays eyes on Jesus, his impulse is to turn away from that miserable sight. But his advisors tell him how good it will be for his public image if he is seen helping Jesus carry his cross. Also, when Jesus accuses him of having murdered thousands of monks, Boniface vehemently denies the allegations and underlines his benevolence by demonstratively kissing a monk in public. But immediately following that instance he comments in an aside on the monk's foul smell. Finally, the scene ends in the Pope's total humiliation as Jesus kicks him in the behind and refuses to let him carry the cross. Boniface VIII explodes in rage: "Christ! Kick me?! Me, a kick!? Me, Boniface?! Me, a monarch?! How dare you?! You saucy fellow, you! You crook! Wait till your dad hears about this! You bum! You superass!" (p. 118).[14] And the scene ends with Boniface dressing himself again in his expensive garments as he sings another solemn hymn.

Mistero Buffo is much more than a simple showcase of traditional popular tales from the Middle Ages. Besides providing today's working class with pride in its traditional cultural heritage, it satirically attacks the modern power structure as well. In the seventies and eighties, the Church still serves the rulers of society, and, Fo seems to argue, the present pope is as publicity conscious as Boniface VIII. *Mistero Buffo* not only points out that those in power derive their position from a false facade of strength and benevolence that hides their often despicable and weak personalities, it also indicates how the satirist-buffoon can contribute to the destruction of that mask of power.

A scene called "Nascita del giullare" ("Birth of the Traveling Player") stands at the center of *Mistero Buffo* and directly links Dario Fo with the tradition initiated by the agitating, antiestablishment figure of the medieval buffoon. In his introduction, the traveling player makes no bones about his intentions:

> Come closer, people, the buffoon has arrived! I'm a buffoon who dances and jumps, who makes you laugh and ridicules your lords! I'll show you how vain and puffed up they are, these fatsoes who make war everywhere and treat us like their slaughterhouse cattle! *I'll expose them, I'll let the hot air out of them, so they . . . pffft! . . . collapse.* Come on, don't be shy, come closer, I'll play the fool who wants to illuminate you! *I'll turn a somersault, I'll sing a song and act out a play! But pay attention to my tongue, see how it flicks, how sharp it is, like a knife!* [p. 72][15]

These words could well be taken as the general statement of purpose of all radical popular theatre artists in the world: to present good entertainment in the form of song, dramatized fiction, movement (acrobatics), and satire directed at the rulers of society. Furthermore, the buffoon emphatically establishes himself as a member of the peasantry as he explains how he became a traveling player. He used to be a farmer until one day his lord came to claim the fertile lands that he was working. When the farmer refused to render the property, the priest and the notary came to convince him of the lord's right in the name of God and the law. When the farmer defied even church and state, the institutional upholders of the lord's hegemony, the landowner sent his army to burn down the estate and to rape the farmer's wife in front of her children. Subsequently, the farmer's wife and children abandoned him, and the villagers ostracized him as a man without honor. On the verge of suicide, the farmer's life is saved by Jesus, Saint Peter, and Saint Mark, who arrive to tell him to go out into the world and dedicate his life to making all the destitute peasants of the world politically conscious by means of satirical laughter.

Humor, farce, and satire are characteristic elements of Fo's work after *Mistero Buffo*. These are indispensable features for drawing the workers to the theatre rather than to an inviting couch in front of the television after the routine of a physically exhausting day on the assembly line. Next to the entertainment value, the treatment of topics that lie close to the working man's heart is an important reason for Fo's popularity. Then there are, of course, Fo's internationally renowned capacities as an actor, which, together with his wife's formidable performing talents, account for much of la Comune's success. Their art has the ability to captivate the audience while at the same time interrupting the action by planned or spontaneous, improvised interludes. If this practice is reminiscent of Brecht, whom Fo acknowledges as his "greatest teacher," the Italian playwright, nevertheless, wants to go beyond the ramifications of Epic Theatre:

> In any case, my way of working is much more deeply rooted in the tradition that I discovered than Brecht, who could not build on it to the same extent . . . That's the big difference: Brecht's plays are more or less the same each night, the mood and the atmosphere in the auditorium do not change. We, however, create theatre that is different every night. With that, I don't mean only the rhythm. We improvise.[16]

Every performance is invariably followed by a discussion between actors and spectators about the play's topic. New insights that emerge from such informal exchanges of opinions are incorporated in subsequent performances. Fo takes collective creation and artistic democracy seriously. Nevertheless, despite the undeniable influence of actors and audience, the dramatic art of il Collettivo Teatrale La Comune bears the ineffaceable stamp of superstar actor-playwright Dario Fo. The humor of Fo's plays serves to increase the entertainment value of the performances but is also an instrument that provides insight into complex contemporary political situations. The laughter evoked by his work thus stems from two principal sources: 1) It is created by comic stock devices derived from the popular theatre tradition, such as double takes, mistaken identities, slapstick, obscene language, facial mimicry (an art in which Fo is second to none). 2) It is produced by political satire and thus has a thoughtful ring to it. His dramatic satires supply dialectical analyses of contemporary history, laying bare all its contradictions and the strategies with which the underdogs in society are being exploited and kept in check by the ruling class. Fo's plays, consequently, are designed to arouse aggression and call for physical action.

The structure of many Fo satires is related to the *mundus inversus* motif that has occurred extensively in popular art and literature throughout Europe from classical times. The most common pictorial representation of this phenomenon is a man entrapped in a globe standing on his head attended by one or more fools. Other illustrations show cosmic reversals or inversions of the normal relations between men and animals (e.g., foxes chasing hunters). The satirical *mundus inversus,* or "world upside-down," usually criticizes a society in which the relation between people and abstract values like social justice, human equality, and honesty has been set on its head. Such satires characteristically show a world of fools and vices in which the Lord of Misrule is the sovereign king.[17]

The narrative structure of several Fo plays borrows from the *mundus inversus* device but employs it for much more militant purposes than the collective, temporary relief from the repressions of society's taboos that carnivalesque festivals provide. *Mundus inversus* satire typically introduces a fool, a naive foreigner, or a child into a world recognizably our own and, with feigned or sincere naïveté or with logic pushed to the extreme, has them expose the ills of our society.

Unlike the popular celebrations that allow the general public to vent its social and political frustrations and to release aggression that might otherwise be turned against the social order and its upholders, Fo's *mundus inversus* satire does not provide catharsis. On the contrary, he regards his satirical theatre as a powerful weapon in the struggle between the social classes. He sees himself as serving the working class to battle what he regards as the bourgeois hegemony. His satire is, then, committed to revealing the essence of economic, social, and cultural institutions through which the ruling class continues to maintain its status quo.

The laughter evoked by Fo's theatre is not evasive, nor does it sublimate social anger. He wants people to keep their rage and to direct it against the social institutions that oppress them. His satire also takes away the fear for the authorities by mockingly deflating their pompousness and by exposing their stupidity. Fo's sharp satirical knives dissect the capitalist power machine into the smallest particles in an attempt to unveil the grotesque elements that hold it together. In that sense, Fo's theatre also encourages the working class while at the same time building up pride for the proletarian cultural heritage.

In *Morte Accidentale di un anarchico* ("Accidental Death of an Anarchist"— 1971), Dario Fo introduces a *mundus-inversus* fool and has him infiltrate the law enforcement system. With his uninhibited behavior, the fool exposes the Italian police as an inefficient organization rotted by corruption and inconsistency that is only barely able to maintain a facade of sternness that hides its innate debility. In the end, the play reveals the Italian police to be led by bullying judges and superintendents who actually are cowards closely linked to paramilitary right-wing extremists.

The radical popular nature of *Morte Accidentale di un anarchico* is evident in the theme, the diction, the satirical style, and the continuous updating of its text. The play topically refers to the "accidental" death of the anarchist railroad worker Giuseppe Pinelli, who, during interrogations about his alleged responsibility for the 1969 bombing of the Agricultural Bank, "suddenly jumped" from a fourth-floor window of the Milan police headquarters. For Fo and other left-wing sympathizers, the Pinelli case became an example of widespread police efforts to discredit radical activities and socialist ideology throughout the Western world. Particularly in Italy, neofascists, aided by accomplices in the police and the military, were responsible for many fatal bomb attacks that cost hundreds of lives and were later attributed in skillfully managed publicity campaigns to left-wing organizations. The newsmedia, then, were also clearly involved in these antileftist attacks, and, more than ever, the radical popular theatre found itself obliged to provide counterinformation. Fo's *Morte Accidentale di un anarchico* was intended as a source of alternative information and also served to encourage the working class in its struggle for dignity and power.

The original idea for *Morte accidentale di un anarchico* was proposed to Fo by Pinelli's lawyers. They decided to collaborate closely on the project: the lawyers would go to court in the mornings and report to Fo in the early afternoon. The playwright would then incorporate the latest findings in the evening's performance even before the newspapers got hold of the information. In this way, the play continued to develop over the eight-year period that it took the Italian legal system to condemn the three fascists who were really responsible for the bank bombing. After each performance of the play, Fo and the other actors would hold debates with the audience about their perception of the case and their opinions of how the play represented it. Over one million people went to see *Morte Accidentale di un anarchico* in two years, and it is safe to say that the play was instrumental in the acquittal of other anarchists charged in similar incidents. Not surprisingly, Fo's activities were hardly appreciated by right-wing elements, and on more than one occasion the playwright and his wife were harassed. Fo has been arrested and jailed, and in 1973 Franca Rame was kidnapped and severely beaten by a fascist group.

With the help of Pinelli's lawyers, Fo obtained official police statements and other documents related to the anarchist's "suicide." He used these as the basis for the speeches of the policemen in the play, but Fo's theatrical and comical instincts prevented it from becoming one of the sterile, dramatized lawsuits that ruined so many other documentary dramas. Being both performer and playwright, Dario Fo never forgets that the theatre's main function is to entertain. Through the outlandish situations and plot complications, the horrible reality remains constantly visible, however. The Italian audience easily recognized Pinelli's main interrogator in Inspector Sportsman, the police spokesman in charge of the coverup in the chief, and Camilla Cederna, the famous independent reporter, in the newspaperwoman. Only the fool played himself: a satirist disguised in many different attires.

The play opens with Inspector Bertozzo's interrogation of the fool, a lunatic accused of falsely appropriating and illegally using the identities of other professionals in order to make a living. Since the fool is an officially certified madman, however, Bertozzo cannot touch him. After the fool has spelled out all the legal loopholes through which he can circumvent the law, Bertozzo leaves the room in utter frustration. In his absence, the fool discovers some files pertaining to the anarchist's "suicide" and decides to assume the role of a Supreme Court judge from Rome come to investigate the irregularities in the affair. He adopts a "stiff-legged" walk and a cold, detached air, dons glasses, and thus equipped enters the office of the chief and Inspector Sportsman. He introduces himself as Dr. Marco Maria Malipiero, first counsel of the high court and claims to have come to help the Milan police straighten out the

Il Collettivo Teatrale la Comune. The superintendent, the maniac, and the constable (l. to r.) in *Accidental Death of an Anarchist,* produced by the Downstage Theatre Company, Wellington New Zealand (1982). Photo by Brian Davis.

inconsistencies in their report of the anarchist's suicide. With sharp analyses, the Fool picks the police version of the incident apart. There was, for instance, the question as to why the window of the interrogation room was open at midnight in December when the weather report listed subzero temperatures. The fool sarcastically comments on this curious fact: "But what do you guys have here anyway? A personal African monsoon that passes through here every night, or is it the 'Gulf Stream' maybe coming through the 'San Marco' tunnel and passing underground through the sewer system?!"[18] Furthermore, the fool wonders out loud how it could ever have been possible that the little anarchist, surrounded by six policemen, managed to jump out a window that was located relatively high off the floor. One of the police officers, trying to help out his superiors who are dumbfounded by this question, suggests that he tried to stop the suicidal anarchist but was unfortunately only able to grab his shoe. Of course, the anarchist had been discovered on the pavement wearing both his shoes.

Morte Accidentale di un anarchico is ultimately a farcical cross-examination of reactionary authorities by a lunatic who manages to verbally and physically abuse the police investigators. As such, the play is clearly a world-upside-down satire. The fun begins when the fool, pretending to be Bertozzo, repeatedly burps into the telephone while talking to Inspector Sportsman. The latter takes offense and knocks Bertozzo out at their next meeting. But the fool is not afraid to insult the authorities to their faces either. At one point he literally calls Bertozzo an idiot and questions his eyesight by pulling down the policeman's lower eyelid. On another occasion, he kicks the chief and Bertozzo in the rear, slaps Inspector Sportsman on the neck, and then innocently points to the chief. The fool even succeeds in getting the chief and Inspector Sportsman to sing the anarchist hymn by arguing that "people would be willing to forgive all the contradictions you've jumped into with both feet—but only if, in exchange, beyond these obstacles, they could catch a glimpse of human heart . . . two humane men who let themselves be moved to tears of compassion; and although still remaining policemen, join the anarchist in singing his own song, just to make him happy. . . ." (p. 28)[19]

With well-aimed pinpricks, the fool effectively deflates the arrogant, loud-mouthed representatives of Italy's power machine and reduces them to gibbering, self-incriminating idiots. This satirical process culminates in a scene that employs one of Fo's favorite comic devices: the inadvertent injection given to a bombastic representative of the law or the establishment. In this case, Bertozzo and the chief are literally punctured by the fool, thus presenting the audience with a hilarious image of deflated authority. When toward the end of the play Bertozzo is about to reveal the disguised fool's true identity and almost explodes with rage at not being allowed to express his suspicions, the fool, now in the attire of a bishop, coolly states:

> An attack I believe. (*He takes a syringe out of his breviary and gets ready to give him an injection.*) Hold him still, this will certainly do him good. It's a benedictine tranquilizer. (*With the swiftness of a cobra he administers the injection, then takes out the syringe and looks at it*). There's a little left; would you like to try some too? (*Without waiting for an answer he injects him with the agility of a gunman. Suffocated lament from the chief.*) [p. 177][20]

The fool not only ridicules representatives of the police force; in his exaggerated disguises he also implicitly satirizes their accomplices and superiors in the legal profession and the Church. In the mode of true low burlesque satire, he explicitly compares judges to shaky old men and shriveled vegetables:

> Being a judge is the best of all occupations! First of all, you hardly ever have to retire. In fact, at the precise moment when an ordinary man, any working person, reaches fifty-five or sixty years of age and already has to be gotten rid of because he's beginning to get a little late, a little slow in his reflexes, the judge, on the contrary is just reaching the peak of his career. A worker on the assembly line or cutting machine is finished after fifty; he causes slow-ups, accidents, and he will have to go; a fifty-five-year-old miner has silicosis. Out, canned, fired, quickly before he can begin to draw his retirement pension. . . . For judges, on the other hand, it's exactly the opposite: the older and more feeble-minded they get, the more important their responsibilities get. They're given absolute powers! You see

a bunch of little old men, made out of cardboard and totally withered . . .
doddering along with faces resembling mushrooms from the Garda valley.
[p. 144][21]

Although not old, the fool walks with a stiff leg when pretending to be Dr.
Malipiero. Moreover, his subsequent disguises contain visual mockeries of
dignitaries. He is forced to relinquish his role of Malipiero when the left-wing
newspaperwoman arrives on the scene. The chief does not want the press to get
any wind of the internal inquiry, and, therefore, the fool proposes to disguise
himself as Marcantonio Banzi Piccini from the scientific division, complete with
glass eye, black patch, wooden hand, and wooden leg. These grotesque
accessories not only reflect satirically on the vulnerability of the power machine,
they also provide opportunities for theatrical slapstick. Every time Piccini provides the chief and the inspector with a brilliant answer to parry a sharp question
by the reporter, the two policemen gratefully shake his hand or slap him on the
back. When the wooden hand comes off, the fool responds indifferently, "You
can keep it. I have another one!" (p. 174), upon which he screws on a feminine
hand.[22] Then the glass eye pops out, and, in a dazzling accumulation of events,
the inspector slips on it, the fool yells at him for having gotten it dirty, a cop
hands him a glass of water to wash it, and, finally, fascinated by a question of the
reporter, the fool swallows the glass eye with the water.

From that moment on, Fo fills the play with even more confusion and
disguises and brings the plot almost to the point of explosion. First Bertozzo
enters the room, unaware of the fool's presence. When he is introduced to
"Piccini" he remarks that the real Piccini and he went to the police academy
together, and that the strange fellow in the room definitely is not his old study
companion. The chief and the inspector, afraid that Bertozzo is going to reveal
the "judge's" identity try to silence their colleague with kicks and slaps, and the
scene develops into a chaotic fight since Bertozzo is tired of being beaten up,
having already received a black eye earlier on. As a result, the fool can no longer
maintain his Piccini role and quickly turns his white collar up, puts on a red
skullcap, "unbuttons his jacket and reveals a gold and silver baroque cross of
dubious authenticity; and finally puts on his finger a ring with an enormous violet
stone" (p. 177) and becomes Father Augustus Bernier, bishop-cop in charge of
the Pope's security.[23] Everyone present respectfully kisses the grotesque ring,
except for Bertozzo who knows the "bishop" is fake. Bertozzo eventually
manages to whip out a gun and forces the fool to reveal himself as a deranged
maniac. The latter, not to be outdone, grabs the bomb that Bertozzo had brought
in for inspection, handcuffs all the policemen and the reporter to a coatrack and
prepares to escape as he informs them that he has recorded the chief's and
Inspector Sportsman's testimony about their responsibility for Pinelli's death.

At that point, the play blows up: in a sudden blackout a cry is heard offstage,
followed by an explosion, and when the lights come up again, the fool is found

smashed on the pavement four floors below. With all the policemen tied to the coatrack they certainly cannot be blamed for this latest suicide. Even the newspaperwoman is prepared to retract all her previous allegations against the police regarding Pinelli's death, as Bertozzo, in his courteous enthusiasm, casually slips his hand out of the handcuff to kiss the young woman's hand.

With Bertozzo's goof, the police alibi is, once again, invalidated, and the fool's death becomes yet another instance of police violence that the authorities want to cover up. The continuous nature of this pattern of oppression is further emphasized by the arrival of the real judge from the Supreme Court in Rome, who has come to reopen the inquiry into the accidental death of the anarchist. The policemen, thinking it is the fool again, assault him and try to pull what they think is a false beard off his face, dragging the coatrack, to which they are still tied, along in the process. Thus, the play appropriately ends in a scene of utter confusion that provides no solution.

The play's open end is necessary for the continuous updating of the plot according to incoming new information about the Pinelli case. The fool's death, furthermore, is not only a convenient coup de theatre to end the plot complications; it also indicates that the Pinelli murder is hardly an isolated incident. It provides a justification for the immense international success of *Morte Accidentale di un Anarchico,* for political murders and "disappearances" occur throughout the world. Fo's play provides the international radical popular theatre with a brilliant creation that is flexible enough to satirize many forms of oppression and power abuse. Some foreign productions of *Morte Accidentale,* however, did not observe the play's radical popular essence so much as they highlighted its farcical elements for commercial purposes. This was obvious, for example, in the extended West End run the play enjoyed in London and the recent Broadway production at the Belasco Theatre, which provoked one reviewer to dismiss the American version as a "hodgepodge, farcical rather than satirical; whatever Swiftian indignation may have lacerated Fo's breast in Italian, in English he emerges as a sort of literary marshmallow, tasteless on principle and gooey at the core."[24]

Fo's original versions of *Morte Accidentale* were dealing with too serious an issue ever to be taken as mere light farce by the Italian audience. Even while laughing at the fool's antics and his clownesque humiliation of the police, the Italian spectators remained constantly aware of the horrible crime that was being exposed. Pinelli's smashed body was constantly present on stage and provided the basis for Fo's labeling the play a "tragic farce" containing a conspicuous "relationship of the tragic to the grotesque."[25] Not a single incident in the play was conceived for gratuitous comic effect. Fo's use of slapstick is reminiscent of Luís Valdez's opinion that everything depends on who slaps whom. Although some of Fo's gags are clearly derived from clown's routines and silent movies, they have been "politicized" making the authoritarian upholders of the power structure the objects of the pranks. By seeing police chiefs and inspectors receive pies and fists in their faces and injections in their exposed buttocks, the audience loses some of its fear of the law enforcers. *Morte Accidentale di un anarchico* clearly establishes itself as a radical popular play by expressing solidarity with the plight of the oppressed proletariat. It does so through speech, action, and explicit statements:

> FOOL: But do you have any idea what a worker is really like? By the time they reach retirement age—and according to the latest statistics, fewer are reaching that age all the time—and when they get there, they're like squeezed-out lemons, larvae with reflexes reduced to the minimum . . . to nothing! [p. 170][26]

The play was also originally written in a northern Italian urban dialect that contained the particular slang expressions and intonations of the Milanese working man. Finally, the fool humiliates the police on behalf of the proletariat and encourages the workers to take action themselves. Through self-referential remarks, the fool establishes the play's self-conscious theatricality and creates an epic distance that keeps the audience aware that it is not merely watching an amusing, self-contained story, unrelated to the reality outside the theatre. With specific statements, the fool reveals himself as a thinly disguised Dario Fo who is not interested in art for art's sake but in serious political realism:

> My hobby is playing roles, different roles each time. Except that I go for the real life theatre, so my theatre company has to be composed of real people, who don't know they're playing roles. On the other hand, I have no money to pay them. I requested a subsidy from the minister of entertainment, but since I have no political backers. . . . [p. 142][27]

Part of Fo's success must be attributed to his realization that the only way to beat the system is to pretend to be part of it. The fool's multiple disguises can be seen as an ironic reflection on the various ways in which the authorities try to cover up *their* actions. Thus, comic deception is used to uncover criminal deception. With his quickness of responding with improvisation to new information and changed circumstances—another hallmark of the radical popular theatre—the fool, then, succeeds in making fools of the police.

In the decade following *Morte Accidentale di un anarchico* Dario Fo has written about twenty other dramatic satires, many of which expose the workings of the capitalist power structure. Like *Morte Accidentale,* most Fo plays are inspired by topical issues, not necessarily restricted to Italy. In 1971, for example, la Comune produced a play about Palestinian guerrilla warfare *(Fedayn),* and in 1973 the troupe did a play called *Guerra di popolo in Cile* ("People's War in Chile") about the events surrounding the overthrow of Salvador Allende. Fo also treated the problem of drug abuse in *La Marjuana della màmma è la più bella* ("Mom Has the Best Pot"—1976) and suggested the use of civil disobedience to protest skyrocketing consumer prices in *Non si paga, non*

Il Collettivo Teatrale La Comune. The two housewives show their wares to the Maoist policeman in this Downstage Theatre production of *We Can't Pay! We Won't Pay!* (1985). Photo by Brian Davis.

si paga! ("We Can't Pay, We Won't Pay!"—1974). This last play is a satirical comedy about two women who join a large group of housewives who decide to raid supermarkets, stuff their shopping bags, and walk out without paying because they can no longer afford to. The women find themselves not only having to justify their actions to the authorities (including a frustrated Maoist police inspector) but also to their macho husbands.

After the mid-seventies, most radical popular theatre groups started including satirical material of macho behavior. They attempted to clarify that sexual oppression within the family was just another way in which the ruling class maintained its control in society. One of the most powerful plays to express the sufferings of women in proletarian households was *Tutta casa, letto e chiesa* ("Household, Bed, and Church Are Everything"), which was written and developed by Dario Fo and Franca Rame between 1977 and 1981. This one-woman show consists of four independent monologues in which different female characters express their most intimate feelings about male oppression. In "Il Risveglio" ("Waking Up") a young woman acts out her daily morning routine before depositing her baby at the day-care center and going to work on the assembly line. While her husband gets in an extra half hour of sleep, she has to clean the baby, cook breakfast, get dressed and washed up herself, and rush to the bus in order to get to the factory on time. On this particular day, her chores are complicated by having awakened too late, by her baby who keeps peeing at inopportune moments, and by the lost house key. The woman becomes all confused and ends up powdering her baby with grated cheese, spraying radiator paint instead of deodorant in her armpit, and putting dishwashing liquid in the refrigerator instead of the milk. When she finally manages to straighten everything out, she notices that her weekly bus ticket has six punches in it, and, shocked, she realizes that it is Sunday and that she does not have to go to work.

"Una Donna Sola" ("A Woman Alone") tells the story of a lonely housewife who is locked up in her home by her husband. She is obviously treated as a sex object by her mutilated brother-in-law, who can move only his hand and penis, by a Peeping Tom across the street, by a breather, by an ostensibly nice student of English who turns out to be also only after her body, and by her possessive husband:

> In order to better protect me, he beats me up first. He keeps me locked up in the house like a battery hen and then . . . he wants to make love! Yes, love! Couldn't care less if I don't feel like it. Always ready I have to be, always ready! Instant. Like Nescafé. Washed, perfumed, shaved, hot, loose, willing, but quiet. Just breathing, that's enough![28]

The monologue skillfully builds up to a climax in which the Woman Alone violently destroys all those who oppress her. She first throws the door shut when the young student's arm protrudes through it fumbling for her body. Subsequently, she pushes her invalid brother-in-law down the staircase in his wheelchair, after which she shoots the Peeping Tom with a rifle and prepares herself to give her husband a similar treatment upon his arrival.

"Abbiamo tutte la stessa storia" ("It's Always the Same Old Story") is a cyclical tale that starts with a woman in bed with a man on top of her and finishes with a fantastic story of a vulgar talking doll that, instead of instilling young girls with motherly instincts, helps them to liberate themselves from traditional female roles and urges them to join other girls in order to fight in solidarity. The last monologue in the sequence is a feminist version of Medea's life story in which the mythical Greek priestess becomes a foreign-born wife to a macho Italian Jason who leaves her for a younger woman. After initially crying and screaming hysterically and contemplating suicide, Medea resolves to take a violent, militant stand and kill her children in order to become a free woman.

Il Fabulazzo Osceno ("Obscene Fables"—1983), one of Dario Fo's most recent creations, also satirizes male sexual behavior. With this one-man play, he returns to the format of *Mistero Buffo* and his research into the medieval proletarian cultural heritage. In "Lucio l'asino" ("Lucio the Ass"), for example, the protagonist, who is also the narrator, tells about a trip he once took to Tessaglia, a country ruled by magic and erotic fantasy. In a mixture of dialects from Bergamo, Brescia, and Cremona in the extreme north of Italy and in his inimitable juicy narrative style full of attention for comic detail, Fo tells about Lucio's arrival in Tessaglia, his sexual encounter with an attractive maid, and his discovery that the wife of his host is really a witch. Lucio watches her prepare a magic potion that turns her into a bird. Despite the warning of the maid, Lucio tries to imitate the witch, but a gust of wind turns the page of the magic book, and, instead of adding pepper to the potion as the recipe requires, he adds two moist farts and some slime from a mountain snail. This alteration causes Lucio to change, not into a bird but into an ass with a human brain and a human sex drive. Fo comically describes how difficult Lucio finds it to walk with four legs:

> So I started to walk: nothing to be done! . . . . I had absolutely no idea how asses walk. . . . So I started alternating legs, sort of like this . . . so, this foot goes first, and the other one comes after. And with every step I took I kept knocking with my knees against those giant balls that I had received as testicles: Oooh, what a pain![29]

Furthermore, Lucio's dirty mind remains activated, and every girl he sees gives him an enormous erection. Thus, Lucio experiences various frustrating adventures until finally a noble lady rents him from a circus where he happened to be employed at the time. She takes him home, and they have a wildly erotic night together. At the end of the story, Lucio becomes human once again after accidentally eating a magic moss rose. Full of hope and desire, he returns to the noble lady, but she rejects him with a clear, antimacho statement:

> I loved you the way you were before because you were an exception. I loved in you what you men have always taught me to love: the potent erection, like a flagpole, important . . . the great potency. On the other hand, men who make love and talk about it like you, there are plenty of those. . . . But an ass who didn't talk but made love like you did before, I had never experienced in my life. [p. 94][30]

At present, il Collettivo Teatrale La Comune continues its myriad artistic activities at the service of radical social change. Dario Fo and Franca Rame still perform throughout Italy before standing-room-only crowds in conventional theatres, nontheatre venues, and occupied factories. They are largely ignored by the establishment press, they receive no financial assistance from the Milan City Council and only a minimal subsidy from the Ministry of Culture. Yet, without a doubt, they are the most popular Italian theatre artists in the twentieth century, and their international reputation continues to grow. They frequently travel abroad to finance their activities at home, which they continue to regard as their priority and which, in terms of sheer spectator figures, are unmatched by any other theatre company in Italy or abroad. Dario Fo and Franca Rame show no sign of weakening in their determination to create highly entertaining and pertinent dramatic satires that deal with the oppression of women and workers.

Their most recent creation is the jointly authored *Coppia aperta* ("Open Marriage"—1984), which is a continuation of *Tutta casa, letto e chiesa*. There is no doubt that Dario Fo and Franca Rame are at the vanguard of the international radical theatre movement. Their work and energy instills the workers of Italy and the world with pride in their cultural heritage and provides radical popular theatre artists everywhere with a powerful example of successful theatre combined with a consistent radical popular focus.

CHAPTER 9

RADICAL POPULAR THEATRE IN FRANCO'S SPAIN AND AFTER

At first sight, the contemporary Spanish radical theatre would seem to take in a rather odd position in the company of the other Western alternative theatre groups. In the previous chapters, I have suggested the existence of quite open links between the sociopolitical events of the mid and late sixties, left-wing concepts of culture, and the emergence of radical theatre in Europe and the United States. These links, although they are acknowledged to have played some role, seem to have been much less of a catalyst in Spain than in the countries north of the Pyrenees. The main reason for that was, of course, the omnipresent repression of the Franco dictatorship. In retrospect, it is rather odd that groups like the San Francisco Mime Troupe, el Teatro Campesino, Bread and Puppet, le Théâtre Populaire de Lorraine, and the 7:84 Theatre Company, who were spearheading the vanguard of the new international alternative theatre movement with popular theatre pieces aimed at the war in Vietnam, exploitation of the working classes, and the general authoritarian structures of postindustrial Western society, seemed to ignore the plight of the Spanish people, who were suffering under a very real fascist dictatorship in Europe's own backyard. While in May 1968 John McGrath was driving his convertible Chevrolet over to Paris to bring a solidarity message from the concerned artists of Great Britain to his comrade Jean-Jacques Lebel, who was occupying the Odéon Theatre with hundreds of other young French radical artists, no one in Western Europe was taking much note of the struggles of the emerging political theatre movement in Spain.

In the late sixties, the antifascist opposition was still deeply traumatized by the heavy repression of the forties. During those early years after the Spanish Civil War, the majority of the Communists, anarchists and socialists—and even a sizeable portion of the Christian Democrats—had been killed or forced into exile. When, under pressure from the other Western countries (the United States in particular), the repression waned in the late fifties, the opposition was not able to settle its ideological differences. This factionary infighting lasted until the early seventies, when it became clear that Franco was about to die and the need arose to present a viable alternative for Spain's leadership after his death. This was the time that ETA, the military wing of the Basque separatists, struck its most devastating blows. In the eighties, ETA has lost much of its popular support, but many people would agree with Joan Baixas of the Catalan theatre group La Claca, that, in the late sixties and early seventies, the Basque terrorists may, ironically, have saved the democracy:

> They "took care of" the police chief of San Sebastian and his entire network of torturers, for example. They killed them, one by one. This act communicated a very clear message of warning: that it was indeed possible to do something [against the repression]. And back then that was extremely important because Franco was already preparing his successors. It seems he had in mind to put the king [Juan Carlos] on top as a figurehead and to perpetuate the movement of his ideology through his men below. Carrero Blanco [the prime minister at the time] was his most serious representative. He had been training people like [Adolfo] Suarez [who became Spain's first prime minister after Franco's death] for years; people who were technically good, but ideologically very much to the right and who understood that the Right needed to change. ETA took care of the affair when Franco was already too old to react. If they had not killed Carrero Blanco, Spain's democracy would look very different today. We would never have had a legal Communist party, for instance.[1]

Apart from ETA's spectacular actions and the often brutally dispersed student demonstrations, the most consistent anti-Franco resistance developed in the cultural field. Catalans like Joan Manuel Serrat and Pi de la Serra and several Basque singers started writing and performing songs in their outlawed regional languages in open defiance of the censors. The regional theatre groups that emerged in the late sixties came to be seen as small nuclei of freedom within an atmosphere of killings, tortures, and sociocultural repression. Paco Obregón of the basque group Teatro Geroa, explains:

> The theatre was like a gesture of liberty at that moment; like a ceremony of freedom. It was a theatre that gave a wink to its audience. Sometimes, all [political] meaning was contained in a gesture that was not in the text nor in the

script, that didn't appear anywhere. It was invented in the last moment, because theatre was alive. That is what gave to the theatre this banner of anti-Franco resistance and celebration of freedom.[2]

In the days when Beatles songs were blasting through the streets of London and Amsterdam and youngsters were experimenting with drugs, sex, and freedom on transcendental planes, their Spanish peers were fighting in the dark against fascism. But not only against the state, emphasizes Obregón:

> This struggle took place more concretely in daily life, in the life of the family, of the village, in forms of entertainment. The freedom that Europe's youth was creating, came here only in the form of a laughable copy. . . . I remember—and this may seem like a joke—in the seventies there was still a fine of 500 pesetas for kissing in the streets. And in this country there are priests who actually fined people [for such offenses] or who did what they could to prevent close dancing in the village square.[3]

The theatre was instrumental in creating ever larger spaces of freedom in Spain, during the final decade of the Franco dictatorship and immediately following it, in the crucial transition period from November 1975 until 1982.

Sam Smiley, one of the few American critics who has paid serious scholarly attention to the contemporary Spanish radical theatre, locates its beginnings in the mid-sixties and characterizes it as "the strongest and most persistent movement which occupies Spain's avant-garde stages."[4] He identifies the following groups as the most important members of Spain's radical theatre movement, which among hispanists is more commonly known as the *Teatro Independiente,* or the independent theatre: els Joglars, els Comediants, and la Claca from Catalonia; Tábano, Goliardos, and Teatro Catarro from Madrid; la Cuadra and Esperpento from Seville; and Akelarre and Teatro Geroa from the Basque country.

Franco's Law on Chamber Theatre and Theatrical Rehearsals, which regulated noncommercial theatre activities, is usually mentioned as one of the crucial factors that, ironically, helped establish the independent theatre movement. The law, which was intended to serve as a tool for the government censors, prohibited more than two performances of any play in any one city. Street theatre performances were completely forbidden. Since commercial theatre enterprises did not risk producing politically sensitive shows, the law was thought to effectively contain all radical theatre activities in Spain. But instead of limiting the radical theatre, it forced the groups to travel throughout the regions in old vans and perform in all provincial towns and villages. Thus, the censors were ultimately responsible for establishing an entire regional cultural communications network that incorporated high schools, universities, and church parishes. Without wanting to, it helped found theatre activities in Bilbao, San

Sebastian, Seville, and Santander, cities which had not had serious theatre before.

All this is not to say that Spain's *Teatro Independiente* suddenly appeared out of the blue. The movement was basically animated by a group of disenchanted professionals who had become fed up with the commercial theatre. With few exceptions, at the end of the sixties, the "official" Spanish theatre was in an enormous slump: its repertory consisted mostly of vaudeville shows and cheap, mildly erotic comedies that catered to a predominantly reactionary bourgeoisie. The remaining artists of Spain's radical theatre came from left-wing university circles and from grass-roots community groups called *teatros de barrio*.[5]

Guillermo Heras, one of the leaders of Madrid's Tábano, started his theatrical career in a *teatro de barrio* that was based in the Concepción district of the capital. His group created plays that were based on the revolutionary Soviet "Blue Blouse" theatre of the early twenties and on *teatro periodico* ("newspaper theatre"), employing techniques derived from Augusto Boal's Theatre of the Oppressed. The "Newspaper theatre" was quite different from the Living Newspapers that the Federal Theatre Project developed during the American Depression years. Whereas the Living Newspapers were often quite realistic, the *Teatro Periodicos* used the aesthetics of Latin American popular theatre based on songs, music, and farce. Radical priests often allowed church facilities to be used as venues for this type of political grass-roots theatre. Guillermo Heras recalls:

> In Madrid there were these small halls that were periodically closed down by the police. These places were full of chess tables or other games. But at other moments, these halls were used for political discussions and cultural dissemination. Films like *Battleship Potemkin* and other such mythical Soviet movies were shown there on small format film projectors. Other spaces crucial to the development of Independent Theatre or clandestine theatre were the senior high schools and the universities. The university sectors worked very hard for the development of this theatre, which in some cases was openly political, directly opposed to the regime, but which in many cases was a cultural theatre.[6]

What happened was that the censors not only prohibited all direct textual references to the current political situation and to the Civil War, but they also forbade absurdist plays like those of Beckett and Ionesco, which they saw as promoting nihilism and the self-destruction of man. Even authors like Tennessee Williams were forbidden for a while. Not to mention, of course, such mythical Spanish playwrights as Ramón Maria del Valle-Inclán and Federico García Lorca.

Most Spanish political theatre groups became quite adapt at circumventing the legal and political impediments imposed by the fascist state. One of the most striking characteristics of the *Teatro Independiente* was the creation of a so-called *metalenguaje*, a code language by which the actors managed to satirize the dictators and the military establishment with what seemed on the surface to be rather banal scenes and dialogues. The plays were, in fact, performed with one enormous wink at the spectators, who, like lucid participants in the conspiracy, knew perfectly well what the actors were really trying to say. Tábano, for example, often located its plays in foreign countries. And after the following scene from *Opera del bandido* ("Bandit's Opera"), a drastically rewritten version of John Gay's *Beggar's Opera,* the audience would go wild and give the company a five-minute standing ovation:

> (*Sound of whistles. The police enter, led by Lockit. The lord hides himself in a trunk. Macky hides behind Jenny.*)
> THE GIRLS: Alarm, alarm, the cops, the cops. Danger! etc.
> LOCKIT: Nobody move or I'll shoot in the air!
> ALL: Please! Not in the air, not in the air![7]

This seemingly absurd audience reaction was in response to the typical reporting of Franco-controlled newspapers, which, whenever some demonstrators had been killed in an antigovernment rally, would feature headlines like: "Police shoots in the air: two people die."

Apart from the general usage of *metalenguaje* and its anti-Franco stance, Spain's radical theatre had the following characteristics:[8]

(1) It was predominantly itinerant. Both because of the legal restrictions and because of their profound belief in theatrical decentralization, many groups owned small vans with which they toured Spain and sometimes other European countries.

(2) Financially, the groups subsisted on whatever they generated through ticket sales. Needless to say, no subsidies could be expected from the Franco government. "We've been hungry a lot," remembers Joan Baixas of the Catalan group la Claca, "at some occasions they even paid us with food, or they gave us 300 pesetas for gas. We had a small van, four spotlights, and more or less five performers."[9]

(3) Most groups subscribed to the promotion of popular theatre. They made a special effort to reach out to those popular sectors of the public who do not habitually attend the theatre. For this purpose, they adopted a policy of afford-able ticket prices and aesthetically accessible and highly entertaining shows that were often taken directly to the target audience's doorstep. Formally, the plays of Spain's *Teatro Independiente* were often inspired by old regional popular tradi-tions of peasant farces, stand-up comics, zarzuelas, musical revues, circus, cabaret, and silent movies.

(4) Certainly at the beginning, the internal structure of the groups was that of a cooperative. In 1972, for example, all members of els Joglars made about sixty-five dollars per month, which, compared to most other companies, was quite a substantial wage.

(5) The *Teatro Independiente* broke, for the first time in Spain's theatrical history, with the class system: they abolished the division between leading actors and general cast; directors and set designers also became unprivileged members of the collective. Names of individual creators rarely appeared on programs or other publications. This attitude prevailed until the late seventies.

(6) Parallel with the egalitarian socioeconomic structure of the groups, the creative process was also usually conducted collectively: actors wrote dialogues, writers acted, and a lot of room was allotted to improvisation. Despite this principle, however, the most resilient groups survived and developed thanks to the leadership provided by one strong artist with often very idiosyncratic artistic visions.

LA CUADRA DE SEVILLA

One of the more interesting groups to have emerged from the grass-roots is undoubtedly la Cuadra de Sevilla. Named after the hall where the company used to rehearse before going public, la Cuadra's type of theatre is predominantly based on the aesthetics of Andalusian popular culture. The group was founded at the end of 1971 by ex-bullfighter Salvador Távora, who had had his first theatrical experience in Juan Bernabé's legendary peasant group Lebrijano, and by several marginally educated workers. With its theatre, la Cuadra wanted more than anything to recuperate the original strength and dignity of the Gypsy-Andalusian culture, which had been falsified through the stereotypes of commercialized flamencos:

> Because of the year in which it was born and because of its way of operating, La Cuadra belongs to the Spanish *Teatro Independiente*. But it has its own unique aesthetic language. At the time, I had absolutely no knowledge of theatrical language. Of course, we shared an ideological affinity with the other groups; we were all anti-Franco. But there were no aesthetic affinities. We felt the necessity to speak, to express ourselves in our own way. In those days, the censors imposed a lot of restrictions, so we created a theatre from the cries of Andalusian songs and from the kicks of its dances; without speaking a word, we discovered a theatre that went way beyond words. And we created it with all those things that we used in our daily lives for survival or subsisting. We used the same lights that we used to illuminate our neighborhoods, the same songs that we had known since we were kids, the same dances with which we had been familiar ever since we were born. And we presented it all with the same aggressiveness that we felt toward certain social sectors and certain political situations. We wanted to make an effective instrument against the dictatorship, but more than that we wanted to rediscover our lost dignity.[10]

La Cuadra de Sevilla has created six theatre pieces to date. *Quejío* ("Moan"— 1972) was the group's first creation, consisting of seven songs and three dances

La Cuadra de Sevilla. The three bullfighters move in on the human bull in *Piel de toro* (1985). Photo by Conxita Cid/Joan Minguell.

that express, through words, shouts, and movement, the oppressiveness of Andalusia's socioeconomic predicament. Then followed *Los Palos* ("The Poles"—1975), *Herramientas* ("Iron Tools"—1977), *Andalucia amarga* ("Bitter Andalusia"—1979), and *Nanas de espinas* ("Thorny Ladies"—1982). In its most recent play, *Piel de toro* ("Skin of the Bull"—1985), la Cuadra and Salvador Távora return to their bullfighting roots. The play itself is basically structured like an allegorical bullfight, complete with all the paraphernalia and motions of this most popular of Andalusian activities.

Despite la Cuadra's professed intentions to revindicate the true, popular essence of Andalusian culture, the company seems to have also curiously capitalized itself on the commercialized images of "Carmen" and flamenco. La Cuadra spends more time performing abroad on government-sponsored tours than any other Spanish company.

THE BASQUE PROVINCES

Basque political theatre is much less an exportable commodity than the original, inoffensive, and quaint Andalusian variety of la Cuadra. That is not to say that Basque theatre is offensive; theatre simply is not and has not been a priority in this staunchly independent region in the north of Spain, where political violence in the form of bomb attacks and executions still occur on an almost daily basis. Paco Obregón of Teatro Geroa explains almost apologetically:

> We've had a very strong political reality here, with deaths, with blood, with an exasperating climate of violence, with a political climate that hardly permits the formation of a [regional Basque] government, which is what's happening now. Theatre here has not responded to it. In the face of this enormous aggressiveness, theatre has fled into escapist, evasive theatre—doing the great universal authors. Our group has done it too. We never had a theatre tradition in the Basque country; we've always followed the fashion. We're getting a bit fed up with that.[11]

During the Franco dictatorship, anything remotely related to original Basque culture was immediately repressed by the authorities. As a result, none of the prominent Basque theatre companies like Cómicos de Legua, Denok, Orain, Akelarre, or Geroa produced any significant original works until well after the dictator's death. Most of these groups created so-called *associaciones de espectadores* ("spectator associations"), organizations similar to the independent theatre clubs that produced Ibsen's and Shaw's first plays in London at the turn of the century. Akelarre, for example, had a "club" of 800 members, for which it performed, once a month, mostly foreign authors like Ionesco, Frisch, Dürrenmatt, Brecht, and Chekhov. Their amateur status permitted them to tackle forbidden texts. Although founded (by Luís Iturri) in 1966, Akelarre (whose name is Basque for "Witch Ceremony") did not create its first major original work until 1977, when it premiered *Irrintzi*. This play, which expresses the recent history of the Basque people in a gloomy accumulation of vignettes in the form of traditional rites, is followed by *Guerra-Ez* ("No to War"—1978), one of the first professionally produced bilingual pieces in Basque theatre history. *Guerra-Ez* deals, in a highly stylized manner, with the Civil War, which for many Basques continues to this day. It explores the causes of the war, its effects on several Basque characters, and, finally, sings a requiem to all those who have fallen, expressing the hope that a war that has been lost can be won through peace.

Akelarre expired quietly in 1982, when its director, Luís Iturri, accepted a job as manager of the municipal Arriaga Theatre in Bilbao. In 1987, the only professional Basque political theatre company with roots that go back to the early days of the *Teatro Independiente* is Teatro Geroa from Durango. Like Akelarre, Geroa mostly produced foreign authors on an amateur basis during the Franco years and the subsequent transition period. It gained national acclaim with its production of Dario Fo's *Accidental Death of an Anarchist* in 1981. Only recently has it started to develop some original Basque texts. In 1985 and 1986, it toured with *Doña Elvira, Imagínate Euskadi* ("Lady Elvira, Imagine a Basque

Country"), a historical tragedy about Lope de Aguirre, a Basque conquistador who assisted in the conquest of Peru, rebelled against the Spanish king, and proclaimed the independent republic of Peru. In the play, which dramatizes the last day of Lope's life, the protagonist comes to realize that he should have fought at home for an independent homeland for the Basques instead of in the hostile foreign lands of South America, which belonged to other people anyway.[12]

Perhaps more interesting than *Doña Elvira* is Geroa's most recent creation, *Grand'Place*. Whereas the former play holds its political discourse about the current Basque situation couched in historical terms, *Grand'Place* places the issues, including ETA terrorism, directly on the stage. The play is, in fact, written by Mario Onaindía, a former member of ETA-militar who was sentenced to death in the infamous Burgos trials of 1970. He spent eight years in prison and was then exiled to Brussels where he lived at the "Grand'Place." He has since returned to the Basque country, where he helped found the left-wing nationalist party, Euskadi Ezkerra. The play is an adaptation from his autobiographical novel by the same title. "It is really the private story of a couple," explains Paco Obregón, who directed the play:

> The man's wife joins him in Brussels from the Basque country. He represents an entire generation of anti-Franco fighters in the Basque country—young people, sincere, who started the armed struggle against the dictatorship. The play shows the encounter of these two people. It ignores the heroic and political aspects and focuses instead on the intimate story of these two individuals, on their personal problems, their internal conflicts in their attempt to construct themselves as a couple, on their mistakes. This hero or martyr is not the protagonist of the play; it is the woman who had always remained in his shadow, who had never appeared in magazines or newspapers. The play gives her human value. Being political, the work shows another side of our history: the sensitive [and crucial] role that women have played and still play in our culture and society, which is so rigid. Within this generation, the story of these two people is a little like a microcosm of what happened back then, of a struggle which was waged not only against the state but also against ourselves, against our own education, against our own customs, against our own traditions, against our parents, our family.[13]

The central set piece in *Grand'Place* is the matrimonial bed where the intimate encounters of the couple in Brussels take place. From there, past and present intermingle in a long series of flashbacks which show us terrorist hijackings, police torture, the woman's loneliness, the world of the parents back home, and the woman's first pregnancy. The play, which was performed in Basque and in Spanish on alternate nights during its Bilbao run in January 1987, shows a fascinating new direction for Basque political theatre, which is finally trying to come to terms with its own reality.

From the preceding account of the *Teatro Independiente* in Andalusia and the

Basque country, one could derive the wrong impression that radical theatre in Spain was relatively tame in political terms. But a closer look at the activities of Tábano from Madrid and particularly els Joglars from Barcelona will prove otherwise.

TÁBANO

The work of Tábano, both in aesthetic and sociopolitical terms, is closer than that of any other Spanish group to the activities of the radical popular theatre in other Western countries. The name *Tábano* means "gadfly" in Spanish and was taken from a phrase which Socrates used in his *Apology:* ". . . for the state is like a big thoroughbred horse, so big that he is big, slow and heavy, and wants a gadfly to wake him up."[14]

Founded by Juan Margallo and several other disenchanted professionals in 1968, Tábano started out with theatrical inprovisations inspired by Artaud's Theatre of Cruelty. But after a year or so of this elitist work, largely for university audiences, the members of Tábano decided they wanted to create a show that would do more justice to their name. They interviewed people in the street, photographed accidents, and investigated popular theatre forms that could give theatrical shape to the realities of life in the Spain of 1970. The result was *Castañuela 70,* the most successful radical popular theatre show of the last decade of the Franco dictatorship.

Aesthetically, *Castañuela 70* was based on a Spanish variety of the musical revue called *Teatro Chino de Manolita Chen* ("The Chinese Theatre of Manolita Chen"), an itinerant and degenerated vaudeville show performed in circus tents that still enjoys a certain popularity in the smaller towns and villages of rural Spain. Guillermo Heras describes it as follows:

> Some old actresses come out and sing some songs to more or less erotic texts. Then you get the snake man, some sort of magician who does terrible tricks, dwarves, or bullfight fire fighters; practically a freak show, really. But it is not known why it is called *Teatro Chino de Manolita Chen*. Manolita Chen was a female impresario who sang Spanish folk songs. It seems that she had an affair with (rather than being married to) a Chinese fellow, whom we don't even know for sure was really Chinese, but whose name was Chen.[15]

Using the framework of this popular freak theatre and in collaboration with las Madres del Cordero, a famous Madrid music group, *Castañuela 70* presents a series of outrageous scenes in which Spanish family life, religion, consumerism, and the dictatorship are sharply satirized. In a scene entitled "Reinar después de morir" ("Reigning After Death"), for example, Tábano takes on the Spanish religious tendency to accept the miseries of life in exchange for happiness and glory in the hereafter. But in this particular case, not God but a television program host takes charge of the matter. He has become so popular that the sole purpose of life for the Spanish people apparently is to be featured as "dead king or queen of the week" in his show. On this particular occasion, the "lucky" ones are doña Juana and her husband don Cosme:

> *(Enter don Cosme, who pushes doña Juana, who is dead, in a wheel chair.)* Good evening, don Cosme. On behalf of myself and of the program "Reigning After Death," I would like to congratulate you: your deceased wife is the winner of this week. Are you happy, don Cosme?
> DON COSME: Yes, sir.
> HOST: Very well, don Cosme. We understand your profound emotion. In just a few moments you will see your wife's head changed into that of an authentic queen, thanks to the precious hands of the noted hairdesigner Mr. Pierre of Hair Salon "Chapital." *(Enter the hairdresser.)* And here we also have the list of gifts for your wife: first of all, a luxury burial complete with red carpet, three priests, and four acolytes. We also have a set of black bracelets, death announcements, a marvelous tomb that fits seven bodies, and black balloons for the kids.
> DON COSME: We really don't deserve all that. You people are too good.[16]

And after crowning and dancing a waltz with doña Juana, the host, assisted by don Cosme and his son, who is in the military and has been introduced as the surprise guest, places the corpse in a jewel-studded coffin and bids her and the television spectators farewell with the words: "Remember this woman, wife, and mother, who, like a queen, is watching you from Heaven" (p. 51).[17]

The strongest references to the dictatorship in *Castañuela 70* appear, undoubtedly, in the scene called "La Caída del imperio Romano" ("Fall of the Roman Empire"), in which an emperor named Meconio is clearly presented as a caricature of Franco. Franco, who reportedly suffered from Parkinsons' disease, and Meconio, *débil and tuberculoso* ("weak and suffering from tuberculosis"), are both equally incapacitated. And the anachronistic Roman Empire of *Castañuela 70* is revealed to be falling because of the corrupting influence of the Americans, just as Franco had allowed the U.S. navy and airforce to install themselves on Spanish territory. The Americans enter "Rome," in the shape of Cianón, who sings: "I am Cianón from Oklahoma, but I live in Washington. I am a strategy expert and nobody touches me, because the dollar is my God. And now, in his divine name, I am bringing you salvation" (p. 53).[18] He goes accompanied by Hippía, a "Flower Power" girl who poses as a pacifist but who really is corrupted by the dollar, drugs, and her lover, CIA(non).

The installations of the American airforce at Torrejón were a hot topic at the time in leftist circles. But because of the censorship, Tábano could not mention the issue directly. "So we talked about Rome instead," explains Guillermo Heras,

and everyone was wearing blue jeans with some sheets over them, because I don't
think that the entire production cost more than 10,000 pesetas [$150]. We have
always built our own sets and sewn our own costumes. . . . Anyway, during one
particular moment of this sketch we wanted to talk about the bases, but the censors
prohibited that; they prohibited the use of the word *bases*. So what we did was:
instead of singing the words of the song, we only sang "lalalalalalala." And the
audience thought that they had forbidden it because the original words were
tremendously political. So they applauded much louder because they thought that
in the original words we were directly mentioning I don't know who.[19]

The news of *Castañuela 70*'s subversiveness spread like wildfire through
Madrid. The two performances that Tábano was allowed to give, were sold out in
no time. The manager of a commercial theatre, the Teatro de la Comedia, heard
about the show and offered his building for an extended run of *Castañuela 70* in
August 1970, when all other theatres are closed for the summer. The show
became the hit of the season. Day in day out, hundreds of people were waiting in
line to get a ticket. Between 21 August and 27 September of that year, Tábano
performed *Castañuela 70* seventy-four times for 51,833 spectators. The run was
stopped not for lack of interest but because the show had become so legendary
that the police decided to stop the performances. It has been historically
documented that they created a nonexisting commando named *Frente revolu-
cionario Marxista-Leninista pensamiento Mao Tse-tung* ("Revolutionary Marx-
ist-Leninist Front, Thoughts of Mao Tse-tung"), which, during the performance
of 27 September, distributed leaflets with highly provocative revolutionary
phrases on them. This was enough reason for the authorities to prohibit any
further performances of *Castañuela 70*.

Forced to silence by the Spanish authorities, Tábano loaded its old van with
props and costumes and crossed the border to play for Spanish emigrant workers
in the countries north of the Pyrenees. For the first time, Tábano was reaching
out to a truly popular target audience. In Spain, like most of the other members
of the *Teatro Independiente,* it had been performing predominantly for an
audience of progressive bourgeois and intellectuals.

The next two creations of Tábano were forbidden in their entirety by the
censors, and the third, *El Retablo del flautista* ("Picture Book of the Flute
Player"—1971), was closed by the police after only one sold-out performance
for 1,500 people. Once more, Tábano was forced into exile, often playing in
exchange for meals only. The group also performed at the Nancy Theatre
Festival of 1973, where the actors met several South American companies. Later
that same year, Tábano embarked on an extended tour to Latin America, where
they were exposed to the harsh political realities and the pragmatic political
theatre of artists like Santiago García of Bogotá, Enrique Buenaventura of Cáli,
and Augusto Boal of São Paulo. They were performing in Caracas as news of
Allende's fall reached them. Four Tábano members were so impressed that they
decided to stay in Latin America. The others returned to Spain with the renewed

resolution to sharpen the aesthetics and the politics of their brand of popular theatre.

One of Tábano's main concerns after its return from Latin America was to develop a truly popular decentralized radical theatre. Given that even outside the commercial circuit, theatre was predominantly limited to Madrid and Barcelona and that its ticket prices excluded access by the popular sectors of the population, Tábano decided to take its theatre to the people. Thus, during its tour of *Opera del bandido* in 1975, Tábano performed 70 percent of the time in independent, noncommercial venues for a total of 35,000 people, 40 percent of whom were workers and 34 percent, students.

With the death of Franco on 20 November 1975, many groups belonging to the *Teatro Independiente* lost their prime raison d'être and began to die a slow and quiet death. Tábano, however, had already long ago discovered that there was a system behind the dictator that would not be simply removed with his death. Over the course of the years the company had redefined itself as a Marxist theatre collective which understood that its connection with the class struggle manifested itself most clearly in the "struggle between bourgeois and proletarian ideology." Consequently, there was still a long road ahead.[20]

In Spain's "predemocratic" years of transition, as they are now often referred to, the political tension was possibly even greater than during the last years of Franco's life. Right-wing and left-wing terrorism intensified and resulted in numerous deaths and the enactment of further repressive legislation to ensure public order. Leftist parties were still outlawed. To accompany these troubled times, Tábano created *Cambio de tercio* ("Change of Fortune"—1976). This comical, musical, melodrama was consciously set in a historical period with strong parallels to the situation of 1976: from the end of the Primo de Rivera dictatorship in 1927 to the proclamation of the Second Spanish Republic on 14 April 1931.

Cambio de tercio was created collectively over a period of eight months. Many discussions and extensive historical research preceded the actual development of the piece. As in the case of *Opera del bandido* and previous Tábano shows, the entire creative process was led by a dramaturgical coordinator. In the first ten years, this task was usually carried out by Luís Matilla or Angel García Pintado. Later, Fermín Cabal and Guillermo Heras took over. After agreeing on the general structure of the show to be created, the coordinator worked out a skeleton script, indicating the main characters. This proposal was again discussed by the entire collective, focusing particularly on the aesthetic, technical, and ideological aspects. After this, each scene was worked out separately in chronological order through improvisations.

The plot of *Cambio de tercio* is basically a love story with many melodramatic complications. Carmen, who had been in love with Nicolás, decides to marry Andrés, a tailor catering to the army. Nicolás, who had been fighting in the War of Morocco for several years, returns on the day of the wedding and spoils the party. After the glory he achieved in North Africa, Spain only presents him with disasters: Carmen is about to be betrothed to someone else; his brother José, a leftwing radical, rejects him, and he eventually becomes jobless. To complicate matters even more, Nicolás kills Carmen's father during the wedding ceremony in church, accusing him of having kept his many letters from Carmen. Consequently, Nicolás ends up in prison. Meanwhile, in an as yet unrelated subplot, several members of the high bourgeoisie and senior officers of the army lament the spread of liberal ideas in the country and found a fascist organization to protect the dictatorship. They bring in Renato Filiberti, an experienced Italian fascist, as an outside consultant and recruit Nicolás, who has just been released from prison, as their hit man. During one of the many violent encounters between extreme right-wing and revolutionary left-wing groups, Nicolás ends up wounding his brother José. The main plan of the fascists is to disguise themselves as government soldiers, to attack the city hall of Guadelajara, and to publicly proclaim a new Spanish republic, hoping thereby to provoke so much patriotic, royalist sentiment that the entire liberal movement will be crushed once and for all. But, unbeknownst to them, elsewhere in the county real army units are also holding up town halls. The entire operation is so successful that within no time the real Second Spanish Republic is proclaimed. The fascists flee the country with suitcases full of money, and Nicolás is left alone, disowned by his family, Carmen, and his opportunistic capitalist friends. As the play's final song explains moralistically, Nicolás "in the end remains alone, as it always happens to those who abandon their class in order to prosper" (pp. 126–27).[21]

The plot of *Cambio de tercio* provided Tábano with abundant opportunities to reflect on the political power struggle that was being waged in Spain in 1976. The company also took advantage of the historical setting to satirize the military whenever they could. For example, in the second scene of the play, as an entire company of army officers is waiting in their underwear to be measured by Andrés the tailor, one general asks him: "Tell me, Mr. Vergador, can bloodstains easily be removed from this type of cloth?" (p. 52).[22]

Cambio de tercio is filled with many such satirical moments, and, together with an energetic burlesque acting style, comic gags taken straight from silent movie comedy capers, an ambience admirably recreated from thirties-style vaudeville, and a series of Brechtian songs that comment on the action and place it in a larger context, it must be ranked as one of the most successful attempts at making radical popular theatre in Spain. Not only in stylistic terms, but also sociopolitically, as the company performed the show 167 times for 70,000 people during a seven-month tour. Many of the venues were organized by labor and neighborhood organizations.

Tábano continued its decentralization efforts for another five years. But gradually the strains of underpayment and constant touring in adverse conditions began to take their toll. The company started doing more repertory work (Brecht, Dario Fo), and the original pieces that it created—*El Nuevo retablillo de las maravillas* ("The New Picture Book of Miracles"—1979) and *Un Tal Macbeth* ("A Certain Macbeth"—1981)—no longer possessed the fresh vitality and the satiric bite of earlier successes like *Castañuela 70* and *Cambio de tercio*. Gradually, many prominent Tábano members began to accept jobs in the mainstream theatre or in branches of the newly created Ministry of Culture under Felipe Gonzales's socialist government. In 1984, Tábano quietly expired when Guillermo Heras became director of the Centro de Nuevas Tendencias Escenicas, a government-sponsored outfit for avant-garde theatre experiments.

Els Joglars

In 1987, the only company that still maintains a highly critical and fully independent outlook in Spain's political theatre landscape is els Joglars ("the Jesters") from Barcelona. Led by the superbly talented Albert Boadella, this company has, over the years, succeeded in creating a political theatre which aesthetically is of the highest international calibre and which sociopolitically has kept Spain's infant democracy on its toes.

Boadella, who founded els Joglars in 1962, originally came from the ranks of the disenchanted professionals. He had completed a classical theatre training at the *Institut d'Art Dramatic* in Barcelona and had come to the conclusion that the Spanish contemporary literary theatre was artistically uninteresting and politically powerless because of the heavy censorship. Boadella's solution was to experiment with silent theatre instead. At first, the newly formed Joglars practiced mime à la Marcel Marceau. No one had ever done this type of theatre before in Spain, and therefore the censors did not quite know how to handle it. After long deliberations, they finally decided to subject it to the same censorship criteria that they applied to circuses and variety shows, criteria more concerned with how decently the performers were dressed than with politics. To be sure, in their apprenticeship years, els Joglars hardly touched politics. Their main priority was to develop their performing skills and to explore an original theatrical language that would be as different from text-based drama as from Marceauesque characters playing with invisible butterflies while being pulled by equally invisible strings.

In 1968, els Joglars went professional and entered the dangerous territory of political theatre with an original creation called *Diari* ("Newspaper"). *Diari* was a kind of theatrically animated Spanish daily, which Joglars performed in mime, page by page. Among other things, it contained thinly veiled references to the government's manipulations of the press. In subsequent creations like *El Joc* ("The Play"—1970), *Cruel ubris* ("Great Cruelty"—1972), and *Mary d'ous* ("Mary of the Eggs"—1973), els Joglars continued sharpening its theatrical style while the political contents became increasingly more daring. Satire, caricature, and parody were the company's chief weapons.

Words, if used at all, continued to play only a minor part in Joglars' work. The only text of *Cruel ubris,* for instance, consisted of the verse: "O Zeus,/La dissortada terra, ferrotge destí/Fuetejat per implacables deus de l'Olimp/Cruel ubris!"—which, loosely translated means, "O Zeus, it is the horrible destiny of this unhappy earth to be whipped by the implacable gods of Mount Olympus; what great cruelty!" These words were repeated ad absurdum whenever a character needed something to say.

One of the central scenes of *Cruel ubris* is "La Tortura" ("The Torture") in which, as the title suggests, a man is being savagely tortured by two agents of the secret police, complete with raincoats, thin moustaches, and dark glasses. The torture is presented like a circus act and also features a sexy female assistant in a glittery bathing suit. After each spectacular hit, which is invariably accompanied by a drum roll, she takes a few quick steps forward, places one hand on her hips and points the other in the air to invite applause. After kicking and punching the detainee in all parts of his body, the cops finally beat him over the head with a piece of wood and stick matches under his nails. The sexy assistant, smiling brightly, subsequently lights the matches while the torturers sarcastically sing "O Zeus, etc." to the tune of "Happy Birthday to You." In the end, the prisoner breaks down and stammeringly confesses the secret he had been keeping all along: "O Zeus,/La dissortada terra, ferrotge destí/etc."[23]

It was remarkable that Joglars got away with this obvious satire of the police. Many a spectator peered anxiously at the exits during the performance for signs of raid. But the censors did not say a thing. "They thought it was all part of a real circus act," explains Albert Boadella. "They were pretty stupid, fortunately. The regime was one big bureaucracy, brutal sometimes, but also terribly idiotic. Everybody shoved responsibility onto the next guy."[24]

In their next play, *Alias Serralonga* (1974), Joglars decided to push its luck even further. In this piece, the company adopted, for the first time, a more or less chronological narrative structure after previously constructing its shows from thematically connected but narratively unrelated sketches. *Alias Serralonga* tells the story of a legendary seventeenth-century Catalan Robin Hood named Serralonga, a popular hero who valiantly fought King Phillip the Fourth of Spain.

Alias Serralonga was performed in the entire theatre building. The action took place simultaneously on the stage, where the king's court was located, and in the auditorium, where the Catalan rebels lived in a tubular tower construction.[25] The play contains several spectacular battles between Serralonga's gang and the royal forces, who were actually depicted as members of Spain's *Guardia Civil*.[26] Other anachronisms, like the king's getting up to listen to the radio news, were clearly intended to remind the audience of the connection between the seventeenth-century action and the twentieth-century reality they were living in.

One of Joglars's trademarks is its fondness for theatrical self-reference, which often finds expression in what can only be called theatrical practical jokes. Thus, after one of the battles of *Alias Serralonga* that included some particularly acrobatic actions up and around the tubular structure, an actor, planted in the audience, yells: "Encore, encore!" Immediately, the company repeats the entire battle scene in slow motion, like the instant replay following a goal in a televized soccer match. The "slow mo" even affects the actors' voices, which become slurred. Also Serralonga's ultimate trial is presented in slow motion and in Latin. The king, who acts as judge, also speaks with a slow, deformed voice, which has the added satirical effect of evoking Franco, whose affliction with Parkinson's disease also had affected his voice and his memory. Not surprisingly, then, the king also repeatedly forgets his lines and is visibly and audibly prompted from backstage.

The end of *Alias Serralonga* constituted a challenge both to Franco's censors and to the Catalan people themselves. For the first time in modern Spain, the entire Catalan national anthem was played on the *sardanne*, the Catalan national instrument. Luckily for Joglars, the censor who was sent to evaluate the show was from Madrid and had never heard the song before, which, by the way, sings the glory of a Catalan peasant revolt of the seventeenth century. The Catalan nationalists in the audience, however, wept when they heard the outlawed melody, and many people rose in a standing ovation. But suddenly this emotionally charged moment was rudely interrupted by an American women who comes running in, dressed in outrageous tourist clothes, shouting: "wonderful, wonderful. Look John, Revolution! How exotic!" She is joined by her husband, who agrees that it is all "absolutely marvelous," and together they hesitantly sing Pete Seeger's "We Shall Overcome" in a pseudoprogressive pose as someone prompts the words "some day, some day" from backstage.[27]

Joglars has never shied away from being polemical or provoking even its partisan Catalan audience. Boadella clarifies:

> What we were trying to say was that when it really comes down to it, the political consciousness of the Catalans is quickly drowned by their comercial instinct. So we left the people completely confused: first we played on their emotions and showed them to be revolutionary and then we blew it all up by attacking them for selling their revolutionism and the whole Catalan coast. They got teary-eyed when they heard their national anthem, but, at the same time, they sold their entire land, their villas, the coast, to foreigners.[28]

Even so, Boadella emphasizes that, politically, the play was immediately understood as an apology for terrorism against Franco: "It was 1974, Franco was still alive, and we were really advocating that he should be killed. It is not like the terrorism of today, which is a luxury. But back then, terrorism was an urgent necessity. ETA was very important during the dictatorship. Shooting a cop was an important thing back then."[29]

Els Joglars came through the Franco dictatorship unscathed, without having a single show closed by the censors. Nevertheless, the company had made a reputation for itself as a highly skilled antifascist cultural resistance unit and as a group of innovators and hilarious theatrical practical jokers that enjoyed a nationwide popularity. It was therefore ironic that Joglar's true political and legal trouble only started after Franco's death, during the precarious early days of the transition.

With the censors adopting a lower profile than before, Joglars decided to open up all its formidable satirical registers, and, this time with quite intelligible words, it lashed out against the military in a play called *La Torna* (1977). "We managed to perform the play forty times," recalls Boadella,

> which was really a miracle, come to think of it. It was extremely popular. But then word got back to the military, and they immediately closed off the theatre building where we were performing. They threw me in jail, and the other actors were summoned to appear in court at a later date, charged with insulting the military. The day before the trial, I escaped through the bathroom window of the prison hospital. Me and some of the actors fled to France, while the others opted to stay for the trial on the advice of their lawyers, who convinced them that there was nothing to worry about. But they ended up being sentenced to two years. Although the play wasn't exactly an insult—it represented the truth—I can imagine that the generals were pissed off. It was amazing, though. The whole affair resulted in such an enormous popular mobilization in our support that at one point one of the military leaders stated publicly that Joglars could well be responsible for a coup d'état. And that this was not all that farfetched became clear only a couple of years later during the shootings in parliament.[30]

The shootings in question accompanied the attempted coup of 23 February 1981 staged by Tejero and Milan del Bosch.

The trial became an international cause célèbre, with actors everywhere in the Western world expressing solidarity. Boadella ended up spending a year in France and was finally allowed to return on the condition that he would not create trouble. But the military protested, and the director of Joglars was thrown in jail again, this time for four months. Eventually, after a little more than a year, the whole affair was solved when King Juan Carlos pardoned the actors.

The word *torna* is Catalan for the small weight that greengrocers use, for example, to find the exact weight of a particular quantity of vegetables. In the Joglars tragicomedy of the same name, the execution of Polish-born lunatic Heinz Chez, who had murdered a policeman, was the *torna* required to sell the clearly politically motivated execution of anarchist guerrilla Puig Antich. Adding the figure of Chez to that of Antich, executing them on the same day—one in Tarragona and the other in Barcelona on 3 March 1974—the authorities tried to manipulate public opinion into believing that both cases were those of common criminals. Under the direction of Albert Boadella, the company researched the case extensively:

Chez had obviously become the victim of a political game. We started talking to his lawyer, and each time we found out more about his life. It seems that he had even been a street performer. He came to Spain, performed on the beaches a bit, stayed in a campground near Tarragona. Then one day a local cop enters the camping and Heinz Chez kills him just like that, with a hunting rifle he had bought the day before. He never explained why. A strange character; it seemed as if he had been the object of a totally predestined fate. Even the night before his execution he was quietly playing a game with the priest who had come to hear his last confession. But Heinz was not interested at all in confessing anything; he only wanted to win the game he was playing. In *La Torna*, we tried to reconstruct his life. We made a commedia dell'arte show, with masks. The only person not wearing a mask was Heinz. We were very meticulous in our research to base everything we said on fact. Thus we discovered, for instance, that it took them more than five minutes to kill Chez. Apparently, the executioner assigned to the case had been thrown in jail in Barcelona for sexually assaulting a minor. So they gave the job to a totally inexperienced guy who had never used the strangling machine before.[31]

In *La Torna*, Joglars have the execution carried out by two spastics. In the play, Joglars also represent the *Guardia Civil* as roosters, and make direct reference to torture techniques being taught at Spain's national police academy. And so the verdict is reached:

(*The military tribunal. The generals have been deliberating for hours. That is, they have been drinking heavily for hours. They all lie in a drunken stupor. A servant-soldier, who has been sent on a wine run, returns with full bottle and some snacks. Slowly, one of the generals gets up. General:* (*With slurred voice.*) Hey you! Get the typewriter! (*Soldier gets the typewriter. General takes an envelope from his inside pocket and slowly opens it. Starts dictating. Soldier mimes typing.*) In this military establishment . . . Date: today . . . We solemnly declare that we consider that we must sentence the plaintiff, Heinz Chez, to the . . . death penalty . . . . (*Hands the paper to the soldier.*) Here! Copy! (*Fade out as General falls asleep. Sound of typing continues on in the dark*).[32]

With *La Torna*, then, Joglars had the double objective of paying hommage to one of the many forgotten victims of Franco's injustice and of pointing out to the Spanish people that they should continue to remain vigilant against all forms of latent fascism in Spanish society. Even the prison terms and subsequent legal hassles have not deterred els Joglars from pursuing their own theatrical crusade against what it considers undesirable social and political excesses. And the company continues to do so in a very powerful and original verbal and nonverbal theatrical idiom that is created after long months of improvisational sessions in an inflatable dome tucked away in the Catalan countryside.

Typically, after touring with one production for an average of a year and a half, the company retreats to its home near Pruit, two hours by car from

Els Joglars. Satire of preschool fascist education in *Olympic Man Movement* (1981). Photo by Josep Gol.

Barcelona. The new piece is developed there from a few original ideas jotted down by Albert Boadella on a piece of paper. Guided by Boadella's brilliant imagination, characters are shaped inprovisationally and are brought to life in short scenes. "I pull the strings," says Boadella, "but the actors aren't marionettes, of course. It is not like the classical theatre where the director tells the actors where and when to enter. I see myself more like a representative of the audience and say things like 'I don't understand that' or 'now, what's happening here?'"[33]

Aesthetically, since *La Torna,* els Joglars has been predominantly exploring the theatricality of public events that, strictly speaking, are not theatre performance. *M-7 Catalonia* (1978), which Boadella created in exile, parodies the framework of a scientific lecture presented in the year 2200 by Nordic scientists who have made an extensive anthropological study of the degenerate people inhabiting Zone Seven of the Mediterranean region: M-7 Catalonia. *Laetius* (1980) presents, in the form of a reportage, the stages of cultural evolution of a new rational being, not quite human, after a hypothetical nuclear holocaust.

In *Olympic Man Movement* (1981), Joglars presented yet another bleak vision of the future, this time in the form of a fascist meeting. This play, which uses a large electronic scoreboard as its most conspicuous set piece, shows a detestable, highly competitive future Spanish society that today's educational and sports institutions are creating. Using large doses of irony, *Olympic Man Movement* succeeded in provoking its audience:

> You see, during the Franco regime we shared a code, a convention with the audience. It was like a church service, if you will. We, the actors, were the celebrants who shared their faith with the congregation. It was a way of giving each other a certain optimism. Catalan *chansons* served a similar purpose. But when Spain embarked on its democratic journey, I no longer had any use for that conspiracy with the audience. I began to amuse myself by annoying and shocking the audience. With *Olympic Man Movement*, the provocation started already in the program notes. The audience didn't know how to take it. Suddenly they see nine fascists appear on stage who hurl all kinds of reactionary messages at them. They were totally flabbergasted and sometimes remained to discuss with us for at least half an hour after the show ended. They said things like: "Yes, but what he says there is ambiguous, and that there maybe too." So I said, "Bullshit! What you just saw was pure, undiluted fascism!" They were hysterical because they considered themselves so-called liberals and democrats.[34]

The artistic perfectionism and the professionalism with which els Joglars prepares its shows is impressive. *Olympic Man Movement* contains a scene, for example, in which four fascists, while roller-skating, reconstruct a painting by Joan Miró to discredit "these sick and degenerate works that are considered the art of today" and to celebrate a romantic landscape painting which "cannot be made while skating, driving, cooking, or dancing, and which does not discriminate, but which can be understood by all."[35] In order to practice for this scene, the actors were coached by some of the best professional roller hockey players in Spain.[36] And in order to work on the mannerisms and speech patterns of his role as an Anglican bishop from Manchester in the play *Teledeum*, Joglars actor Jaume Collell had himself invited to tea on several occasions by an Anglican priest in Barcelona.

Teledeum (1984) is a hilarious satire on institutionalized Western religions and their exploitation of the mass media. It is presented in the form of a technical rehearsal for a direct international television broadcast of an ecumenical concelebration that is to take place the following day. The church service starts off in the most solemn fashion but progressively deteriorates as the voice of the director (played by Albert Boadella himself) interrupts the action more and more frequently.[37]

Els Joglars. As part of the ecumenical concelebration in *Teledeum* (1984), each representative gives a sermon in the style of his or her denomination. Here Jaume Collell appears as the Anglican bishop. Photo by Josep Gol.

The concelebrants, a Belgian Jehova's Witness, a German Mormon, an Italian Catholic archbishop, the aforementioned Anglican bishop, and a nun belonging to a new American Catholic order that allows women to become priests, gradually turn into caricatures of themselves as they start bickering among themselves, loudly complaining if a particular sermon lasts too long and fighting for the most favorable camera angles. From start to finish, *Teledeum* is filled to the brim with satirical references to minutely studied behaviorisms of the Christian pastors and with gags based on the curious particulars of the various Christian rites. At one point, for example, the scene is suddenly filled with an enormous smoke cloud from which the different church dignitaries emerge teary eyed and coughing heavily: the assistant to the television director had bought the wrong brand of incense.

In this day and age when popes and evangelists of all denominations preach to international television audiences via satellite from glittery altars that have small artificial waterfalls running down from them, or supported by the backup vocals of angelic choirs dressed in virginal white, *Teledeum* seems to have made a timely appearance. But the play's humor was lost on Spain's still influential Catholic hierarchy and its conservative lay allies. *Teledeum* caused scandals and violent reactions almost everywhere it was performed. "All bishops and priests in Spain protested against the play," comments Albert Boadella. "Extreme right-wing groups have thrown Molotov cocktails at the Joglars truck. They have shot at the theatre building with shotguns. They organized a fanatical rally outside the theatre in Cáceres where we were performing. The police had to close off the entire downtown area. And when the audience came out of the theatre, they were attacked."[38]

At the moment, Boadella is facing three court cases in connection with *Teledeum*. A Valencia lawyer and ex-member of the neofascist organization Fuerza Nueva has charged him with violating the liberty of conscience clause in the Spanish constitution, with profanity, and with aggravated blasphemy. The same individual has also charged Boadella with violations of the constitutional articles that protect the Spanish armed forces and the Catholic religion in *Virtuosos de Fontainebleau* (1986), the latest Joglars provocation.

Virtuosos is announced, on posters and program notes, as a classical concert by the famous French chamber ensemble "Virtuosos de Fontainebleau" to cele-brate Spain's entry into the European Community, because, after all, "What is better than classical music to symbolize the cultural synthesis of the great Europe?"[39] The "concert" starts convincingly enough. A Catalan interpreter introduces the individual virtuosos, who then begin the evening with Antoine de Vivaldon's "Tempête de la mer." In order to obtain a high level of authenticity, the actors studied for several months at the Barcelona Conservatory, and "Ladi" Costa, the company's sound technician, installed ingenious potent but almost invisible loudspeakers under each musician's chair through which separate soundtracks of each instrument are played. This setup is so persuasive, in fact, that during many a performance spectators could be heard whispering, "Gosh, it's a real concert!" And, indeed, during the first fifteen minutes or so, the performers stay perfectly within the conventions of a classical music recital, imitating minutely the facial expressions, body postures, and instrument hand-ling of professional musicians in a symphony orchestra. But halfway through the second piece, Mozart's Symphony no. 40 in G Minor (K 360), the musicians suddenly stop and animatedly discuss, in fake French, whether the piece is perhaps too difficult for this backward provincial Catalan audience. They decide that is is and opt to insert a brief pedagogical interlude in which they introduce their instruments and play a few popular folk tunes. From that moment on, the concert conventions start coming apart by the seams and, in a rapid succession of anarchic improvisations, explode into complete chaos.

Els Joglars. *Virtuosos de Fontainebleau* (1987).
The musicians, thinking their music too difficult for the provincial audience,
play something simple while lecturing briefly about their instruments.

The musicians, in a display of classical haute cuisine, ceremoniously prepare le
Coq Français.

The French "Virtuosos" first arrogantly insult what they call the *pueblo tribú español,* the tribal Spanish people. Feigning to lower themselves to the cultural level of their audience, the "civilized" musicians explain the concept of polyphony by illustrating it with a cacaphony of corporal noises, ranging from soprano burping and sneezing to alto yawning and spitting and bass nose blowing and farting. Subsequently, they proceed to show what high culture is all about. They cook a rooster on stage in an exhibition of haute cuisine, which, they claim, is structurally comparable to classical music. Immediately following this gastronomic ritual, the musicians bring out their pet dogs (rolled-up wigs in reality), with which they commit all kinds of perverse acts. Antonio, the Andalusian stagehand, walks inadvertently onto the stage with a stack of chairs and ends up being sexually assaulted by the two female musicians. One of them decides to play a Tchaikovsky violin concierto with her instrument pressed against the stagehand's crotch, to which the latter responds in ecstasy: "Culture is very easy!"[40]

Virtuosos alternates excerpts of serious music with continuous verbal attacks on Spanish culture and glorification of the French. The bass player, for example, argues:

> We, ze French, have helped mucha ze Spanish culture. Picasso: Paris; Buñuel: Paris; Goya: Paris; Pablo Casals: Perpignan; Machado: Coulioure. But you: Tamtam! (*makes gesture of shooting*) ze Spanish poets: Garcia Lorca, quirchk! Cervantes, quirchk! You Spanish come to Lourdes to search for miracles and afterwards you leave us with all ze shit. You even send us ETA terrorists! Vive la France! Vive l'Europe! (*points at the audience*) Hahaha! You? Europeans? Hahaha!

The end of the play brings an authentic cultural war as the Catalan interpreter, who has had all he can take from the Virtuosos, enters in the guise of a traditional Catalan *tambour* and chases the French away with his threatening drumrolls.[41] He is aided by Antonio, who appears inside the statue of the popular Virgin of Zaragoza. But the French are not that easily defeated and counter the attack by bringing in some cultural and historical symbols of their own: Napoleon and Louis XIV in drag, who lipsynchs Edith Piaf's "Non, je ne regrette rien." In the meantime, the Catalan drummer has jumped into the auditorium and distributes citrus fruits, typical products of the Spanish Mediterranean coast, encouraging the spectators to use the (plastic) oranges and lemons as projectiles to bombard the French with. An uneasy truce is eventually negotiated, and, in the finale, both Catalans and French play the famous Jota de la Dolores folkdance together, as Salvador Dali and an oversized caricature of Jordi Pujol, the president of the Catalan autonomous government, also make a last minute appearance.

Albert Boadella claims that *Virtuosos de Fountainebleau* is more than a simple anti-French satire:

Antonio, dressed as the highly revered Virgin of Zaragoza, joins the *tambour* and the Virtuosos in their encore.

Louis XIV lipsynchs Piaf.

Salvador Dali highlights the final scene.

The French musicians represent the concept of Europe and the Common Market. They have also brought us the notion of culture as a commodity, European cultural consumerism. The French, in our eyes, also betray their Mediterranean character. They have always chosen the side of the Nordics, because that is where traditionally the economic power resides. It is really a story about the north-south division. This is obvious even in the two Spanish characters of the play: the interpreter is from the economically powerful north, and Antonio is a migrant from the empoverished south.[42]

For Boadella, France represents the European synthesis in which the new Spanish technocrats like to see their country integrated as well. But in Boadella's eyes, that European lifestyle is hardly anything to aspire to:

It is deadened by super refrigerators and other advanced electrical appliances and by their little, neatly organized houses. All that consumerism hasn't quite taken over here yet. And the Spanish people still have passion. They are sometimes still capable of killing for their passion. That is not bad. I prefer it. I love it when I get into trouble with *Teledeum*, for example. Because there is a reaction, and it shows that the society is still alive. Something like that would never happen in Sweden, for example. The audience here can still be taken in by a theater show and present you with unpredictable reactions afterwards. During *Olympic Man*, for example, in several venues, the audience got up and started insulting the actors. That is wonderful.[43]

Boadella obviously derives great pleasure from his art, and so do hundreds of thousands of Spaniards. Els Joglars have been playing to sell-out crowds for many, many years now. The group is so popular, in fact, that it is one of the few political theatre companies in the West that manages to survive without any significant official subsidy. Boadella is not worried about getting sucked in by the system either, because, he says, "I have such a great time doing what I'm not doing that no amount of money in the world could buy me that same quality of pleasure."[44] He is not too concerned about the *Teledeum* trials either, which could cost him a six-year prison sentence: "I'm not prepared to go to jail. I want the government to know that if they don't take a decision that prevents [my conviction] that I'll happily become the first cultural exile under the Socialist administration."[45]

Boadella and els Joglars never compromise, not to art and not to politics. For twenty-five years now, they have been creating ever larger spaces of liberty in Spanish society. And doing it with theatre that is great by the world's best standards.

CHAPTER 10

CONCLUSION

GENERAL CHARACTERISTICS OF RADICAL POPULAR THEATRE

Looking back over almost twenty years of radical popular theatre in the West, we can distinguish the following general features that characterized at least the early stages of its development.

I. With the exception of Spain's radical theatre, which was more antifascist than class oriented, it established itself in an area in which the majority of the inhabitants is made up of agricultural or industrial laborers, and it elects this population as its target audience.

The radical popular theatre is aware that even in the pre-1968 communion-type popular theatre, the working classes were largely excluded from most artistic experiences. Even according to the most optimistic calculations, at most 5 percent of the audience in a communion-type popular theatre consisted of blue-collar workers, and less than one percent were peasants. Obviously, with such statistics, any countercultural initiative seemed doomed from the start. The post-1968 radical popular theatre realized that it needed to develop new strategies to attract larger numbers of these traditionally nontheatre audiences to its performances. The working classes did not attend the theatre on a regular basis because they were intimidated by the classical theatre buildings designed for the bourgeoisie: plush seats, thick red velvet curtains, ushers in official-looking uniforms, and exorbitant ticket prices. The communion-type popular theatre had tried to eliminate most of these social and psychological obstacles but basically continued to play a bourgeois repertoire. Secondly, many workers are physically too tired to go out after a long day's work; night shifts, overtime, and weekend jobs complicate matters even more. Under these circumstances, the convenience of having one's own entertainment at home in the form of color television, video, and, in the not-too-distant future, an almost limitless choice of cable and satellite channels, will effectively prevent many workers and peasants from donning clean clothes after a hard day's work and traveling to the nearest theatre.

The first measure that the radical popular theatre took was to implant itself visibly in the social habitat of its target audience in order to learn its customs, language, and culture, to express solidarity with its plight, and to break down traditional social barriers that may exist between artists and the general public. In the beginning stages of such an implantation, small nuclei of committed actors would rent a house or rehearsal space in a working-class neighborhood or a rural village. Often, they would also take a local job to pay for food and rent until municipal or federal subsidies and ticket sales would allow them to work full time on their theatrical productions.

II. The radical popular theatre aggressively recruits a nontheatre audience that consists of workers, peasants, white-collar employees, students, housewives, unemployed youth, and children.

The radical popular theatre reaches out to the nontheatre audience by means of free admission (or the charging of minimal contributions) to their shows, which it often performs under makeshift conditions in the target audience's working and living environment. The theatrical spaces used by radical popular theatre groups are only rarely fixed locations preconceived as playhouses. If they possess their own theatre, the groups usually built it themselves by converting buildings that used to have some functional connection with their target audience: a neighborhood cinema gone bankrupt, an abandoned warehouse, etc. In most cases, however, popular theatre troupes do not have their own permanent performance space and tour through the region in which they have elected to base themselves, presenting their plays in makeshift theatres set up in social meeting places that are frequented by the target audience: the smoky pub on the corner, the workingmen's club, the village square on a hot summer's evening, or the neighborhood cultural center. In a very real sense, the radical popular theatre presents itself as an integral part of the working-class social atmosphere. It has learned to adapt itself to the impediments that the differing circumstances of each performance present. It employs a wide range of techniques to break through such physical and social barriers as smoke, noise, beerdrinking, and the latest soccer predictions. Most performances of the radical popular theatre are preceded by catchy music from an accordion player, rock group, or a small marching band. Sometimes, a joke-cracking comedian or an uninhibited clown tries to break the ice. Also, during the performance of the actual play, a relaxed interaction between actors and audience is maintained: dramatic characters move offstage in order to directly address individual spectators. Theatrical illusion is constantly challenged and never really given a chance to establish itself. The audience is made to feel part of a game.

In its anti-illusionist aspect, the contemporary radical theatre is clearly indebted to Brecht's epic theatre. The playful acting style of the popular theatre is derived from epic acting, although the atmosphere surrounding a popular play is usually much more jovial and festive than the rather sterile and serious Brechtian creations. Most contemporary radical popular plays contain songs that serve a narrative and analytical purpose quite similar to Brecht's. Like Brecht's, the anti-illusionist devices of the contemporary radical popular theatre prevent the audience from getting too wrapped up in the action of the play, lest they forget that the actual social changes must be implemented outside the theatre.

The radical popular theatre has a high standard of professionalism, and here lies one of the main differences with earlier attempts at making radical theatre, which were predominantly amateur and agitprop. Although they often perform in makeshift theatre spaces, radical troupes realize that their newly gained audience is demanding and must be treated to high-quality shows that are entertaining and speak to the interests of the spectators. Therefore, the radical popular theatre is conscious of the habits, the prejudices, and the attitudes of the audience it has chosen to work for. Naturally, ticket prices are kept to a minimum and do not exceed the price of other types of working-class entertainment like soccer matches, boxing, or the cinema. Partly for logistical reasons, several troupes have, at one time or other, cooperated with left-wing political parties or unions in order to secure sufficient funding for professionally mounted shows and to attract the largest possible working-class audience. The publicity channels of these political organizations proved quite effective in the establishment of a reputation for previously unknown radical troupes. It was convenient to be able to rely on the contacts of local union representatives or on members of socialist or Communist parties in small rural communities or in some heavily industrialized section of town to announce the imminent performance of a popular play. However, this type of collaboration did not always proceed without conflicts; in some instances it caused such severe ideological disputes that it resulted in irreparable breaks.

Just as government subsidies lead to economic and ideological dependence on authorities, no matter how liberal the latter may be, in the same way financial and organizational support from unions and political parties tends to diminish the artistic integrity of radical troupes.[1] Several left-wing theatre companies that decided to work together with the cultural sections of socialist and Communist parties soon found themselves in conflict with certain dogmatic ideas on the political function of art. The radical popular theatre considered itself to be involved in the consciousness-raising of industrial and agricultural laborers and requested for themselves the freedom to create plays that it thought to be most

attractive and effective. Dogmatic left-wing party leaders, however, saw no
essential function for art in the class struggle and wanted to subordinate the
artistic activities of the theatre people to the decrees of the party's executive
committee. Thus, wherever left-wing parties and unions regarded cultural action
as insignificant for class struggle, radical troupes ended the collaboration.[2] They
saw a much more dynamic function for themselves in the complex, dialectic
relation between base and superstructure; in their view, art is not only determined
by socioeconomic circumstances, but it also exercises a relative influence in
return.

III. The radical popular theatre usually creates its plays
more or less collectively.

In the true spirit of 1968, most radical troupes try to avoid the cultivation of
stardom and the development of individual artistic reputations. Their creative
methods have undergone strong modifications that vary from group to group,
although most subscribe to some form of collective creation. The figure of the
lone playwright, writing his dialogues and stage directions all by himself and for
an audience and a troupe he does not know, is virtually nonexistent in the radical
popular theatre. At times, actors in the radical popular theatre tried to create
plays by means of pure improvisation, without a dramatist. But clearly in the
text-based variety of radical popular theatre, the best results were created when a
competent literary artist collaborated with a director and actors through the
various stages of a play's construction. Typically, the playwright first designs the
skeletal structure and the basic plot of a play that may be substantially trans-
formed during improvisational sessions. The playwright then goes back to work
with specific suggestions from actors, director, set designer, and representatives
from the target audience. In the case of less verbally oriented theatres like Bread
and Puppet and Joglars, a strong visual artist can be seen as fulfilling a similar
function to that of the playwright: he creates the initial images and provides the
collective creative process with its basic structure. The final product consists of
dramatic situations and/or dialogues that are flexible enough to be adapted to
ever-changing topical circumstances. Very often, the published version of a
popular play credits the entire troupe as the creators and not an individual
dramatist. Even internationally known radical playwrights like Dario Fo and
John McGrath do not conceive of themselves in quite the same terms as their
mainstream counterparts. They are extremely aware of the fact that creating a
popular play is much more than simply writing a text, because it also involves
careful consideration of the kind of audience they are writing for, the type of
space in which the play is going to be performed, and the quantity and type of
publicity that is available. Their plays are far from being idiosyncratic expressions of individual artistic sensibilities.

IV. The creation of the play is preceded or accompanied by an extensive period of research into its subject matter.

The themes of radical popular plays are usually related to specific problems that affect the target audience, and the plays often provide analyses or historical illuminations of its socioeconomic predicament. This research period often involves elaborate interviews with members of the target audience and tryouts of impromptu sketches or preliminary scenes of the upcoming play.

Radical troupes make a point of carefully documenting the facts of their plays. They often base their creations on actual historical events or on traditional regional legends. For example, le Théâtre Populaire de Lorraine did a play on the bankruptcy of Lorraine's iron mines. Before the actual creation of the play, the company members painstakingly investigated all the economic and social aspects of the Lorraine steel industry. The radical popular theatre also provides alternative news coverage of the facts that the mass media misrepresent or flatly ignore. As a result, the radical popular theatre feels a strong responsibility to be true to the facts and to make sure that they are carefully documented. In the preparatory stages of a new play, radical troupes usually cooperate closely with representatives of their target audiences in order to grasp emotional aspects of the issues in question. They play preliminary versions of scenes for a select audience and invite suggestions for change. Consequently, the target audience also feels involved in the creative process; spectators become aware that the play is for them and, in a very real sense, by them.

V. Even the full-length final draft of the radical popular play is rarely definitive.

The radical popular theatre responds to dynamic political situations of which the particulars differ from performance to performance and from locale to locale. Thus, typically, the performances of the radical popular theatre are followed by animated discussions between cast members and spectators, and pertinent comments and criticisms are incorporated in an unfixed script that is continually updated.

Radical popular plays must be flexible enough to respond to the changing conditions of every new audience. The names, the physiques and the attitudes of the oppressors differ from village to village, and a small change in gesture, makeup, or accent can make a character more easily recognizable to the public. Furthermore, actors and authors themselves learn from the audience after the show. When the play is over, they often sit down on the edge of the stage or go down to the cafeteria or bar and mix with the spectators, asking them what they thought of a particular character or situation.

*VI. The radical popular theatre considers its plays to be
nonpermanent creations and opposes mass production and commercial
distribution of drama.*

If texts of radical popular plays are printed at all, it is often done in the
cheapest possible way (often simply mimeographed) and for the convenience of
the audience only, not to make a profit or to flirt with immortality. Getting plays
into print is not one of the radical popular theatre's priorities. Believing in the
dynamics of history and the capacity of the people to affect it, it prefers that its
plays be nonpermanent, changeable creations as well. Furthermore, the radical
popular theatre tries to avoid the cultivation of artistic immortality. Nor does it
produce art for material profit. It consciously avoids contact with large publishing houses, for it opposes the mass production of art. Most of the printing of
radical popular plays is done either privately or by relatively small, progressive
publishing houses. Dario Fo, for example, publishes all his plays under license
of his theatre production company La Comune, and John McGrath publishes his
plays with the progressive Pluto Press. Texts are sold together with T-shirts and
posters for the audience's convenience and to raise additional funding for the
troupe.

*VII. The radical popular theatre sharply distinguishes itself
from populist entertainment.*

There is no denying that sexually suggestive situation comedies, soap operas,
and melodramas are extremely well liked in working-class circles. They appeal
to cheap sentimentality and sexist attitudes, reinforcing rather than questioning
social values and prejudices. As such, these dramatic phenomena belong to what
Paolo Freire called "cultural action for domination," which lures the oppressed
people into social integration rather than contention. In an interesting study, J.R.
Goodlad points out that populist drama of the type described above is conservative in nature and clearly serves to maintain the social and political status
quo.[3] Although the radical popular theatre sometimes draws on forms and
characters derived from populist drama, its objectives are totally different. Intent
on upsetting the status quo, the radical popular theatre uses slapstick situations
and absurd character behavior to provoke pensive laughter in the Brechtian
sense. It wants to provide its audience with new insights into its predicament and
to reveal the real faces behind the masks of the authorities.

*VIII. Formally, the radical popular theatre draws on the traditional artistic
forms of the working classes, while also incorporating elements of
contemporary popular culture.*

The radical popular theatre makes ample use of traditional popular forms of
art that are indigenous to the areas in which it has based itself. Following

Mao's suggestions, it also employs the richness of local slang and dialect to authenticate the dialogues of its plays. Thus, plots are often based on or refer to legends and symbols that are still living in the communities of their target audience.

During the centuries of bourgeois supremacy, popular art has been systematically suppressed, expropriated, and denigrated. The language of the proletariat is commonly presented as an inferior form of expression, whereas in actuality it is every bit as valid a means of communication as the "standard" language spoken by the radio announcer or the member of Parliament. Most sociolinguists agree that the standard norms for pronunciation and lexicon are set by that segment of society that holds the economic and political power. The same goes for cultural standards: street songs or bawdy peasant farces are not necessarily less rich in artistic quality than the arias and drawing-room comedies with which the bourgeoisie amuses itself, but they have been labeled as vulgar following decades of ruling-class manipulation of public taste. The radical popular theatre makes a sustained effort to reverse this process of cultural oppression, and consequently its plays revive age-old types of popular art. Often, radical popular plays are the fruits of extensive cultural research to revive ancient forms of oral literature, farces, medieval improvisational theatre, folk songs, legends, or popular folk heroes over which centuries of aristocratic and bourgeois hegemony have thrown a veil of oblivion. Performed professionally by skilled actors and singers, these forgotten types of popular songs, dances, and dramas regain something of their proper respectability. In this fashion, the radical popular theatre shows its audience that the old traditions are nothing to be ashamed of, but instead constitute a cultural heritage that is as valid as that of the bourgeoisie. Furthermore, the radical popular theatre feels that forms of folk art are useful sources for regionalist and class emancipation in the indispensable cultural prelude to all social change. Thus the Scottish branch of the 7:84 Theatre Company has used forms like the *Ceilidh* when they performed in the Highlands and the Hebrides Islands, or the *Noson Llawen* in Wales. They also include Gaelic songs, dances and Scottish fiddling in their performances. Similarly, lo Teatre de la Carriera consistently mixes French with Provençal in its dialogues and sets contemporary political themes to the form of, for example, the traditional Provençal pastoral. Also the Mexican-American Teatro Campesino has bilingual dialogues in its plays and uses forms and symbols derived from the Mexican Hispanic and Indian cultural heritage.

Apart from traditional forms of popular folk art, the radical popular theatre has also found it useful to work with more modern elements of contemporary popular culture. Westerns, gangster movies, musical revues, vaudeville shows, stand-up comic routines, sentimental songs, and the various types of contemporary rock music (heavy metal, new wave, punk, reggae) provide a ready frame of cultural reference for an audience that is not familiar with the more conventional traditions of the theatre.

IX. Humor in the form of comedy and satire is the radical popular theatre's
essential language.

One of the main priorities of the radical popular theatre is that its plays should be entertaining and fun. Laughter and humor serve the double function of attracting nontheatre audiences to the performance and of revealing the more absurd aspects of capitalist society. A working man, not used to attending the theatre to begin with, will certainly not leave his home to go see a "serious" play—he wants to enjoy himself. The radical popular theatre has recognized the capacity for laughter in the oppressed classes, and, consequently, their plays are often conceived in the comic mode. But the humor of radical popular plays is seldom gratuitous; although they contain situation comedy derived from traditional peasant farces and the like and although they contain a fair amount of slapstick, these elements are usually linked to specific political circumstances. The laughter provoked by the radical popular theatre, then, clearly serves a political purpose.

The radical popular theatre employs satirical techniques to expose the workings of the social power structure, often presenting its representatives grotesquely in order to ridicule them. The laughter elicited by the sight of a policeman or a judge caught with his pants down is not intended to result in the sublimation of social anger. The rage at an unbearable social situation should persist at all times and should be rechanneled into political action. Radical popular dramatic satire helps the working classes understand that the status quo is perpetuated by means of a repressive apparatus, the operators of which are not as invincible as they seem.

Satire is, then, an essential ingredient of radical popular plays. It satisfies two basic requirements of the radical popular theatre: entertainment and political criticism. Radical popular dramatic satire can be defined as the demystifying of capitalist exploitation with a grin. No artistic mode more effectively reduces bourgeois institutions and their representatives than satire. In this fondness for satire, the radical popular theatre is supported by Lenin and Mao. Lenin was a great admirer of Mayakovsky's satiric irony, and Mao Tse-tung stressed the need for satire in artistic attacks against fascists and reactionaries.[4] Mao even suggested a distinction between satire that criticizes the limitations and flaws of the popular masses and satire that denigrates the bourgeois class enemy. Satire that attacks the comrades should be gentle and sprinkled with pedagogical elements, whereas satire that ridicules the enemy should be a weapon that strikes with unscrupulous efficiency. Marxists, in general, regard satire as a useful arm in the struggle between the social classes. For them, the contradictions in social reality form the source of satirical inspiration; it is the eminent task of satire to expose the persistent presence of anachronistic elements in a given historical situation. In the Marxist view, satire is committed to reveal the essence of outdated economic and social relations by which the ruling class continues to maintain the status quo, and, in that sense, satire fulfills a revolutionary task.[5]

The often proclaimed objective of satire in the radical popular theatre is to communicate a profounder truth than the facts supplied by the official channels of public information controlled by the ruling class. Satire in the radical popular theatre serves the purpose of changing the audience's perspective on situations and persons that were previously unchallenged. By means of various types of exaggeration and irony, satire exposes the contradictions in society.[6] Satire can reverse the effect of integration propaganda that is constantly diffused by the bourgeois-controlled media, whose purpose it is to support and propagate the dominant ideology in society, and incites its audience to accept "unquestioningly and uncomplainingly the social conundrums of the present and not challenge the authority of those who perpetuate the dominant and ongoing social institutions."[7]

The popular masses, being perhaps less adept at analyzing the propagandistic value of the mass media than the more highly educated bourgeoisie, are more prone to fall victim to information manipulation. Through satire, the radical popular theatre attempts to undermine the authority of bourgeois institutions by inflating or deflating their representatives out of proportion. For this purpose, it makes use of the techniques of high and low burlesque. The former describes the satiric victim in gigantic or exaggeratedly virtuous terms in order to prove that he is exactly the opposite; the latter presents the satiric victim in association with animals or the lowest, most vulgar humans imaginable.

Several theorists claim that satire is essentially conservative in nature and that it serves as a beneficial verbal release for aggressions that might otherwise be expressed in the form of physical violence. But radical popular satire is more serious business than mock warfare that intends to sublimate the audience's need for rebellion.[8] Satire in the radical popular theatre analyzes current social conditions and lays bare the means by which the people are exploited. At times, the radical popular theatre also announces alternatives for social change by means of *mundus inversus* satire that has a naive fool enter a fictional world that is recognizably our own. Thus, the maniac in Dario Fo's *Accidental Death of an Anarchist* manages, with his uncorrupted logic and lack of inhibitions, to expose the hypocrisy and crookedness of those who are supposedly in charge of protecting the people's interests.[9]

Satire often appears in conjunction with comedy, because pure and unrelieved invective is commonly considered unattractive and wearisome over an extended period. Thus, the rage and pensive laughter of satire is often interchanged with the lighter merriment of a comic plot. In the final analysis, however, satiric elements prevail over the comic ones in the radical popular theatre. Comedy traditionally works toward resolution of disorder and social integration, whereas satire and radical popular theatre present the disorder without a resolution or emphatically impose a fake one. Radical popular dramatic satires seldom have happy endings, and, if they do contain positive resolutions, they are either transparently accidental or obviously fantastic. The real happy endings of satires and militant popular plays must, by necessity, be created outside the perimeters of their fictional, artistic form—through the political actions of the audience.

Reasons for the Decline of Radical Popular Theatre in the West

Making up the balance after close to two decades of radical popular theatre, it is justified to ask how successful the troupes have been in achieving their main objective. Have their efforts indeed led to noticeable changes in society? At first sight, it would seem that the Western world has grown politically more conservative than when the radical popular theatre first started its activities in the late sixties. If anything, today's youth is disillusioned and apathetic rather than militant and prepared to overthrow the capitalist system. Students at universities in Europe and the United States are concerned more with grades and the hope of getting a well-paying job than with solidarity for the oppressed people elsewhere in the world. Furthermore, violent racism is emerging again all over the Western world. Protests now take the form of individual expressions of discontent in unconventional hairdos and outfits, not in massive, collective demonstrations in the street. Are we to conclude, then, that the cultural efforts of the radical popular theatre to raise the consciousness of the masses have all been for nought? John McGrath, artistic director of Britain's 7:84 Theatre Company, denies it:

> I think that there's no doubt that there is a difference: in straightforward political terms of appreciation. Popular theatre is now a reality. The attack on the English 7:84, for example, is being met by a fantastic audience support, from the whole Labour Party, the trade unions, and thousands of people from the working class. And in 1968, when we began, those people would never have supported theatre in this way. And that is not only because of us, but of the whole movement trying to engage with people on their own land.[10]

However, even in these words, McGrath points more to the social and cultural establishment of radical popular theatre than to its political effectiveness. The fact that radical popular theatre is now more widely accepted than before is as much (or more) a function of aesthetic and organizational compromises on the part of the troupes as one of changed attitudes in the public.

Most radical troupes started out with forms of militant, agitprop street theatre in the late sixties and early seventies. Although most of the companies have maintained a progressive and regionalist outlook, many gradually dropped their agitprop label in order to pursue more enduring artistic forms. In 1987, most of the groups discussed in this book are no longer headquartered in rural or industrialized areas. In Europe in particular, troupes managed to acquire permanent theatre buildings and relatively large government subsidies. As a result,

in the seventies the theatre fringe expanded drastically and often became incorporated into the cultural establishment itself. "Fringes" and "Off-Off" became
"in" places frequented by trendy young urban professionals. Through the years,
the creativity and the professionalism of the radical troupes improved to the
extent that their type of political drama came to be widely accepted as a
legitimate form of art. Consequently, many radical troupes started receiving state
and local subsidies based on artistic merit, and gradually their concern for
political issues became overshadowed by concern for their material and artistic
perpetuation. Nowadays, the majority of their audience no longer consists of
workers but of the ever-expanding middle classes.

In the early days, the radical popular theatre was driven by social anger and
revolutionary fervor, and finances never really were an issue. Back then, theatre
was a political weapon first and a means of artistic expression second. Radical
troupes felt that they needed to respond directly to rapidly changing political and
social circumstances. As soon as a new issue came up, plays were created
quickly and efficiently with little regard for finesse. But in the mid seventies—in
some cases even earlier—a gradual change started taking place: many groups
reorganized; militant members, frustrated with the lack of immediate results,
left; and artistic form became more of a priority. Following this development, the
radical popular theatre became institutionalized and its forms legitimized, and
soon the first subsidies started coming in. Today, the annual budget of most of
the radical troupes in question comes, for an important part, from government
contributions. Thus the radical popular theatre is in the ironic situation of being
financially dependent on the ruling class that it ideologically claims to oppose.
The explanation of this paradox is multifaceted and must address two questions:
(1) why the state bothers to finance subversive cultural activities and (2) why
radical left-wing artists accept money (and implicitly imposed restrictions) from
the state. The particulars of the rationale for the state's decision to finance the
radical popular theatre differ from place to place. However, in most cases, the
government's arguments seem to be that it can remove the sting from the radical
popular theatre's social criticism by improving the financial comfort of the
troupes and their members.[11]

Theatre people argue that the state has an obligation to support popular theatre
as a social service. Although the subsidies to radical popular theatre companies
nowhere approach the astronomical sums allotted to symphony orchestras, operas, and classical repertory theatre companies, there can be no doubt that the
increased financial backing improved the day-to-day living conditions of the
artists in question. Charles Tordjman of le Théâtre Populaire de Lorraine candidly admits that a correlation exists between improved economic conditions and
diminished artistic and political militancy:

> Actually, in a certain way we are no longer fighting. Maybe having become an
> institution, having the means that allow us to live without fear of tomorrow,

softens the [aesthetic] forms because it softens the people. When people get into more comfortable circumstances, they become more interested in other things because the urgency is gone.[12]

Comfortably installed in the spacious municipal auditorium of Thionville and with a subsidy of over three million Francs a year, TPL has seen its proletarian attendance dwindle to 10 percent of its total audience, whereas in the early seventies its audiences used to be made up of more than 80 percent workers. It is now no longer TPL's priority to provide a predominantly working-class audience with cultural confidence. Instead, the company wants to create "un théâtre élitaire pour tout le monde," an elitist theatre accessible to everyone. Also the Grips Theater in Berlin, although more faithful to its proletarian concerns and the radical popular theatre form, has changed the focus of its plays from class politics to a more psychological perspective. After years of struggling with right-wing politicians who regarded Grips as communist indoctrinators of their children, the troupe is now extensively subsidized by Berlin's conservative CDU city government. By supporting Grips, the Right wants to prove how tolerant it is. More surprisingly, however, Grips does not really seem to mind collaborating with the CDU in its political publicity game:

> They recognize that Grips is a special cultural aspect of Berlin with which Berlin has something extraordinary to offer. We have become an export product. We have performed all over the world, and we are constantly invited by Goethe Institutes everywhere. We are now so firmly established that our fiercest enemies . . . are now quiet and treat us exactly the same as all other theatres.[13]

The Western governments, then, in most cases resolved to fund rather than oppose radical troupes and succeeded in blunting their social criticism and in absorbing them into the cultural establishment. After years of living and working in the margin of society, many radical troupes gradually adopted a more pragmatic attitude toward government funding. Joan Holden of the San Francisco Mime Troupe coolly explains, "The fact is that the enemy has the money. If you want to do anything, you have to get the money from them in one way or another."[14] Dan Chumley, codirector of the Mime Troupe, agrees with her:

> There's simply no way we can earn our own way anymore, unless we tour 36 weeks of the year and raise our ticket prices way above what our audiences can afford. . . . Besides, radical theater needs to take its rightful space alongside establishment theater. And, to those who ask whether we will ever bite the hand that feeds us, I can assure you that we haven't lost our teeth or our will.[15]

The San Francisco Mime Troupe directors and their colleagues in most other radical companies realize that it is impossible to participate in a capitalist society and remain pure. As a result, the radical popular theatre is now, on the whole, more willing to make certain compromises than before. Spokespersons of the various radical troupes defend this change in attitude by arguing that capitalism is full of contradictions, and that history is dialectic and does not stand still; back in the late sixties the radical popular theatre responded to conditions that have now ceased to exist. Circumstances have changed as well as the nature of oppression in the West and, concurrently, so have the theatrical forms with which the radical popular theatre responds to the times. Although this may be true, socioeconomic and psychological factors must also be considered in the changed attitude of the radical popular theatre.

The people that have been involved in the radical popular theatre since its beginnings in the late sixties are now approaching middle age. And, according to Gloriamalia Flores of el Teatro Campesino, the age factor must be considered in explaining the new outlook of the radical popular theatre:

> As far as labor camps and parks are concerned, we don't do that kind of thing anymore. It is very strenuous to perform in those places. And also you should realize that our people are getting older and responsibilities get more heavy. People that were used to sleeping on the floor and sharing bathroom facilities, now can't do that anymore. They have husbands and wives and babies and families. The commune situation is gone, and people just need their privacy. You know, things that we used to be able to do when we were young just can't happen anymore. Things change when you get older. You expect more, you need more comfort.[16]

Tired of scraping by on poverty-level salaries, radical popular theatre artists more willingly accept grants and subsidies from official sources. But also the increasing artistic desire to mount more sophisticated shows demands budget expansions. Joan Holden expresses the feelings of many radical popular theatre artists when she passionately declares that "I have been writing plays for fifteen years, only to be shouted by actors into the wind. I want to write plays to be seen indoors, under lights, where there are more possibilities. And I can only do that if we make more money. Similarly for the actors. It is the logic of artistic development."[17] Most people in the radical popular theatre feel, then, that the only way for the movement to survive is to get bigger, to get more artistic recognition and to obtain financial security, because economically and psychologically it has been such a long and tiresome struggle that people would otherwise simply give up.

Over the course of the past fifteen years, many artists have dropped out of the radical popular theatre movement, including some of its most prominent leaders. Ron Davis (who founded the San Francisco Mime Troupe), Luis Matilla (who founded Tábano), Claude Alranq (who started lo Teatre de la Carriera) and Jacques Kraemer (who founded le Théâtre Populaire de Lorraine) all left their troupes in frustration. Other groups, notably in West Germany, disbanded altogether. Moreover, many of the radical troupes discussed here have been on the point of breaking up at one point or other in their history. Obviously, with so much intense work and so little moral and material reward, burnout is a real problem for the radical popular theatre. Some troupes have tried to deal with this desertion by discontinuing their full-time core of actors and by becoming production companies instead. They engage actors for one show at a time. 7:84, la Comune, and el Teatro Campesino operate on this basis. But many of their free-lance actors return for other productions. Even troupes with permanent acting companies like Grips, la Carriera, Joglars, and Bread and Puppet have people come and go. Leaders like Volker Ludwig, Catherine and Hélène Bonafé, Albert Boadella, and Peter Schumann provide the expertise and the artistic continuity; young actors and musicians, who usually do not stay longer than five years, provide the necessary fresh blood.[18]

In the midst of skyrocketing budgets, the Bread and Puppet Theater is one of the few radical troupes that continues to refuse any form of government subsidy. It continues to operate a low-budget enterprise that generates its finances solely from private donations and ticket sales. Relying heavily on complex set pieces, the company recycles scrap material to put on its visually striking shows with very little money. Thanks to Peter Schumann's inventiveness and craftmanship, Bread and Puppet remains one of the purest and most independent troupes in the radical popular theatre landscape. Also Dario Fo's and Franca Rame's production company la Comune and Albert Boadella's els Joglars continue to operate without any substantial government funding, but they have become so successful that they can easily afford not being subsidized. Despite their relative economic independence from the powers that be, even Bread and Puppet, Joglars, and la Comune cannot avoid working in bourgeois venues. For financial reasons they have to complement their nontheatre activities with performances in the established theatre. The Bread and Puppet Theater tours the college circuit in the eastern United States in winter and performs in Europe during the early summer. Els Joglars performs in commercial (albeit often decentralized) venues throughout Spain, and Dario Fo and Franca Rame do not object to having their plays produced by profit-seeking commercial companies, and they themselves must now be counted among the highest paid stage actors in the world.

In addition to playing the bourgeois theatre circuit, many radical troupes have appeared on television and at many major international theatre festivals as well. Catherine Bonafé remarks that lo Teatre de la Carriera goes to these official functions not only for the money but also for the artistic recognition, which is important for the morale of both the actors and the partisan audience at home. Like la Carriera, most other radical troupes still prefer to play for working-class audiences and continue to consider themselves ideologically opposed to bourgeois culture. But in order to balance their ever-increasing budgets, they are forced to make excursions into the bourgeois theatre.

If the present developments are any indication, the radical theatre will, undoubtedly, continue to make more and more compromises. What with the growing dependence on subsidies and income from bourgeois venues and with the increasing desire for comfort and artistic recognition, the slowly aging radical popular theatre artists will be more and more tempted to perform outside the explicitly proletarian domain. Radical troupes will continue to perform in labor clubs and community centers of rural and urban proletarian districts, but they know full well that official recognition is only obtained on the established stages of the major cities. Furthermore, disillusion and frustration constitute a real danger for those who work in the radical popular theatre. The long-term political results of their work are hard to measure and seem to be negated—on the surface at least—by the increasing depoliticization of public life. Very likely, then, the radical popular theatre will continue its two-sidedness. John McGrath does not necessarily see that as a drawback:

> I think that the radical popular theatre could actually become a very important part of theatre as a whole. As long as it doesn't get taken over by the smart asses it will be all right. As long as the power remains with the groups, with the people, and it is talking to the working classes. . . . And you can't really stay out of these bourgeois theatres because they are very good places to make theatre in. We can't afford to turn our backs on all bourgeois theatre, that's crazy! What we've got to try and do is to convince the people in them that the audiences we bring to the theatre are more important than the audiences that they usually bring in. If we transform the theatre buildings, the attitudes of the people that run them and the audiences, then the future of popular theatre is enormous, actually.[19]

Most leaders of the contemporary radical popular theatre seem to agree with McGrath's argument.

In the second half of the eighties, the radical popular theatre seems to have drastically redefined its original orientation. If cooptation is perhaps too strong a word for its current attitude, the radical popular theatre in the West certainly has become more pragmatic over the years and has stabilized itself in the form of institutions. It is determined to expand its activities inside the cultural establishment, for whom the radical theatre artists have become valuable assets. For many years, they have been forced to work at all creative and organizational facets of theatre under the most demanding conditions and with extremely limited means. Certainly in that sense, the radical popular theatre has been one of the toughest theatre schools imaginable.

In practical political terms, one of the greatest mistakes that the radical popular theatre in the West has made is its failure to expand beyond the limits of the individual groups. Despite the public rejection of individual stardom and the promotion of collectivity, almost all the groups discussed in this book have concentrated on internal artistic development and reputation building for the collective. Participation in major international festivals became an important priority. Obviously, the groups in question have many ideological, sociopolitical, and aesthetic characteristics in common. It is therefore striking that they never really bothered establishing close cooperative links interregionally and internationally. Thus it is possible, for example, that lo Teatre de la Carriera has never really heard of the 7:84 Theatre Company and vice versa. A conscious international radical popular theatre movement was never properly organized.

Secondly the radical popular theatre's performance orientation can be seen as another contributing factor to its relative political ineffectiveness. It is a mistake to assume that a play is automatically a success in political terms if it is received at the end with a ten-minute standing ovation. The only truthful conclusion that can be drawn from enthusiastic applause is that the audience has been well entertained, not that it has been adequately informed, agitated, and motivated to take political action. Just like Bertolt Brecht the political activist became the victim of Brecht the artist, the radical popular theatre in the West is subject to a similar danger. Its flaw has been to miscalculate the importance of the spectator, despite its professions to the contrary. The emphasis in the production (and the reception, for that matter) of Western political theatre has always been and continues to be on the artist as creator and performer, and on the duration of the transmission of communicative signs that constitute the actual performance or the theatrical text. The moment the spectator walks out of the venue or the reader closes the book, he ceases to be of interest.

Part of the problem with the radical popular theatre in the West in the post-1968 period is that, in most cases, it is very much a theatre of highly educated outsiders coming in to perform *for* a working class audience. Despite its efforts to tap the remnants of regional proletarian cultural forms, the radical popular theatre has done very little to help revive homegrown artistic activities in the working-class communities themselves. In a recent comment, Professor Timothy Wiles appropriately wondered whether "workers really need or want this kind of theatrical art" and whether "they occasionally feel talked down to by its oversimplifications."[20]

All aesthetic innovations in twentieth-century political theatre were alleged attempts at improving the communication of the political message. Shaw's discussion plays, agitprop slogans, Brecht's epic acting style and his now famous *Verfremdungseffekte,* Piscator's multimedia theatre, and Hochhut's documentary drama all presupposed that the performing actor is the only possible agent for bringing about the desired political effect. But theirs is, in essence, a top-down attitude that casts the spectator in a passive, receptive role. Moreover, all the new aesthetic and strategic elements that were designed to create a more effective political theatre had no firm empirical basis and, in the final analysis, amount to nothing more than speculation. If Brecht claimed that his epic theatre would cause his audience to become less emotionally involved in the play and would therefore be more receptive to its political analysis, he may well have succeeded in changing certain audience reception patterns, but he had no absolute way of measuring the deeper, long-term sociopolitical impact of his works. As it turns out, in today's productions of Brecht's plays all over the world, the *Verfremdungseffekt* has become a purely aesthetic element in an expanded system of theatrical conventions; as yet another form of self-conscious theatricality, it has become part and parcel of postmodern theatre in the same way as the aside and the soliloquy were inherent elements of Elizabethan theatre.

In the absence of any absolutely reliable scheme to measure the effects of a *drama performance* on its audience, the truly committed theatre artist must look for practical alternatives. In this respect, the recent experiences of the radical popular theatre in the Third World could provide its Western counterpart with valuable inspiration. Working under often violently repressive conditions and in extreme poverty, Third World radical theatre artists have no time to waste on speculation and experimentation. They need immediately effective solutions. With its emphasis on *process* and *networking* rather than (or in combination with) *performances,* the Third World theatre of liberation, as it could perhaps best be called, seems to have found the key.[21]

Theatre of liberation practitioners, then, do not limit their activities to performances in middle-class or working-class venues only. They stay with their target group for however long necessary: a few days or several months. They realize that for political theatre to be effective, a lifetime commitment of artists and target group is required. Through the workshop processes of people's theatre, they help the poor discover their own creativity and, by extension, their own collective potential for social change.

The Filipino radical theatre company PETA is one of the world's leaders in the practice of theatre of liberation. Its members combine highly professional performance skills with total dedication to grass-roots cultural organizing. Consequently, they no longer call themselves actors but *ators,* which stands for Artist-Teacher-Organizer-Researcher. Over the past fifteen years, PETA and professional theatre workers elsewhere in the Philippines have established a nationwide network of community theatre groups run by industrial workers, fishermen, peasants, and students. At the time of the fall of the Marcos dictatorship in February 1986, this Philippine theatre of liberation network comprised close to three hundred groups that were highly instrumental in the mobilization of the popular masses in Manila and elsewhere in this archipelago.[22] Since the late seventies, PETA has also been extending its networking activities to neighboring countries in the Southeast Asian region. PETA ators have conducted theatre of liberation workshops in countries like India, Bangla Desh, Thailand, Indonesia, Papua New Guinea, and Sri Lanka.

The Filipino brand of radical popular theatre emerges, then, as the model for an exciting new concept of political theatre.[23] It is a kind of theatre that may not be as aesthetically sophisticated as, say, Brecht's, McGrath's, or Dario Fo's. But

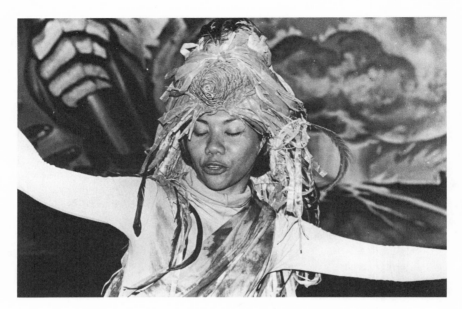

PETA. "The Mythical Bird of Freedom," a dance in *Nukleyar II* (1986).

PETA. Guardian angels of the powers that be in *Nukleyar II* (1986).

its tireless practitioners, several of whom have died or have been tortured, command the greatest respect, both in their artistic and in their political capacity. Although admittedly the circumstances differ greatly, the radical popular theatre in the West can learn from the courage, the commitment, and the strategies of its Third World colleagues. Surely, the theatre of liberation can pride itself on some very tangible results, and that—and not aesthetic or literary value—should be the most important criterion by which to measure political theatre.

APPENDIX
SOME FACTS ABOUT
THE TROUPES

THE SAN FRANCISCO MIME TROUPE

Artistic Director: Joan Holden and Dan Chumley.

Administrative Address: 855 Treat Street, San Francisco, California 94110. Phone: (415) 285-1717.

Permanent Theatre Building: None. Company owns the premises at 855 Treat Street, which also includes a storage and rehearsal space.

Permanent Acting Company: Six men (including four musicians who double as actors) and three women.

Annual Budget: $500,000 (1986).

Founded in: 1959 by Ron G. Davis, followed by a major reorganization in 1970.

Present Organizational Structure: Theatre collective. Today's Mime Troupe structure is much more stratified than the collective of the early seventies. Back then, the actors doubled as bookkeepers and publicists. The business jobs were rotated. Starting in 1978, a full-time administrative staff was installed.

Major Productions since 1968: (Unless otherwise indicated, all plays are written by Joan Holden.)

1968: *Ruzzante, or the Veteran* (collective); *The Farce of Pathelin* (anonymous); *Gutter Puppets* ("Meter Maid," "Little Black Panther, "Meat") (collective).

1969: *Congress of the Whitewashers* (Brecht); *The Third Estate.*

1970: *La Siete; The Independent Female, or a Man Has His Pride; Eco Man; Telephone, or Ripping Off Ma Bell.*

1971: *The Dragon Lady's Revenge; Clown Show.*("Highway Robbery" and "Soledad").

1972: *Highrises; Frozen Wages; American Dreamer.*

1973: *San Fran Scandals; The Mother* (Gorki/Brecht).

1974: *The Great Air Robbery.*

1975: *Frijoles, or Beans To You; Power Play.*

1976: *False Promises/Nos Engañaron.*

1977: *Hotel Universe.*

1978: *Electrobucks.*
1979: *Squash; We Can't Pay, We Won't Pay* (Dario Fo), *T.V. Dinner.*
1980: *Fact Person.*
1981: *Factwino Meets the Moral Majority; Americans, or Last Tango in Huehuetenango; Ghosts.*
1982: *Factwino vs. Armageddonman.*
1983: *Secrets in the Sand; The Uprising of Fuente Ovejuna.*
1984: *Steeltown* (indoors); *1985* (parkshow).
1985: *Factwino: The Opera* (indoors); *Crossing Borders* (parkshow).
1986: *Spain/'36* (indoor show in collaboration with the Los Angeles Theatre Center); *Hotel Universe* (parkshow); *Mozamgola Caper* (parkshow).

Published Plays:

Davis, R. G. *The San Francisco Mime Troupe: The First Ten Years.* Palo Alto, California: Ramparts Press, 1975 (includes *l'Amant Militaire* and excerpts from *The Minstrel Show, or Civil Rights in a Cracker Barrel*).
Foster, Rick, ed. *West Coast Plays 10.* Berkeley: California Theater Council, 1981 (includes *Hotel Universe* and *Ghosts*).
Hurwitt, Robert, ed. *West Coast Plays 15/16.* Berkeley: California Theater Council, 1983 (includes *Factwino* trilogy).
The San Francisco Mime Troupe. *By Popular Demand.* San Francisco: San Francisco Mime Troupe, 1980 (includes *San Fran Scandals; The Independent Female, or a Man has his Pride,* and *Dragon Lady's Revenge*).

Secondary Literature:

Cohn, Ruby. "Joan Holden and the San Francisco Mime Troupe." *The Drama Review* 24, no. 2 (1980):41–50.
Gordon, Mel. "The San Francisco Mime Troupe's *The Mother*." *The Drama Review* 19, no. 2 (1975):94–101.
Holden, Joan. "Satire and Politics in America; or, Why Is That President Still Smiling?" *The Drama Review* 19 (1975):104–8.
Kleb, William. "Hotel Universe: Playwriting and the San Francisco Mime Troupe." *Theater* 9 (1978):15–21.
Shank, Adele E. "The San Francisco Mime Troupe's *Americans, or Last Tango in Huehuetenango*." *The Drama Review* 25, no. 3 (1981): 81–83.
Shank, Theodore. "Political Theater: The San Francisco Mime Troupe." *The Drama Review* 18, no. 1 (1974):110–17.

EL TEATRO CAMPESINO

Artistic Director: Luis Valdez.
Administrative Director: Gloriamalia Flores.
Administrative Address: P.O. Box 1278, San Juan Bautista, California 95045. Phone: (408) 623-2444.
Permanent Theatre Building: El Teatro Campesino Playhouse, 705 Fourth Street, San Juan Bautista.
Permanent Acting Company: Core company of 13.
Annual Budget: Between $240,000 and $300,000 (1984).
Founded in: 1965 by Luis Valdez.
Present Organizational Structure: Luis Valdez and the core company members handle artistic matters. The board of directors, made up of Luis Valdez, his wife Lupe and Gloriamalia Flores decide on financial matters.

Major Productions since 1968: (Unless otherwise indicated, all plays are written by Luis Valdez.)

1968: *The Shrunken Head of Pancho Villa; La Conquista de México.*
1969: *No saco nada de la escuela; The Militants.*
1970: *Huelgistas; Vietnam Campesino.*
1971: *Soldado Razo; Bernabé; La Virgen del Tepeyac* (performed every Christmas since 1971).
1972: *Calavares; El dia de los muertos.*
1973: *The Dark Root of a Scream; La gran carpa de los rasquachis.*
1974: *El Baile de los gigantes.*
1975: *El Fin del mundo; El Corrido; La Carpa* (second version); *La Pastorela* (performed every December in the old mission of San Juan Bautista since 1975).
1976: *El Fin del mundo* (second version).
1977: *El Corrido de Jesús Pelado Rasquachi.*
1978: *Zoot Suit.*
1981: *Mundo; Rose of the Rancho* (David Belasco, R. W. Tully).
1982: *Bandido.*
1983: *Soldier Boy* (Severo Perez and Judith Schiffer Perez).
1984: *Corridos.*
1985: Revival of *The Dark Root of a Scream, Soldado Razo,* and *Bernabé.*
1986: *I Don't Have to Show You No Stinking Badges.*

Published Plays:

Garza, Roberto J., ed. *Contemporary Chicano Theatre.* Notre Dame, Ind.: University of Notre Dame Press, 1976 (includes *Bernabé*).

Valdez, Luis. *Actos.* Fresno: El Teatro Campesino, 1971.

Secondary Literature:

Bagby, B. "El Teatro Campesino; Interviews with Luis Valdez." *Tulane Drama Review* 36 (1967):70–80.

Brokaw, John W. "Teatro Chicano: Some Reflections." *Educational Theatre Journal* 29 (1977):535–44.

Burger, Gerd; Rating, Arnulf; and Rielke, Gerhard. "Erkentnisse über den Abfall." *Theater Heute* (1977):31–35.

Church, Dan M. "Activist Theater in Minority Agricultural Milieux: California's El Teatro Campesino and Provence's Lo Teatre de la Carriera." in *Proceedings Comparative Literature Symposium.* Lubbock: Texas Tech Press, 1985, pp. 57–70.

Copeland, Roger F. "Review of Campesino's Performance of *La Carpa de los Rasquachis,* Chelsea Theater, The Brooklyn Academy of Music, New York City, 9 April 1973." *Educational Theater Journal* 25 (1973):376.

Copelin, David. "Chicano Theatre." *The Drama Review* 17, no. 4 (1973):73–89.

Herms, Dieter and Projektgruppe Regensburg. "Das befreiende Gelächter, Interview mit Luis Valdez über El Teatro Campesino." *Theater Heute* (1972):29–32.

Huerta, Jorge A. "Luis Valdez's *Zoot Suit:* A New Direction for Chicano Theater?" *Latin American Theater Review* 13 (1980):69–76.

Kanellos, Nicolás. "Chicano Theater in the Seventies." *Theater* 12 (1980):33–37.

Kourilsky, Françoise. "El Teatro Campesino." *Travail Théâtral* 7 (1972):56–71.

Monod, Richard. "Le Campesino exporté." *Travail Théâtral* 5 (1971):135–38.

Morton, Carlos. "The Teatro Campesino." *The Drama Review* 18, no. 4 (1974):71–76.

———. "An Interview With Luis Valdez." *Latin American Theatre Review* 15, (1982):73–76.

Rahner, Christiane G. M. "The Background of Chicano Theater and the Artistic and Political Development of Teatro Campesino." M. A. thesis, University of California at San Diego, 1980.

Sommers, Joseph and Ybarra-Frausto, Tomás, eds. *Modern Chicano Writers: A Collection of Critical Essays*. Englewood Cliffs, N.J.: Prentice-Hall, 1979.

THE BREAD AND PUPPET THEATER

Artistic Director: Peter Schumann.

Administrative Director: Elka Schumann.

Administrative Address: Road 2, Glover, Vermont 05839. Phone: 525-3031.

Permanent Theatre Building: None. The company owns Old Dopp Farm, Route 122 in Glover, Vermont, where they have a studio, the Bread and Puppet Museum, and a large outdoor space.

Permanent Acting Company: Approximately twelve "puppetteers" (including Peter Schumann) live on or near the Schumann farm in Glover.

Annual Budget: Details unavailable.

Founded in: 1961 by Peter Schumann.

Present Organizational Structure: Elka Schumann, Peter's wife, handles financial matters and public relations. Peter Schumann is in charge of the artistic creations. He designs the basic concept of all plays, which are then further developed by the entire company.

Major Productions since 1968: (Unless otherwise indicated, all plays are created by Peter Schumann.)

1968: *Fire; A Man Says Goodbye to His Mother; Grey Lady Cantata.*

1969: *The Cry of the People for Meat; Theatre of War; Blue Raven Beauty.*

1970: *Mississippi; Eating and Drinking in the Year of Our Lord; The Difficult Life of Uncle Fatso.*

1971: *The First Grey Lady Cantata; The Birdcatcher in Hell; Emilia; The Dead Man Rises; A Description of Vermont's First Paper-Maché Cathedral; Ghengis Khan and the Women; Poisons, Worries and Screams.*

1972: *The Christmas Story; Coney Island Cycle; That Simple Light May Rise Out of Complicated Darkness.*

1973: *The King; The White-Washing of the Dirty Sheets of Attica; The Theater of Uncle Fatso; The Domestic Resurrection Circus* (a two-day extravaganza that is performed every summer).

1974: *Hallelujah; Laos; Grey Lady Cantatas nos. 4 and 5; Harvey McLeod; The Revenge of the Law and Attica; Stations of the Cross.*

1975: *Ishi Workshops; Grey Lady Cantata no. 6.*

1976: *Pageant; Jesu, Meine Freude; The Mountain Man of Chile; White Horse Butcher;* Domestic Resurrection theme: "Bicentennial."

1977: *Joan of Arc; Ballad of Masaniello;* Domestic Resurrection theme: "Masaniello."

1979: *Ah! or the First Washerwoman Cantata; The Washerwoman Nativity;* Domestic Resurrection theme: "Washerwomen."

1980: *Goya; This is; Stations of the Cross; Histoire du Pain.*

1981: *Woyzeck* (Georg Büchner); *Venus Rising from the Water;* Domestic Resurrection theme: "The Fight Against the End of the World."

1982: *The Story of One Who Set out to Study Fear; Diagonal Man; The Life and Death of Charlotte Salomon; Thunderstorm of the Youngest Child;* Domestic Resurrection theme: "Saint Francis of Assisi."

1983: *Washerwoman's Nativity; The End Falls before the Beginning; Insurrection Oratorio;* Domestic Resurrection theme: "Domestic Insurrection."

1984: *The Door; The Nativity and Resurrection of Archbishop Romero of El Salvador;*
Domestic Resurrection theme: "Central America and Liberation Theology."
1985: *Romero Pageant; Ex Voto; The Daily News Nativity;* Domestic Resurrection theme:
"Nicaragua."
1986: *Puerto Rico;* Domestic Resurrection theme: "Hunger."

Published Plays:

Playscripts of Bread and Puppet productions do not exist but the following attempts at
performance documentation are quite useful:

The Bread and Puppet Theater. "Scenes from the Difficult Life of Uncle Fatso." *The
Drama Review* 14, no. 3 (1970):6–35.

Brecht, Stefan. "Peter Schumann's Bread and Puppet Theatre." *The Drama Review* 14,
no. 3 (1970):44–90 (includes a detailed description of *The Cry of the People for
Meat).*

Dennison, George. "Fire." *The Drama Review* 14, no. 3 (1970):35–44.

Guma, Greg, ed. *Bread and Puppet: Stories of Struggle and Faith from Central America.*
Burlington, Vt.: Green Valley Film and Art, 1985 (includes a detailed description
with color photographs of the 1984 Domestic Resurrection Circus).

Towsen, John. "The Bread and Puppet Theatre: The Stations of the Cross." In *The New
Theatre: Performance Documentation.* Edited by Michael Kirby. New York: New
York University Press, 1974: 141–54.

Secondary Literature:

Argelander, Ron. "Bread and Puppet's Domestic Resurrection: The War is Over." *Soho
Weekly News,* 19 August 1976.

Bell, John. "The Fight against the End of the World." *Theaterwork,* September/October
1982, pp. 20–27.

Blanc, Maurice. "Clowning with the Life Force." *Village Voice,* 5 September 1968, p.
393.

Braithwaite, Chris. "Schumann Sides with Witch Doctors." *Weekly News,* 23 November
1982, p. 9.

Dort, Bernard. "l'Amérique ou l'utopie de la mort blanche: le Bread and Puppet." *Travail
Théâtral* 24/25 (1976):177–80.

Dupavillon, Christian. *Bread and Puppet Theater.* Paris: Alain Bouret, 1978.

Gussow, Mel. "Theater: Bread and Puppet Troupe." *New York Times,* 17 September
1972.

———. "Theater: 'Goya' on War." *New York Times,* 4 March 1981.

Karasek, H. and Hardtmann, Th. "Traumatische Genauigkeit—Das Bread and Puppet
zeigt *Grey Lady Cantata* und *Vogelfänger in der Hölle." Theater Heute* 2
(1972):28–31.

Kourilsky, Françoise. *Le Bread and Puppet Theatre.* Lausanne: La Cité, 1970.

———. "Dada and Circus: Bread and Puppet Theatre." *The Drama Review* 18, no. 1
(1974):104–9.

McColm, Del. " 'Ishi' Opens Bicentennial Celebration." *The Davis Enterprise,* 22 May
1975, p. 6.

Munk, Erika. " 'Tis the Reason." *Village Voice,* 27 December 1983, p. 100.

Schumann, Peter and Greene, Wayne. *Puppen und Masken: Das Bread and Puppet
Theater, ein Arbeitsbericht.* Frankfurt am Main: Fischer, 1973.

Sobieski, Lynn. "The Bread and Puppet Theater's *Woyzeck." The Drama Review* 25, no.
2 (1981):55–62.

Sterrit, David. "Many-Sided Bread and Puppet Man." *Christian Science Monitor,* 9
February 1973, pp. 18–23.

Le Théâtre Populaire de Lorraine

Artistic Director: Charles Tordjman.
Administrative Address: Rue Pasteur, 57100 Thionville, France. Phone: (8) 253-33-95.
Permanent Theatre Building: Municipal Theatre, Thionville (1350 seats); Théâtre du Saulcy, Metz (100 seats).
Permanent Acting Company: None.
Annual Budget: State subsidy of 1.5 million francs, municipal subsidy of 660,000 francs, ticket sales of 1 million francs. Total budget: 3.16 million francs (1984).
Founded in: 1963 by Jacques Kraemer.
Present Organizational Structure: TPL is a production company with a permanent staff of seven, including administrators, technicians, and artists. Charles Tordjman makes most of the artistic and economic decisions.
Major Productions since 1968:
1968: Several pieces by Brecht.
1969: *Splendeur et misère de Minette la bonne Lorraine* (Jacques Kraemer).
1970: *Candide* (Voltaire).
1971: *La Liquidation de Monsieur Joseph K.* (Kraemer).
1972: *Les Immigrés* (Kraemer).
1973: *Jacotte ou les plaisirs de la vie quotidienne* (Kraemer).
1974: *Le Retour du Graully* (Kraemer).
1975: *Noëlle de joie* (Kraemer).
1976: *Pourtant le soleil est là* (Kraemer); *Histoires de l'oncle Jacob* (Kraemer).
1977: *Minette la bonne Lorraine* (Kraemer); *C'était. . . .* (Charles Tordjman)
1978: *Déménagement* (Anne-Marie Brucher); *Intimité* (Tordjman).
1979: *Cage* (Kraemer); *La Punaise* (Mayakovsky).
1980: *Flaminal Valaire* (Maurice Regnaut); *Les Basses-terres* (Moni Grego and A.-M. Brucher).
1981: *XVIIIe Fureur du théâtre* (writers of the eighteenth century); *En Revoir* (Tordjman).
1982: *Camerawoman* (Christine Combe); *Le Juif Süss* (Kraemer); *Le Chantier* (Tordjman).
1983: *Les Voies aériennes* (selected American poets); *Bistrot* (Aristide Demonico); *Léonie est en avance/Gibier de potence* (Georges Feydeau).
1984: *La Fiancée de l'eau* (Tahar Ben Jelloun).
Published Plays:
Ben Jelloun, Tahar. *La Fiancée de l'eau.* Le Paradou: Actes Sud, 1984.
Kraemer, Jacques. *Splendeur et misère de Minette, la bonne Lorraine.* Paris: Editions du Seuil, 1970.
———. *Les Immigrés.* Paris: P. J. Oswald, 1973.
———. *La Liquidation de M. Joseph K./Jacotte ou les plaisirs de la vie quotidienne.* Paris: P. J. Oswald, 1974.
———. *Noëlle de joie.* Paris: P. J. Oswald, 1975.
———. *Le Retour du Graully.* Paris: P. J. Oswald, 1975.
———. *Histoires de l'oncle Jacob / Les Ciseaux d'Anastasie.* In *Avant-Scène* 601 (1977): 3–29.
———. *Minette, la bonne Lorraine.* In *Avant-Scène* 623 (1978):3–35.
Tordjman, Charles. *Intimité.* In *Avant-Scène* 646 (1979):3–20.
———. *Le Chantier.* Paris: Edilig, 1982.
Secondary Literature:
Ertel, Evelyne. "Essai d'analyse d'un échec." *Travail Théâtral* 21 (1975):86–90.
Mignon, Paul-Louis. "Jacques Kraemer." *Avant-Scène* 601 (1977): 6–7.

────. "TPL: un auteur, une troupe." *Avant-Scène* 601 (1977): 30–31.
Le Théâtre Populaire de Lorraine. "Notre Expérience." *Travail Théâtral* 8 (1972):57–75.
van Erven, Eugène. "The Satirical Methods of the Regional Political Theater in France."
   In *Legacy of Thespis: Drama Past and Present,* edited by K. V. Hartigan.
   Lanham, Md: University Press of America, 1984.

Lo Teatre de la Carriera

Artistic Direction: Marie-Hélène Bonafé.
Administrative Address: 4, Boulevard Victor Hugo, 13200 Arles, France. Phone: (90)
   96-84-71.
Permanent Theatre Building: None. The premises at the Boulevard Victor Hugo serve as
   rehearsal space.
Permanent Acting Company: Four males and four females.
Annual Budget: Details are unavailable.
Founded in: 1969 (by Claude Alranq)
Present Organizational Structure: Theatre collective. Catherine and Marie-Hélène
   Bonafé used to alternate the artistic direction of each new project until Catherine's
   departure in 1986. For example, in 1983, Catherine was in charge of the budgeting
   and direction of *Miracle! Miracle!;* Marie-Hélène was in charge of the collaboration with Le Campagnol on *L'Enclave des papes;* in February 1985, Catherine was
   in charge of the creation of a show on the music hall of Marseilles. Productions are
   very much developed in a collective way: all actors and actresses contribute to the
   writing, the set design, and the composition of musical scores.
Major Productions since 1968:
1969: Agitprop sketches in the streets.
1970: *Mort et résurrection de M. Occitania* (Claude Alranq).
1972: *La Guerre du vin* (Alranq).
1973: *Une Heure pour le Chili* (Alranq).
1974: *Tabò ou la dernière Ste. Barbe* (Alranq).
1975: *La Pastorale de Fos* (Alranq).
1976: *La Liberté ou la mort* (Alranq).
1977: *Dans le lit du Rhône* (Alranq); *Les Cévennes* (troupe).
1978: *La Fille d'Occitania* (Alranq); *Bogre de Carnaval* (troupe); *La Galine* (M.-H.
   Bonafé); *Saisons de Femme* (C. Bonafé and Annette Clément); *St. Jean, bouche
   d'or* (Jacques Clerc, Christian Coulomb, René Fernandez, and Maurice Tuech).
1980: *Porte à Porte* (M.-H. Bonafé); *Le Miroir des Jours* (troupe).
1981: *L'Estrangier* (Clément).
1982: *Yerma* (Federico Garcia Lorca).
1983: *Miracle! Miracle!* (C. Bonafé and Michèle Rochin); *L'Eau qui danse* (M.-H.
   Bonafé and Doumée).
1984: *L'Enclave des papes ou la nouvelle villégiature* (Vincenzo Cerami).
1985: *Les Folies de Marseille* (troupe).
Published Plays:
Alranq, Claude. *Tabò ou la dernière Ste. Barbe.* Paris: P. J. Oswald, 1974.
────. *La Pastorale de Fos.* Paris: P. J. Oswald, 1975.
────. *La Liberté ou la mort.* Paris: P. J. Oswald, 1976.
────. *Mort et résurrection de M. Occitania.* Arles: by the author, 1976.
────. *La Fille d'Occitania.* Le Paradou: Editions Actes/Sud, 1978.
Lo Teatre de la Carriera. *Ecrits des femmes.* Paris: Solin, 1980.

Secondary Literature:
Church, Dan. M. "State Subsidies and Militant Regionalism in Contemporary French Theater." *Contemporary French Civilization* 6, no. 3 (1982):342–60.
Deutsch, Michel. "Le Théâtre de la Carriera." *Travail Théâtral* 18/19 (1975):131–42.
van Erven, Eugène. "l'Ail sur le pain culturel français: un entretien avec Catherine Bonafé de Lo Teatre de la Carriera." *Contemporary French Civilization* 9, no. 1 (1985):54–75.
Verdeil, Jean. "Le Théâtre de la Carriera." *Travail Théâtral* 9 (1972):126–34.

THE 7:84 THEATRE COMPANY

Artistic Director: John McGrath.
Administrative Address: England: 31, Clerkenwell Close, London EC1 ROAT. Phone: (01) 253-4049. Scotland: 31, Albany Street, Edinburgh. Phone: (031) 557-2442.
Permanent Theatre Building: None.
Permanent Acting Company: 7:84 (England) employs three permanent actors, and 7:84 (Scotland) employs Elisabeth MacLennan, McGrath's wife, as a permanent actress.
Annual Budget: 7:84 Scotland: £120,000 (1985) (Scottish Art Council).
Founded in: 1971 by John McGrath.
Present Organizational Structure: John McGrath oversees the artistic and financial operations of both companies. Both companies have separate budgets, however, and solicit subsidies from different institutions. Both the English 7:84 and the Scottish 7:84 are production companies with their own technical and administrative staff and stage equipment. One or two members of each company make policy decisions together with John McGrath. Actors and directors are engaged for one show at a time and have no vote in general company decisions.
Major Productions since 1968: (Unless otherwise indicated, all plays are written by John McGrath.)
1971: *Trees in the Wind; Apricots and Thermidor* (Trevor Griffith).
1972: *Plugged into History; Out of Sight; Occupations* (Griffith); *Underneath; The Ballygombeen Bequest* (John Arden and Margaretta D'Arcy); *Sergeant Musgrave Dances On* (Arden, adapted by McGrath).
7:84-Scotland
1973: *The Cheviot, the Stag and the Black, Black Oil.*
1974: *The Game's a Bogey; Boom.*
1975: *My Pal and Me; Capital Follies* (David MacLennan and John Bett); *Little Red Hen.*
1976: *Honour Your Partners* (MacLennan); *Out of Our Heads.*
1977: *Thought for Today* (MacLennan); *Trembling Giant; His Master's Voice* (David Anderson).
1979: *Joe's Drum.*
1980: *Swings and Roundabouts; Blood Red Roses.*
1981: *The Catch or Red Herrings in the Minch.*
1982: *Clydebuilt* (A Season of Scottish Popular Theatre); *Screw the Bobbin* (7:84 Scotland and Chris Hannan).
1984: *The Ragged Trousered Philanthropists* (adapted by Archie Hind from Robert Tressell's novel).
1985: *The Baby and the Bathwater; The Albannach; In Time of Strife* (Joe Corrie).
7:84-England

1973: *Man Friday* (Adrian Mitchell); *The Reign of Terror; The Great Money Trick* (7:84 England).
1975: *Fish in the Sea; Lay Off; Yobbo Nowt.*
1976: *Relegated* (Shane Connaughton); *The Rat Trap; Our Land, Our Lives* (Steve Gooch).
1977: *Wreckers* (David Edgar); *Trembling Giant; Joe of England.*
1978: *Underneath; Vandaleur's Folly* (Margaretta D'Arcy and John Arden).
1979: *Big Square Fields; Bitter Apples; Trees in the Wind.*
1980: *SUS* (Barrie Keeffe); *One Big Blow* (John Burrows).
1981: *Night Class.*
1982: *Trafford Tanzi* (Claire Luckham); *Rejoice!*
1983: *V-Signs / Jimmy Riddle* (Peter Cox).
1984: *School for Emigrants* (7:84 England).
Published Plays:
Edgar, David. *Wreckers.* London: Methuen, 1977.
McGrath, John. *The Game's a Bogey.* London: Pluto Press, 1975.
———. *Fish in the Sea.* London: Pluto Press, 1977.
———. *Little Red Hen.* London: Pluto Press, 1977.
———. *Yobbo Nowt.* London: Pluto Press, 1978.
———. *Joe's Drum.* Aberdeen: Aberdeen People's Press, 1979.
———. *The Cheviot, the Stag and the Black, Black Oil.* London: Eyre Methuen, 1981.
———. *Two Plays for the Eighties: Blood Red Roses and Swings and Roundabouts.* Aberdeen: Aberdeen People's Press, 1981.
Secondary Literature:
Beacham, Richard. "Political Satire in Great Britain: the 7:84 Company." *Theater* 10 (1979): 49–53.
Bigsby, C. W. E. "The Contemporary Anxiety: Contemporary Socialist Theatre in England." *Modern Drama* 24 (1981):393–403.
McGrath, John. *A Good Night Out.* London: Methuen, 1981.
Shank, Theodore. "Troupes Anglaises de théâtre différent." *Travail Théâtral* 22 (1976):3–16.
van Erven, Eugène. "7:84 in '85: Fourteen Years of Popular Theater for the British Proletariat." *Minnesota Review* (February 1987): 103–16.
———. "Theatre for the People: An Interview with John McGrath of the 7:84 Theatre Company." *Minnesota Review* (February 1987):117–22.

DAS GRIPS THEATER

Artistic Director: Volker Ludwig.
Administrative Address: Altonauerstrasse 22, 1000 Berlin 21, Federal Republic of Germany. Phone: 393-3012 or 391-4004.
Permanent Theatre Building: Das Grips Theater, Hansaplatz, 1000 Berlin 21.
Permanent Acting Company: Approximately fifteen full-time actors and musicians.
Annual Budget: 2.2 million Deutschmarks (1984).
Founded in: 1968 by several members of the Reichskabarett, among whom Volker Ludwig.
Present Organizational Structure: Private theatre that is formally headed by Volker Ludwig as financial and artistic director. The company's policies are made by a board that consists of Volker Ludwig, three elected actors, one musician, one author, and one director.

Major Productions since 1968:
1968: *Die Reise nach Pitschepatsch* (Rainer Hachfeld and Volker Ludwig).
1969: *Maximilian Pfeiferling* (Carsten Krieger and Ludwig).
1970: *Mugnog-Kinder!* (Hachfeld and Ludwig).
1971: *Balle Malle, Hupe und Arthur* (troupe); *Trummi Kaputt* (Ludwig).
1972: *Mannomann* (Rainer Lücker and Ludwig).
1973: *Dof bleibt dof* (Ulrich Gressieker, Lücker, and Ludwig); *Ruhe im Karton!* (Stefan Reisner and Ludwig); *Ein Fest bei Papadakis* (Christian Sorge and Ludwig).
1974: *Die Ruckzuckmaschine* (Lücker, Reisner, and Ludwig); *Nashörner schiessen nicht* (Jörg Friedrich and Ludwig).
1975: *Mensch Mädchen* (Reisner and Ludwig); *Das hälste ja im Kopf nicht aus* (Detlef Michel and Ludwig).
1976: *Kannst du zaubern, Opa?* (Reisner and Hachfeld); *Banana* (Hachfeld and Lücker).
1977: *Vatermutterkind* (Lücker and Ludwig); *. . . Und raus bist du!* (Christian Veit and Wolfgang Kolneder); *Wasser im Eimer* (Lücker and Reisner).
1978: *Die schönste Zeit im Leben* (Michel and Ludwig); *Max und Milli* (Ludwig).
1979: *Spaghetti mit Ketchup* (Hachfeld).
1980: *Stärker als Superman* (Roy Kift); *Eine Linke Geschichte* (Michel and Ludwig); *Heile, heile Segen* (Ludwig and Veit).
1981: *Alles Plastik* (Michel and Ludwig); *Dicke Luft* (Lücker and Ludwig).
1982: *Friede, Freude, Pustekuchen* (Lücker and Reisner).
1983: *Institut für Lebensmut* (a new cabaret written by Hachfeld, Michel, and Ludwig).
1984: *Der Spinner* (Henning Spangenberg and Ludwig); *Voll auf der Rolle* (Leonie Ossoski).

Published Plays:
Ludwig, Volker. *Nashörner schiessen nicht.* Frankfurt:Verlag der Autoren, 1973.
Ludwig, Volker and Michel, Detlef. *Eine linke Geschichte.* Berlin: Grips Theater, 1980.
Ludwig, Volker and Michel, Detlef. *Alles Plastik.* Berlin: Grips Theater, 1981.
Ludwig, Volker and Spangenberg, Henning. *Der Spinner.* Berlin: Grips Theater, 1984.

Secondary Literature:
Fischer, Gerhard. "The Youth Theatre of Grips." *Modern Drama* 23 (1981): 448–71.
Kolneder, Wolfgang; Ludwig, Volker; and Wagenbach, Klaus. *Das Grips Theater: Geschichte und Geschichten, Erfahrungen und Gespräche aus einem Kinder- und Jugendtheater.* Berlin: Klaus Wagenbach, 1979.
Lefèvre, Gérard. "A Propos de *Faut pas s'laisser faire.*" *Travail Théâtral* 15 (1974):3–61.
———. "La Situation du Gripstheater." *Travail Théâtral* 20 (1975):58–68.
———. "Le Réalisme tonique du Gripstheater." *Travail Théâtral* 28/29 (1977):103–6.
Paul, Arno. "The West German Theatre Miracle." *The Drama Review* 24, no. 1 (1980):3–24.

IL COLLETTIVO TEATRALE LA COMUNE

Artistic Director: Dario Fo and Franca Rame.
Administrative Address: Viale Piave 11, 20129 Milano, Italy. Phone: (02) 783204 or 783435
Permanent Theatre Building: None since the "Palazzina Liberty" closed in 1982.
Permanent Acting Company: La Comune is basically a production company with Fo and Rame as the only two permanent performers.

Annual Budget: La Comune receives the lowest possible state subsidy (70 million lire). Exact figures of La Comune's annual budget are unavailable.

Founded in: 1970 by Dario Fo and Franca Rame.

Present Organizational Structure: Actor-managed company. Dario Fo and Franca Rame make all the artistic and financial decisions and are the nominal owners of the company. They employ an administrative staff of approximately eight.

Major Productions since 1968: (Unless otherwise indicated, all plays are written by Dario Fo.)

1968: *Grande Pantomima con bandiere e pupazzi piccoli e medi.*

1969: *Mistero Buffo; Ci ragione e canto no. 2; l'Operaio conosce trecento parole, il padrone mille: per questo lui è il padrone; Legami pure che tanto spacco tutto lo stesso.*

1970: *Vorrei morire anche stasera sedovessi sapere che non è servito a niente; Morte accidentale di un anarchico.*

1971: *Tutti uniti, tutti insieme . . . ma scusa, quello non è il padrone?; Fedayn.*

1972: *Ordine per dio.ooo.ooo!!!; Pum, pum! chie è? La Polizia!*

1973: *Ci ragione e canto no. 3; Guerra di popolo in Cile.*

1974: *Ballate e canzoni; Non si paga, non si paga!*

1975: *Il Fanfani rapito.*

1976: *La Marjuana della mamma è la più bella; La Giullarata.*

1977: *Tutta casa, letto e chiesa* (with Franca Rame).

1978: *La Storia di un soldato.*

1979: *Storia della tigre ed altre storie.*

1980: *Clacson, trombette e pernacchi.*

1981: *Tutta casa, letto e chiesa—nuova edizione; l'Opera dello Sghignazzo.*

1982: *Fabulazzo osceno.*

1983: *Coppia Aperta* (with Franca Rame).

1984: *Quasi per caso una donna: Elisabetta.*

Published Plays:

Most of the plays listed above have been published, in the year of production, by the company's own publishing outfit, Edizione Franca Rame La Comune. The following titles have been translated into German and English:

Fo, Dario. *Accidental Death of an Anarchist.* Adapted by Gavin Richards. London: Pluto Press, 1980.

———. *Ulrike Meinhof/Tomorrow's News.* Translated by Tony Mitchell. In *Gambit* 9, no. 36 (1980).

———. *Female Parts.* Translated by Margaret Kunzle and adapted by Olwen Wymark. London: Pluto Press, 1981.

———. *Can't Pay? Won't Pay!* Translated by Lino Pertile and adapted by Bill Colvill and Robert Walker. London: Pluto Press, 1982.

———. *Obszöne Fabeln/Mistero Buffo.* Translated by Peter O. Chotjewitz. Berlin: Rotbuch Verlag, 1984.

———. *Trumpets and Raspberries.* Translated and adapted by R. C. McAvoy and A.-M. Giugni. London: Pluto Press, 1984.

Secondary Literature:

Ballerini, Luigi and Risso, Giuseppi. "Dario Fo explains." *The Drama Review* 22, no. 1 (March 1978):34–48.

Bayón, Miguel. "Forza Fo." *Cambio 16* 573 (1982):152–53.

———. "Fo, esperanza y caridad." *Cambio 16* 581 (1983):96.

Cowan, Suzanne. "The Throw-Away Theatre of Dario Fo." *The Drama Review* 19 (1975):102–13.

————. *The Militant Theatre of Dario Fo*. Ph.D. dissertation, University of Minnesota, 1977.

————. "Dario Fo: Bibliography, Biography, Playography." *Theatre Quarterly* Checklist 17 (1978).

————."Dario Fo, Politics and Satire." *Theater* 10 (spring 1979):7–11.

Dort, Bernard. "Dario Fo: un acteur épique." *Travail Théâtral* 15 (1974):112–18.

Fo, Dario. "Entretien." *Travail Théâtral* 14 (1974):3–30.

————. "Les Intellectuels et la culture." *Travail Théâtral* 31 (1978):64–67.

————. "Dialogue with an Audience." *Theatre Quarterly* 9, no. 35 (1979):11–16.

————. "Ueber das Lachen in einer Gesellschaft die nicht zum Lachen ist." *Linkskurve* 1 (1981):11–14.

————. "Popular Culture." *Theater* 14, no. 3 (1983):50–54.

————. "Aspects of Popular Theatre." *New Theatre Quarterly* 1, no. 2 (1985):131–37.

Fo, Dario and Rame, Franca. *Theatre Workshops at Riverside Studios, London*. London: Red Notes, 1983.

Gill, Brendan. "Belasco Fiasco." *New Yorker,* 3 December 1984: 182.

Grant, Steve and Mitchell, Tony. "An Interview with Dario Fo and Franca Rame." *Theater* 14, no. 3 (1983):43–49.

Groves, David. "Fo Interviewed." *Act* (New Zealand) 7, no. 2 (1982):18–20.

————. "Laughter Has Become a Sghignazzo." *Act* (New Zealand) 7, no. 2 (1982):16–18.

Heer, Hannes. *Dario Fo Ueber Dario Fo*. Köln: Prometh, 1980.

Jungblut, Helga. *Das politische Theater Dario Fos*. Frankfurt am Main: Lang, 1978.

Mitchell, Tony. "Dario Fo's *Mistero Buffo:* Popular Theatre, the Giullari, and the Grotesque." *Theatre Quarterly* 9, no. 35 (1979):1–10.

————. "Dario Fo—the Histrionics of Class Struggle." *Gambit* 9, no. 36 (1980):55–60.

————. "Open House with Dario Fo and Franca Rame." *Theater* 15, no. 3 (1984):65–68.

————. *Dario Fo: People's Court Jester*. London: Methuen, 1986.

Schechter, Joel. "Dario Fo's Obscene Fables." *Theater* 14, no. 1 (1982):87–90.

Sogliuzzo, A. Richard. "Dario Fo: Puppets for a Proletarian Revolution." *The Drama Review* 16, no. 3 (1972):72–77.

Torres, Alberto F. "El Vodevil politico." *Cambio 16* 523 (1982):127.

Els Joglars

Artistic Director: Albert Boadella

Administrative Address: Avinguada dels Paisos Catalans, 1, Apartado 55, Vic (Barcelona), Spain. Phone: (93) 885-3315.

Permanent Theatre Building: None, but the company owns a large country house and an inflatable dome rehearsal space near Pruit (Barcelona province).

Permanent Acting Company: Nine permanent actors (seven males, two females), three technicians, and three administrative assistants.

Annual Budget: 100 million pesetas ($800,000—10% state subsidy, 90% ticket sales) (1986).

Founded in: 1962 by Albert Boadella, Antoni Font, and Carlota Soldevilla.

Present Organizational Structure: Albert Boadella currently makes all the artistic and financial decisions. Before 1978, the company was a collective.

Major Productions since 1968: (Unless otherwise indicated, all plays are created by Boadella.)

1968: *El Diari*
1970: *El Joc*
1972: *Cruel ubris*
1973: *Mary d'Ous*
1974: *Alias Serralonga*
1977: *La Torna*
1978: *M-7 Catalònia*
1979: *l'Odisea*
1980: *Laetius*
1981: *Olympic Man Movement*
1983–84: *Teledeum*
1985–86: *Virtuosos de Fontainebleau*

Published Plays:

Ayesa, Guillermo. *Joglars: una historia*. Barcelona: Editorial La Gaya Ciencia, 1978. Contains detailed descriptions of performances of *El Joc, Cruel ubris, Alias Serralonga,* and *La Torna*.

Boadella, Albert. *M-7 Catalònia/Operació Ubú*. Barcelona: Edicions 62, 1985.

Collell, Jaume. *El Via crucis de Teledeum*. Barcelona: El Llamo, 1985. Contains a detailed description of *Teledeum*.

Els Joglars. *La Torna*. In *Pipirijaina* (textos) 8-9 (September 1978).

———. *Olympic Man Movement* (bilingual version in Spanish and Catalan). In *Pipirijaina* 21 (March 1982):44–107.

Secondary Literature:

Abellan, Joan. "Los espectáculos del año: M-7 Catalònia: ¿Demoler un belén?" *Pipirijaina* 10 (September-October 1979):55-57.

———. "Els Joglars en perspectiva." *Pipirijaina* 21 (March 1982):2–11.

Boadella, Albert. "Els Joglars, 23 años, mayoría de edad." *Cuadernos El Público* 4 (May 1985):70–71.

Fàbregas, Xavier et al. "Laetius o el camino hacía el holocausto atómico." *Pipirijaina* 16 (September-October 1980):16–17.

———. *20 Anys d'Els Joglars*. Barcelona: Monografies del Centre Dramàtic de la Generalitat de Catalunya, 1982.

———. "*Teledeum* desde la optica del monaguillo." *El Público* 4 (January 1984):5–7.

Gisbert, Joan Manuel. "l'Odissea: el vientre de Els Joglars fecundo sigue." *Pipirijaina* 11 (November-December 1979):49–51.

López Mozo, Jerónimo. "20 años en la moviola de papel." *Pipirijaina* 21 (March 1982):12–27.

Perer de Olaguer. "Unos Cómicos incordiantes." *El Dominical,* 24 January 1982:4–14.

Perez Coterillo, Moíses. "Hay mucho más teatro fuera de los teatros que dentro." *Pipirijaina* 21 (March 1982):28–43.

———. "Bufones laicos del siglo que viene." *El Público* 4 (January 1984):8–9.

———, ed. *Pipirijaina* 6 (January-February 1978). Complete issue dedicated to the *La Torna* case. Also numbers 7, 8, and 9 of *Pipirijaina* contain many articles by and about the Els Joglars trials, exile, and imprisonment.

Pintado, Angel García. "Texto o no Texto: ¿Es esa la cuestión?" *Pipirijaina* 16 (September-October 1980):18–24.

Población, Felix. "*Virtuosos de Fontainebleau:* Europa en solfa." *El Público* 27 (December 1985):6–12.

NOTES

CHAPTER 2

1. This explanation of the term *popular* is derived from Augusto Boal's writings on the topic. See, for example, his article "Sobre Teatro Popular y Teatro Antipopular" in *Popular Theatre for Social Change in Latin America,* ed. Gerardo Luzuriaga (Los Angeles: UCLA Latin American Center Publications, 1978), pp. 24–41.

2. J. R. Goodlad, *A Sociology of Popular Drama* (New York: Heineman, 1971).

3. Goodlad, *Popular Drama;* Julius Bab, *Das Theater im Lichte der Soziologie* (Leipzig: Hirschfeld, 1931); and Jean Duvignaud, *Spectacle et société* (Paris: Denoël, Gonthier, 1970).

4. See Piga T. Domingo, "El Teatro popular: consideraciones históricas e ideológicas," in Luzuriaga, *Popular Theatre,* pp. 4–13; and Vera Lee, *Quest for a Public* (Cambridge, Mass: Schenkman, 1970), pp. 4–5.

5. See the section on the San Francisco Mime Troupe in chapter 4 and the section on Dario Fo's *Mistero Buffo* in chapter 8 for a more detailed discussion of how commedia dell'arte was acquired by the ruling class to serve its own purposes.

6. See Piga T. Domingo, "Teatro popular"; Vera Lee, *Quest for a Public;* and Romain Rolland, *Le Théâtre du peuple, essai esthéthique d'un théâtre nouveau* (Paris: Michel, 1926).

7. Denis Diderot, quoted by Romain Rolland, *Théâtre du peuple,* pp. 69–70. All further references to this work appear in the text. Translations are by Barrett H. Clark and are published in *The Theory of the Modern Stage,* ed. Eric Bentley (Harmondsworth, Middlesex: Penguin, 1968).

8. Romain Rolland wrote some twenty plays on the theme of revolutionary heroism, several of which were based on the French Revolution. *Les Loups* ["The Wolves"— 1898), *Le Quatorze Juillet* ["July 14th"—1902), and *Robespierre* (1938) are the best known.

9. Pottecher's theatre still exists and produces a new play every year under the direction of his daughter, Madame Chan-Pottecher.

10. Cecil W. Davies, *Theatre for the People: the Story of the Volksbühne* (Austin: University of Texas Press, 1977), p. 21. For more information on the German Volksbühne see also Gernot Schley's *Die freie Bühne in Berlin* (Berlin: Haude & Spenersche, 1967).

11. Davies, *Theatre for the People,* p. 103.

12. Ibid., p. 105.

13. Erwin Piscator himself wrote detailed descriptions of these productions in *Das politische Theater* (Hamburg: Rowohlt, 1963).

14. Raphael Samuel, "Workers' Theatre 1926–36," in *Performance and Politics in Popular Drama,* ed. David Bradby, Louis James, and Bernard Sharratt (Cambridge: Cambridge University Press, 1980), p. 216.

15. In this context, the Blue Blouse Movement must be mentioned. As Frantisek Deák described it, the Blue Blouse was "overtly political, it employed avant-garde as well as popular techniques. Energetically (and successfully) striving to reach a mass audience, it was created by both theatrical specialists and previously untrained personnel." ("Blue Blouse," *The Drama Review* 17, no. 1 (T 57, March 1973): 35–46).

16. Malcolm Goldstein, *The Political Stage: American Drama and Theatre of the Great Depression* (New York: Oxford University Press, 1974), p. 32.

17. Ibid., p. 60.

18. Ibid., p. 59.

19. Sam Smiley, *The Drama of Attack, Didactic Plays of the American Depression* (Columbia: University of Missouri Press, 1972), p. 27. This book provides an authoritative account and detailed aesthetic analysis of America's radical theatre of the thirties.

20. Ibid., p. 28.

21. See Goldstein, *Political Stage,* pp. 242–90, for a detailed account of the Federal Theatre project.

22. See Smiley, *Drama of Attack,* chapters 3 and 7, for an analysis of Living Newspapers.

23. Professor Timothy Wiles has kindly pointed out to me that despite similar politics, aesthetics, and organizational structures, the proletarian theatre of the twenties and thirties was different from the type that emerged after the sixties in that it tended to see technological progress as a potentially positive factor in the improvement of the working man's condition. "The post-'68 generation," Professor Wiles argues appropriately in a recent critique of my work, "has much more fear of science and of modernization models in general. It argues for regionalism, ecological solutions, even for antique local languages, mythologies, and sometimes, mysticism."

24. Kenneth Tynan, quoted by John McGrath in *A Good Night Out* (London: Methuen, 1981), pp. 45–46.

25. The term nonpublic was coined by the French critic Francis Jeanson.

26. See Bernard Dort, *Théâtre public* (Paris: Editions du Seuil, 1967).

27. This figure applies to most European countries. For more statistics on proletarian presence in the established theatre audiences see Bernard Dort's *Théâtre public;* J. R. Goodlad's *Sociology of Popular Drama;* Richard Demarcy, *Eléments d'une sociologie du spectacle* (Paris: UGE, 1973); and Wolfgang Ismayr, *Das politische Theater in Westdeutschland* (Meisenheim am Glan: Anton Hain, 1977).

28. For a more detailed account of the Théâtre National Populaire, see Vera Lee, *Quest for a Public.*

29. Jean Vilar, *Le Théâtre service public* (Paris: Gallimard, 1971), p. 173.

30. In an interview with *Théâtre populaire* 15 (1955), Jean-Paul Sartre criticized Vilar's Théâtre Nationale Populaire for not reaching out exclusively to the working classes. By being subsidized, Sartre argued, the T.N.P. cannot afford to produce explicitly radical plays and, consequently, attracts only lower-middle-class spectators and no blue-collar workers.

31. Emile Copfermann, *Le Théâtre populaire pourquoi?* (Paris: Maspero, 1965), p. 9. My translation.

CHAPTER 3

1. Stephen Spender, *The Year of the Young Rebels* (New York: Random House, 1969), pp. 89–90.

2. Alain Touraine, *The May Movement* (New York: Random House, 1971), p. 23.

3. One of the more spectacular actions taken in this context was the *Aktie Tomaat* ("Operation Tomato") that rocked Dutch theatres in the fall of 1969. After a performance of Shakespeare's *Tempest* by one of Holland's main repertory companies, student-actors of the academy for the performing arts started throwing tomatoes at their established colleagues to express dissatisfaction with their choice of plays and their general bourgeois attitude.

4. Emile Copfermann, "Quelque chose a changé . . . ," *Partisans* 47 (1969), p. 10. My translation.

5. Jean-Jacques Lebel, *Procès du Festival d'Avignon, Supermarché de la culture* (Paris: Editions Pierre Belfond, 1968), p. 11. My translation.

6. V. I. Lenin, *On Culture and Cultural Revolution* (Moscow: Progress Publishers, 1966), pp. 166–67.

7. According to A. V. Lunacharsky, "Lenin and the Arts," in Lenin's *On Culture and Cultural Revolution*, p. 257.

8. For example, commedia dell'arte derived its characters and plot patterns from Italian peasant farces.

9. Antonio Gramsci quoted by A. R. Buzzi, *La Théorie politique d'Antonio Gramsci* (Louvain: Editions Nauwelaerts, 1967), p. 73. My translation.

10. "The family, which was itself the historical product of definite economic constellations, created, through the process of child rearing, the type of character structure which supported the political and economic order of the society as a whole." Quoted from Wilhelm Reich's *The Sexual Revolution* by Paul A. Robinson in his book *The Freudian Left: Wilhelm Reich, Geza Roheim, Herbert Marcuse* (New York: Harper and Row, 1969), p. 45.

11. Reich actively encouraged premarital sexual intercourse and advocated the social and sexual equality of men and women. One of the first riots in Paris was specifically related to Wilhelm Reich: after an informal lecture on Reich's ideas on sexual liberation, male students occupied an all-women dormitory on the campus of Nanterre University.

12. Herbert Marcuse, *One-dimensional Man* (Boston: Beacon Press, 1964), p. xiii.

13. Ibid., p. 10.

14. The term *counterculture* was coined by Theodore Roszak in his book *The Making of a Counter Culture* (London: Faber & Faber, 1968).

15. Thus the West German students publicly attacked the right-wing newspaper tycoon Axel Springer as an obvious representative and distributor of the dominant ideology.

16. Che Guevara found this out himself when his guerrilla operation in Bolivia failed due to the lack of peasant support. Likewise, Catherine Bonafé of lo Teatre de la Carriera (see chapter 5) mentions the suspicion of rural Occitanian population when her radical troupe first settled in a small village not far from Montpellier. It took them a long time to overcome the latent local animosity.

17. Bonnie S. McDougall, ed., *Mao Zedong's Talks at the Yan'An Conference on Literature and Art: A Translation of the 1943 Text with Commentary* (Ann Arbor: Center for Chinese Studies of the University of Michigan, 1980), p. 69.

18. Ibid., p. 59.

19. Ibid., pp. 67–68.

20. In all fairness it should be mentioned that non-Maoist directors like Jacques Copeau and Jean Dasté had practiced similar popular theatre techniques much earlier.

21. Paolo Freire, "The Adult Literacy Process as Cultural Action," *Harvard Educational Review* 40 (1970), p. 211. Inspired by Freire, militant popular theatre groups help to raise the consciousness of the oppressed people in society through Cultural Action: their dramatic art is designed to unmask the myths thanks to which the ruling class stays in power.

22. Paolo Freire, "Political Action and Conscientization," *Harvard Educational Review* 40 (1970), pp. 471–72.

23. Ibid., p. 452.

24. This was, at least, Jean-Jacques Lebel's contention.

25. John McGrath, *A Good Night Out* (London: Methuen, 1981), p. 21.

26. Ibid., pp. 21–22.

CHAPTER 4

1. Jean-Jacques Lebel, *Procès du Festival d'Avignon: Supermarché de la culture* (Paris: P. Belford, 1968).

2. For a detailed discussion of the Living Theatre's major productions, see Margaret Croydon, *Lunatics, Lovers and Poets* (New York: Delta Books, 1974), pp. 89–135.

3. The panel discussion is reprinted, in French, in the Parisian magazine *Partisans* 47 (April-May 1969), pp. 87–108.

4. R. G. Davis, *The San Francisco Mime Troupe: The First Ten Years* (Palo Alto: Ramparts Press, 1975), p. 28.

5. Ibid., p. 18.

6. Ibid., p. 31.

7. See chapter 8 for a similar reappropriation of commedia dell'arte in Dario Fo's theatre.

8. Davis, *San Francisco Mime Troupe*, p. 86.

9. Satire is traditionally less respected than comedy. In his *Comedy* (London: Hutchinson's University Library, 1948), L. J. Potts expresses the opinion that "comedy, as well as tragedy, is not only in a different class from satire, but also in a higher class; and that when a satirist develops into a comic writer his mind has become more mature and his work more truthful" (p. 155). Judgments like these are based on the aesthetic criterion that high-quality literature should strive for universal rather than ephemeral topics. Satire, of course, has traditionally kept itself at a distance from transcendental concerns. Its topical referentiality is, indeed, one of its defining characteristics. As Edward W. Rosenheim puts it, "The Satiric is lost when the object of attack is entirely imaginary or when, as a phenomenon so persistently recurrent and widespread as to be regarded 'universal,' it cannot, without further qualifications, be assigned specific historical identity." "The Satiric Spectrum," in *Modern Essays in Criticism: Satire,* ed. Ronald Paulson (Englewood Cliffs, N.J.: Prentice-Hall, 1971), p. 318.

10. Northrop Frye, *Anatomy of Criticism: Four Essays* (Princeton: Princeton University Press, 1957), pp. 223–39.

11. Davis, *San Francisco Mime Troupe,* p. 49.

12. Ibid., p. 63.

13. *L'Amant Militaire* in Davis, *San Francisco Mime Troupe,* p. 174. All further references to this work appear in the text.

14. Davis, *San Francisco Mime Troupe,* p. 151.

15. Interview with Joan Holden, San Francisco, 17 August 1984.

16. Ibid.

17. The San Francisco Mime Troupe, *By Popular Demand* (San Francisco: San Francisco Mime Troupe, 1980), p. 161.

18. *San Fran Scandals* in *By Popular Demand,* p. 89. All further references to this work appear in the text.

19. See William Kleb, "Hotel Universe: Playwriting and the San Francisco Mime Troupe," *Theater* 9 (spring 1978), pp. 15–21.

20. See chapter 8 for a more detailed discussion of Dario Fo.

21. Holden interview.

22. Ibid.

23. See Adele E. Shank, "The San Francisco Mime Troupe's *Americans, or Last Tango in Huehuetenango,*" *TDR* 25 (1981), pp. 81–83.

24. The San Francisco Mime Troupe, *1985* (unpublished typescript), p. 2. All further quotations from this work appear in the text.

25. Holden interview.

26. Ibid.

27. Beth Bagby, "El Teatro Campesino: Interviews with Luis Valdez," *TDR* 11 (1967), p. 73.

28. Ibid.

29. Luis Valdez, *Actos* (San Juan Bautista, Calif.: Cucaracha Press, 1971), p. 14. All further references to this work appear in the text.

30. See Dieter Herms et al., "Das befreiende Gelächter: Interview mit Luis Valdez über El Teatro campesino," *Theater Heute* 13 (September 1972), pp. 29–32.

31. Bagby, "Interviews with Luis Valdez," p. 77.

32. See Barclay Goldsmith, "Brecht and Chicano Theater," in *Modern Chicano Writers: A Collection of Critical Essays,* ed. Joseph Sommers and Tomás Ybarra-Frausto (Englewood Cliffs, N.J.: Prentice-Hall, 1979), pp. 167–75.

33. Françoise Kourilsky, "El Teatro Campesino," *Travail Théâtral* 7 (1972), p. 66. My translation.

34. Kourilsky, p. 67. My translation.

35. Luis Valdez and Stan Steiner, eds., *Atzlán: An Anthology of Mexican American Literature* (New York: Knopf, 1973), p. 4.

36. Nicolás Kanellos, "Folklore in Chicano Theatre and Chicano Theatre as Folklore," in *Popular Theatre for Social Change in Latin America,* ed. Gerardo Luzuriaga (Los Angeles: UCLA Latin American Center Publications, 1978), p. 168.

37. Roberto J. Garza, "Historical Antecedents to Chicano Theatre," in *Contemporary Chicano Theatre,* ed. Roberto J. Garza (Notre Dame, Ind.: University of Notre Dame Press, 1976), pp. 1–5.

38. Roger F. Copeland, "Review of Campesino's Performance of *La carpa de los Rasquachis,* Chelsea Theatre, The Brooklyn Academy of Music, New York City, 9 April 1973," *Educational Theatre Journal* 25 (1973), p. 376.

39. Gerd Burger, Arnulf Rating, and Gerhard Riecke, "Erkenntnisse über den Abfall. El Teatro Campesino und sein Stück 'La Carpa de los Rasquachis,' " *Theater Heute* (1977), p. 34.

40. For an eyewitness description of this controversial performance, see Theodore Shank, "A Return to Mayan and Aztec Roots," *TDR* 18 (December 1974), pp. 56–70.

41. Ibid., p. 66.

42. Luis Valdez, *Bernabé* in Garza, *Contemporary Chicano Theatre* (Notre Dame, Ind.: University of Notre Dame Press, 1976), p. 29. All further references to this work appear in the text.

43. My translation. Original: "Eres el último y el primero. El último de un gran noble linaje de hombres que conocí en tiempos antiguos; y el primero de la raza nueva de los siglos heredará la Tierra para todos. Tu cara es memoria cosmica, Bernabé: me recuerda de una humanidad entera, de tus mismos ojos, tu piel, tu sangre. Ellos también querían a la Tierra y honraban a su padre sobre todo lo demas."

44. For a more detailed discussion of *Zoot Suit* see Jorge A. Huerta, "Luis Valdez's *Zoot Suit:* A New Direction for Chicano Theatre?" *Latin-American Theater Review* (summer 1980), pp. 69–76; and Carlos Morton, "An Interview with Luis Valdez," *Latin-American Theater Review* (spring 1982), pp. 73–76.

45. The movie version of *Zoot Suit* never became a commercial success in the United States. In Mexico and Spain, however, it seems to have become a cult movie of sorts that has acquired a large following.

46. The play is a melodrama that deals with the meteoric rise and fall of Tiburcio Vasquez, a legendary gentleman-robber who operated in California. The objective of the play is to bring back to life a popular Mexican hero in a homage filled with song and dance. It is an attempt to add legitimacy to Mexican-American popular culture and to rewrite part of American history, which has systematically excluded any Mexican-American heroes.

47. Luis Valdez's latest movie project is *La Bamba,* the filmed life story of Chicano rock and roll star Ritchie Valens (Valenzuela).

48. Luis Valdez, program notes to *Rose of the Rancho.* A calavera extravaganza is a boisterous outdoor parade featuring skulls, skeletons, and specter-like figures symbolizing death.

49. Ibid.

50. The play was written by Severo Pérez and his wife Judith, and premiered in the fall of 1982.

51. In the fall of 1984, *Los Corridos* was having a successful run at San Diego's Globe Theatre.

52. *Los Angeles Times,* 2 February 1986, p. 42.

53. Interview with Gloriamalia Flores, San Juan Bautista, Calif., 15 August 1984.

54. Interview with Peter Schumann at Goddard College, Plainfield, Vt., 28 December 1983.

55. Ibid.

56. For a detailed description of this powerful play, see George Dennison, "Fire," *TDR* 14 (1970), pp. 36–44.

57. For a detailed description of this play see "The Bread and Puppet Theatre: The Stations of the Cross," in *The New Theatre: Performance Documentation,* ed. Michael Kirby (New York: New York University Press, 1974), pp. 141–54.

58. David Sterritt, "Many-Sided Bread and Puppet Man," *Christian Science Monitor,* 9 February 1973, p. 20.

59. Peter Schumann, "Introduction: Puppetry and Politics," in *Bread and Puppet: Stories of Struggle and Faith from Central America,* ed. Greg Guma (Burlington, Vt.: Green Valley Film and Art, 1985), p. 12.

60. Schumann interview.

61. Christian Dupavillon, *Bread and Puppet Theater: Spectacles en noir et blanc* (Paris: Alain Bouret, 1978), p. 8.

62. Schumann interview.

63. Ibid.

64. This march took place on 22 October 1983. See "Marching for peace in London," *The Chronicle* (Burlington, Vt.), 2 November 1983, pp. 18–20.

65. Schumann interview.

66. See appendix for further details.

CHAPTER 5

1. Maurice Blanc, "Clowning with the Lifeforce," *Village Voice,* 5 September 1968, p. 393.

2. Françoise Kourilsky, "El Teatro Campesino," *Travail Théâtral*, no. 7 (April-June 1972), p. 57. My translation.

3. Jean-Jacques Lebel, "Notes on Political Street Theatre, Paris: 1968, 1969," *TDR* 13, no. 4 (1969), p. 112.

4. Ibid., p. 116.

5. Jean-Louis Mignon, "Jacques Kraemer," *Avant-Scène* 601 (January 1977), p. 7. My translation.

6. Interview with Charles Tordjman, Thionville, France, 16 May 1984. My translation. Original: "Je ne crois pas que Mao, Gramsci et Marcuse étaient dans le coup. *Minette* a été crée spontanément bien qu'influencée par des idées qui étaient dans l'air. Et bien sûr elle avait l'ambition de démonter les mécanismes du capitalisme. Donc une sorte de transposition de la théorie Marxiste. Les gens qui étaient peut-être dans le coup c'était plutôt des gens comme Althusser et Brecht. Parce que *Minette* a été un peu écrite sur l'idée du *Aufhaltsame Aufstieg des Arturo Ui*."

7. See particularly scene 6, where this similarity is emphasized in a conversation between an interior decorator and the boss. The latter orders a decorated ceiling for his establishment because, he argues, "Dans la position horizontale, on ne voit que cela," i.e., in a horizontal position that is the only thing one really sees. Jacques Kraemer, *Splendeur et misère de Minette, la bonne Lorraine* (Paris: Editions du Seuil, 1970), p. 40. All further references to this work appear in the text.

8. My translation. Original: "Grâce à ses initiatives hardies, Monsieur Joseph soutiendra vertueusement de nombreuses familles. . . . Le vertueux M'sieur Joseph, toujours désintéressé, sacrifie ses loisirs pour le développement de notre vallée."

9. My translation. Original: "Bouleversant! Une idylle se noue entre Jo et une jeune fille pauvre: oui, les princes épousent encore des bergères."

10. ". . . Le seul ton convenable était le burlesque. Ce ton se retrouve dans le jeu clownesque des comédiens . . . ," *Minette*, p. 120. My translation: "The only suitable tone for the play was the burlesque. It can be found in the clownesque acting style of the actors."

11. My translation. Original: "Dans le château de M'sieur Joseph un bar et des tabourets structurés comme des chevalements de puits de mine . . . un fauteuil évoque les deux principales machines que l'on trouve au fond des mines de fer."

12. The procedures in question are: *flottage* ("floating"), *lévigation* ("levigation"), and *triage électromagnétique* ("electromagnetic separation"). See *Minette*, pp. 26–27.

13. The treatment of immigrant workers was hinted at but not developed in *Minette* in the character of Salah.

14. Jacques Kraemer, *Les Immigrés* (Paris: P. J. Oswald, 1973), pp. 25–26. All further references to this work appear in the text.

15. My translation. Original: "créatures hybrides, ni hommes, ni bêtes (cependant humaines) découvertes dans un lointain pays."

16. See "Présentation," in *Les Immigrés*, p. 9.

17. My translation. Original: "PROPRIETAIRE I: Dites-moi, vous qui les connaissez bien, ils ne commettent pas trop de déprédations, car j'y tiens, moi, à ma villa. PROPRIETAIRE II: Pas du tout, vous savez, on raconte beaucoup de choses sur eux, mais en réalité, ils sont très calmes. D'ailleurs, quand ils rentrent, ils ne pensent qu'à dormir. Ils s'écroulent sur les paillasses et dorment. . . . PROPRIETAIRE I: Et comment se chauffent-ils? PROPRIETAIRE II: La chaleur animale."

18. Jacques Kraemer, *La Liquidation de Monsieur Joseph K./Jacotte ou les plaisirs de la vie quotidienne* (Paris: P. J. Oswald, 1974), p. 77. All further references to this work appear in the text. My translation. Original: "On peut y lire une critique du théâtre métaphysique, du théâtre de l'absurde. On retrouve dans la mise en scène l'accessoire obligatoire de ce genre de théâtre: la poubelle."

19. My translation. Original: "Au lieu d'avoir à suivre dans un confort intellectuel relatif la prise de conscience du héros, le spectateur se trouve obligé de prendre ses distances par rapport à la non évolution du personnage. Cette forme est mise en oeuvre dans les plus grandes pièces de Brecht. . . . Elle vise à produire une nouvelle conscience spectatrice. *La Liquidation* tente de s'inscrire dans cette démarche. Ce qu'elle donne à voir, c'est une conscience aveugle et mystifiée; un homme encore incapable d'accéder à la connaissance des causes politiques et à l'exigence d'une stratégie collective."

20. ". . . voir quelqu'un ne pas voir, c'est la meilleure façon de voir intensément ce qu'il ne voit pas." Roland Barthes, *Mythologies,* quoted in the program of *La Liquidation de Monsieur Joseph K.* My translation: "To watch someone not see is the best way of seeing intensely what he does not see."

21. My translation. Original: "Chansonnette de Joseph K. sur le gros et le petit negoce: J'étais un petit commerçant/ J'ai dû déposer mon bilan/ Un des 6 929/Qui dans l'année soixante et neuf/ Ont vu la fin de leur négoce/ Dévorés par les Gobkoloss/ Comment le petit boutiquier/ Ne serait-il pas liquidé?"

22. Ever since it was satirized as pimps in *Minette,* the "Patronat" of the mining industry had waged a relentless campaign to destroy TPL. Through Parisian contacts it managed to bring about a significant reduction in central government and local subsidies for the troupe, and it organized a boycott by the regional press and by national and regional radio and television. TPL has fought back in many ways. *La Liquidation de Monsieur Joseph K.* stands at the center of these efforts and constitutes a testimony of their difficulties.

23. See for example the combination of satire and expressionism in O'Neill's *Hairy Ape* and Elmer Rice's *Adding Machine.*

24. Jacques Kraemer, *Noëlle de Joie* (Paris: P. J. Oswald, 1975), scene 8, pp. 27–29. All further references to this work appear in the text.

25. Tordjman interview. My translation. Original: "La proportion du public ouvrier a faibli. On est à dix pour cent maintenant, ce qui n'est pas mal d'ailleurs. On a quitté un peu le schéma dans la tête qui dicte qu'il faut absolument avoir un public ouvrier à tout prix."

26. Jacques Kraemer, "Minette, la bonne Lorraine," *Avant-Scène* 623 (1978), p. 4. All further references to this work appear in the text. My translation. Original: "une fantastique créature, sujette à toutes les métamorphoses, receptacle de toute une symbolique: la terre, la mère, la fécondité, la splendeur de la chair, la décrépitude, la mort . . . Minette sera comme un personnage de cauchemar adamovien, subira toutes les mutilations possibles."

27. My translation. Original: "Il sourd là-bas une mélodie inouïe, un son sismique des profondeurs sylvestres. . . . Appel attirant, affolant, angoissant. . . . Lame de fonds, crevasse d'ombre. Mousse. Le jeu du temps et de la matière."

28. See pages 19 and 20 of the new version, which correspond to pp. 91–93 of the original.

29. "Le Corse" has completely disappeared in the new play.

30. Jacques Kraemer left TPL in 1983, burnt out after twenty years of struggling daily for legitimization with the regional authorities. See also *Atac/ Informations* 85 (1981), pp. 38–39, for an interview with TPL actor René Loyon, who discusses Jacques Kraemer's authoritarian dominance in the troupe.

31. In 1983 and 1984, fifty people have died in France through racist violence.

32. Tordjman interview. My translation. Original: "J'ai jamais vu cela de ma vie, j'ai jamais vu des gens arriver au théâtre avec des Djelabahs s'asseoir à côté d'un Français et commencer à parler de ce que c'est son pays. J'ai vraiment eu l'impression qu'on a réussi avec ce projet à faire un petit pas en avant. D'une certaine façon c'était du vrai théâtre

populaire. On a joué la pièce de Ben Jelloun un mois, mais on aurait pu la jouer trois mois. Parce que je crois qu'on avait trouvé un nouvel enracinement dans le public."

33. In this respect, lo Teatre de la Carriera invites a comparison with el Teatro Campesino, another bilingual popular theatre group that also started out performing for rural audiences. See D. M. Church, "Activist Theater in Minority Agricultural Milieux: California's El Teatro Campesino and Provence's Lo Teatre de la Carriera," in *Proceedings Comparative Literature Symposium* (Lubbock: Texas Tech Press, 1985), pp. 57–70.

34. Lo Teatre de la Carriera, *Ecrit des Femmes* (Paris: Editions Solin, 1980).

35. Ironically, this steel industry was relocated from Lorraine, a development against which TPL had protested in its *Minette* plays.

36. Eugène A. van Erven, "l'Ail sur le pain culturel Français: un entretien avec Catherine Bonafé de Lo Teatre de la Carriera," *Contemporary French Civilization*, 9, no. 1 (1985), p. 61. My translation.

37. Chichois is also a stock character in the popular opera tradition of Marseilles.

38. Lo Teatre de la Carriera, *La Pastorale de Fos* (Paris: P. J. Oswald, 1975), pp. 76–77. All further references to this work appear in the text. My translation. Original: "Sur les chantiers nous sommes tous des boumians, bons à tordre, bons à jeter, tant que nous étions divisés. . . . Les travailleurs noirs . . . et les travailleurs blancs . . . et ceux de la terre . . . et ceux de la mer . . . les Pierrots, les Augustes, et les Hercules . . . et les Pamparigoustiens . . . Et les Boumians. Tous ensemble . . . nous vaincrons."

39. My translation. Original: "Ce soir, nous allons jouer, en famille, une petite leçon d'économie. Bouchez-vous tous les trous. Sauf les oreilles, bien entendu. Bouchez-les bien. C'est très bien. Je baisse le chauffage. J'augmente les prix. . . . Et si vous n'êtes pas contents, nom d'un chien, c'est la faute aux grévistes! Et si vous n'êtes pas contents, nom d'un chien, c'est la faute aux Boumians! Un coup, deux coups! Frappez sur les grévistes! Un coup, deux coups! Frappez sur les Boumians!"

40. My translation. Original: "toujours un peu plus déformé et son nez s'est allongé."

41. Lo teatre de la Carriera, *Mort et résurrection de M. Occitania* (Arles: by the authors, 1976), p. 68. All further references to this work appear in the text. My translation. Original: "siatz malautas vosautres atanben. Avatz sa malatié. Pissatz roge d'aquela viticultura tugada."

42. My translation. Original: "Etre de l'opposition, c'est dur. J'y suis pour vous. Mais sans trop, pour ne pas attirer dans le Midi les foudres de la rancune gouvernementale, pondérément pour faire le chantage aux subventions, mais suffisamment pour changer la vie. Tout mon art est dans la mesure. Mes études de pharmacien m'ont préparé plus que toute autre profession à ma carrière politique. Mais je demeure viticulteur par mes parents. Je suis donc en vous comme vous êtes en moi . . . vous défendre, c'est me défendre."

43. My translation. Original: "[M. Métaneuf], les mots ne seront jamais assez forts pour dire le bien que vous avez fait et que vous faites encore. Grâce à vous nous avons maintenant de magnifiques bureaux de chômage. Les fauteuils y sont moëlleux, les moquettes intimes, les hôtesses charmantes . . . et les nombreux chômeurs peuvent y venir et revenir. Ils sont toujours bien acceuillis."

44. Claude Alranq, *La Fille d'Occitania* (Le Paradou: Editions Actes/Sud, 1978), pp. 20–21. All further references to this work appear in the text. My translation. Original: 'Paris adieu! Quatre ans ma claque! Des comprimés pour se lever tôt, des cachets pour s'endormir, des excitants pour tenir . . . des talons pour péter haut! Des soustinges aéro! Et des slips petit-bateau! . . . Des maquillages pour s'oublier et des revues pour rêver! Paris ras le bol!"

45. van Erven, "l'Ail sur le pain culturel français," p. 64.

46. For more detailed discussions of theatrical decentralization in France see Judith Graves Miller, *Theatre and Revolution in France since 1968* (Lexington, Ky.: French Forum Publishers, 1977); Vera Lee, *Quest for a Public* (Cambridge, Mass.: Schenkman, 1970); and Dan M. Church, "State Subsidies and Militant Regionalism in Contemporary French Theater," *Contemporary French Civilization*, VI (1982): 342–60.

47. Before becoming minister of culture, Jack Lang had been involved in the regional theatre of Nancy, where he had also cofounded the world-famous international Theatre Festival.

48. It is interesting to note that both the Théâtre du Campagnol and the Théâtre de l'Est Parisien also consider themselves to be popular theatre groups that do most of their work in response to the needs of the neighborhoods in which they are implanted. Operating in the Parisian metropolitan area, however, has considerably enhanced their chances of getting exposure and money.

CHAPTER 6

1. See Catherine Itzin's *Stages of the Revolution* (London: Eyre Methuen, 1980) for a panoramic description of the British radical theatre scene.

2. John McGrath, *A Good Night Out* (London: Methuen, 1981).

3. Eugène A. van Erven, "Theatre for the People: An Interview with John McGrath of the 7:84 Theatre Company," *Minnesota Review* N.S. 27 (fall 1986), p. 118.

4. van Erven, "Theatre for the People," p. 118.

5. Simon Trussler, ed., *New Theatre Voices of the Seventies* (London: Eyre Methuen, 1981), p. 106.

6. John McGrath, *The Cheviot, the Stag and the Black, Black Oil* (London: Eyre Methuen, 1981), p. 76.

7. John McGrath, *Trees in the Wind* (unpublished manuscript), p. 1.10. All further references to this work appear in the text.

8. McGrath, *A Good Night Out*, p. 52.

9. McGrath, *A Good Night Out*, pp. 30–31.

10. John McGrath, *Soft or a Girl* (unpublished manuscript), p. 52. All further references to this work appear in the text.

11. McGrath, *A Good Night Out*, p. 29.

12. John McGrath, *Fish in the Sea* (London: Pluto Press, 1977), preface. All further references to this work appear in the text.

13. McGrath, *A Good Night Out*, p. 30.

14. In this respect, *The Cheviot, The Stag and the Black, Black Oil* is reminiscent of lo Teatre de la Carriera's *Pastorale de Fos* which also utilized a traditional dramatic structure to express the effects of modern industrialization on a predominantly rural Occitanian area.

15. McGrath, *The Cheviot*, p.x. All further references to this work appear in the text.

16. Compare this to the similar satirical treatment of the exploitation of Occitanian wine in La Carriera's *Mort et Résurrection de M. Occitania*.

17. Interview with Robert Rae, London, 25 June 1983.

18. Rae interview.

19. Ibid.

20. Ibid.

21. Ibid.

22. Blurb on the program bill of *The Ragged Trousered Philanthropists*.

CHAPTER 7

1. For a panoramic discussion of West Germany's *Freie Gruppen,* see Dietmar Roberg's *Theater muss wie Fussball sein* (Berlin: Rotbuch Verlag, 1981).

2. Interview with Wolfgang Anrath, Munich, 8 June 1984. My translation. Original: "In Januar '68 bin ich mit Strassentheater angefangen. Die Hauptaktionen des Strassentheaters richteten sich damals hauptsächlich gegen die Notstandsgesetze. Was wir damals machten, war mit Originaltexten aus dem Faschismus und Texten aus diesen Notstandsgesetzen. So haben wir dann eine Szenenkollage gemacht und Kommentare noch dazu und haben einfach diese dokumentarischen texten in Aktion umgesetzt. Wir sind mit der Strassenbahn und dem Omnibus herumgefahren und haben überall gespielt. Bis Mai '68 haben wir dann immer Veränderungen gemacht wenn die neue Situation darum bat."

3. Interview with Volker Ludwig, West Berlin, 15 June 1984. My translation. Original: "Wir verstehen uns eigentlich nicht so sehr als ein Theater für eine bestimmte Altersgruppe als eben doch eine bestimmte Form von politischem Theater. Und diese Form, die wir für Kinder und Jugendliche machen, wäre genau so vortzusetzen wie Theater für Erwachsene, und das wird vielleicht auch kommen. Wir haben es in einem Stück versucht, *Eine Linke Geschichte;* das ist ein Stück über uns selbst, ein sehr grosser Erfolg. Das ist eben die Geschichte über zwei Studenten die sich in 1966 bei einer Vietnamdemonstration kennengelernt haben und wir verfolgen ihre politischen Entwicklung. Wir sehen also eine klare Verbindung zwischen dem radikalen Kindertheater und dem radikalen Volkstheater für Erwachsene. Und unseres Theater wird auch so aufgenommen. Das heisst, wir sind abends immer aussverkauft mit unseren Jugenstücken zu denen auch das normale Theaterpublikum kommt aus Mangel eines anderen zeitkritischen Theaters."

4. Ludwig interview. My translation. Original: "In 1967 haben wir unser erstes Vietnam-Programm gemacht. Die Leuten glaubten uns einfach die Tatsachen nicht. Berlin ist nun eben eine extrem Amerika-freundliche Stadt wegen der Blokade und der Luftbrücke. Deswegen war auch die Polarisierung so stark in Berlin. Aber nach einer Weile wurde dieses Theater ein riesiger Erfolg; es wurde schick links zu sein. Wir kriegten sogar gute Kritiken der *Bildzeitung,* obwohl die Programme immer brutaler wurden. Also nach einer Weile sahen wir keinen Sinn mehr drin für solch ein Publikum Kabarett zu machen."

5. Ludwig interview. My translation. Original: "Das Kabarett war viel intellektueller, das war für Studenten, das hatte seine Funktion. Wir wollten eben an die ganzen Bevölkerung heran und das ging nur durch das Kinder- und Jugendtheater. Das Kindertheater erreicht man in Schulklassen und die Schulklassen waren gerade—durch die mit uns gleichzeitig bewusstgewordenen jungen Lehrer—offener geworden."

6. Ludwig interview. My translation. Original: "Der grosse Vorteil, den wir haben ist natürlich, dass wir aus dem Kabarett kommen, das heisst: beim Kabarett lernt man Timing. Man weiss, die Totsünde ist erstmal zu langweilen. Wenn man die Leute nicht unterhält, darf man kein Geld nehmen. Das Wichtigste ist mal Entertainment. Auch bei der San Francisco Mime Troupe, die hier bei uns vor ein Paar Jahr gespielt hat, war das klar. Oder bei Molière: er sagte, 'Wenn man mit Tränen rührt, fliesst der ganze Inhalt weg; mit Lachen muss erst verstanden werden.' Es soll also kein Lachen aus Schadenfreude sein sondern ein erkennendes Lachen. Dazu lernt man im Kabarett nicht zu lang zu werden und auch sich auf ein bestimmtes Publikum zu richten. Und auch diese Sachen mit Songs zu übersetzen. Ich bin sicher, dass Grips ohne die Kabaretts tradition nie ein Erfolg geworden wäre."

7. Arno Paul, "Zu einigen Strukturelementen der GRIPS-Dramaturgie," in *Das Grips Theater: Geschichte und Geschichten, Erfahrungen und Gespräche aus einem Kinder- und Jugendtheater,* ed. Wolfgang Kolneder, Volker Ludwig, and Klaus Wagenbach (Berlin: Verlag Klaus Wagenbach, 1979).

8. Ludwig interview. My translation. Original: "Wir stehen auch darauf, dass ein Autor bis zum letzten Tag dabeisein muss und sich vom Schauspieler viel sagen lassen muss. Die Schauspieler haben ja inzwischen auch soviel Erfahrung, dass die wissen was klappen wird und was nicht. Also es geht so: es wird ein Thema vorgeschlagen auf einer Vollversammlung. Das wird dann angenommen oder nicht. Man kann dann immer rufen wenn man Probleme hat. Die Autoren werden dann beauftragt ein Stück zu schreiben. Wenn ein Grundschema des Stücks da ist, wird es besetzt und wird eine Produktionsgruppe gebildet: Techniker, Regisseure, Schauspieler, Musiker, usw. Diese Gruppe recherchiert dann gemeinsam mit den Autoren. Das heisst, wir haben eine Arbeitsteilung wie in anderen Theatern, aber es wird viel intensiver miteinander gearbeitet."

9. Volker Ludwig, *Nashörner schiessen nicht* (Frankfurt: Verlag der Autoren, 1973), p. 7. All further references to this work appear in the text. My translation. Original: "Ich werde mal was Besseres! Wo man viel Geld verdient und befehlen kann. . . . Und wo man mit einem dicken Auto herumfährt und nicht mit so 'nem blöden Fahrrad wie du! Und wo man in einer weissen Villa wohnt und nicht in so einer Bruchbude wie wir!"

10. My translation. Original: "Da gibt es doch Leute, die sagen dir glatt,/ Dass jeder die gleichen Chancen hat!/ Wenn du Schuhputzer bist und schuftest ganz schwer,/ Wer weiss, eines Tages biste Mihilionär!/ Natürlich! So etwas gab es schon!/ Doch die Chance hat einer von einer Million!/ Der eine hat viel Geld, er braucht nur zur Bank,/ Der andere spielt Lotto sein Leben lang./ Die Kinder der Feinen studieren fast immer,/ Die Andern ha'm nicht mal ein eigenes Zimmer./ Denn gleiche Chancen, die gab es noch nie. . . ."

11. My translation. Original: "Iih! Das ist doch die Stinkgegend, wo die Leute in Rattenlöchern wohnen! . . . *(zur Mutter)* Hast du selber gesagt! Und das sie sich nie waschen, auch! Und das sie alles klauen!"

12. My translation. Original: "wenn Ratten aus der Ottostrasse beissen, dann tut das eben weh!"

13. My translation. Original: "Du musst viel essen, damit die Kinder viel kaufen! Jeden Tag neu! Kaufen, kaufen, kaufen! . . . Dazu machen wir doch den Film! Die müssen wollen! Und dann kaufen sie. Ob sie wollen oder nicht. Stellt euch das mal vor! Das ist ja das Tolle unserer Arbeit: wenn wir gut sind, können wir erreichen, dass Millionen Leute etwas kaufen, was sie eigentlich gar nicht wollen."

14. My translation. Original: "Nashörner schiessen nicht! Die machen was ganz anderes! Nashörner fressen Gras! . . . Und können ganz schnell laufen! . . . Aber wenn man ihnen weh tut oder sie bescheissen will, dann werden sie unheimlich wütend! Dann spiessen sie alles mit ihrem grossen Horn auf!"

15. Volker Ludwig and Henning Spangenberg, *Der Spinner* (Berlin: Grips Theater, 1984), p. 20. All further references to this work appear in the text. My translation. Original: "Der ist überhaupt kein richtiger Mensch, ist der. Der hat nur Geld und Termine im Kopf, und dass alles immer schief geht, und dass alle anderen bescheuert sind ausser er selber."

16. My translation. Original: "Verdammt noch mal! Hörst du jetzt endlich auf damit! . . . Davon wird man ja verrückt!"

17. My translation. Original: ". . . überall habe ich die Menschen von Hunger krepieren und im Dreck ersticken sehen, mein Lieber. So sieht deine Traumwelt in

Wirklichkeit aus. Du lebst doch hier wie im Paradies! Wenn du grösser bist, kannst du dir die Welt begucken. Abenteuer gibt's da genug. Aber Spinner brauchen die da nicht. Da musst du erst mal was lernen! Was können! Was mitbringen! Lass dich doch nicht verblöden von diesem ganzen Fernseh- und Kino- und Werbedreck!"

18. My translation. Original: "Du bist gar nicht richtig da! Eine Null bist du! Ein Nichts! Was kannst du überhaupt, he? In die Röhre starren! Cola saufen! Kekse fressen. Das vielleicht. Mensch, du bist doch wie tot! . . . Mein Gott, womit habe ich das verdient?—Hau bloss ab! *(Oliver steht herum)* Hau ab, habe ich gesagt!! *(Oliver ab).*"

19. My translation. Original: "PIA: Weisste: einfach nur so herumreisen in der Welt und glotzen, ist doch langweilig. Kostet nur Geld. Aber wenn ich was kann, was die Afrikaner oder die Indianer brauchen, dann freuen sie sich, wenn ich komme."

20. Volker Ludwig und Detlef Michel, *Alles Plastik* (Berlin: Grips Theater, 1981), p. 59. All further references to this work are from this edition. My translation. Original: "Die ganze Welt verrottet/ und erstickt/ Weil'n Haufen Spiesser auf die Tube drückt/ Wer das erkennt/ und weiter pennt/ Und sicht nicht wehrt/ der lebt verkehrt!!!"

21. Ludwig interview. My translation. Original: "Weil die Kinder noch verpflicht in der Schule sind, kommen die mit der ganzen Gruppe, aber die Jugendliche, um die herbeizuführen, muss man wirklich wissen für wen man es macht. Wir haben uns entschlossen Theater zu machen für die Unterprivilegierten, die überhaupt das Theater nicht kennen. Nur Fussball und Disko. Manche kommen auch zu uns ins Theater und wollen nur Krawall machen und wissen dann gar nicht was sie sehen. Die müssen wir erst mal kriegen, und das eben mit Mitteln, mit denen sie sich identifizieren können: die Sprache, die Haltung, die Sprüche, alles muss genau stimmen. Und die sind dann total verblüfft wie kleine Kinder. Die schreien dann auch mit; und wenn wir die fragen, ob ihnen ein Stück gefallen hat oder nicht; dann können die das nicht sagen. Aber sie sagen dann, 'Es hat mir nicht gefallen dass dieser Bursche das gesagt hat,' oder, 'Das ist ein Schleimer.' In der Pause sagen die dann, 'Das ist besser als Kino,' und, "Wann geht denn der Film weiter?' weil das das einzige ist was sie kennen. Und was wir in diesen Jugendstücken erreichen wollen, ist sie zu ermutigen. Unser Theater wird darum auch Mutmach-Theater genannt. Das heisst, die Jugend steht im Mittelpunkt des Stückes und sie erreicht ganz kleine Schritte mehr als in der Wirklichkeit, aber so klein dass sie sich identifizieren können und doch etwas mehr Selbstbewusstsein kriegen."

22. Interview with Gerd Hunger, West Berlin, 14 June 1984. My translation. Original: "Die haben ein festes Haus, eine Arbeitsteilung, die es bei uns nicht gibt, Leute an der Kasse, Bühnenarbeiter, Beleuchtungstechniker, Schauspieler, Regisseure, Dramaturgen. . . . Grips geht auch öfters auf Tournee, aber die Sensation ist, wenn die Rote Grütze kommt: die liefern immer ihr Stück ab, aber wir machen ein Theaterfest. Bei Grips ist es mittlerweise so, dass die sehr Theater geworden sind. Bei uns ist das alles viel offener. Es gibt verschiedene Meinungen über die Stücke und man kann die konträren Meinungen auch aussprechen. Bei Grips arbeiten die Schauspieler auch nicht länger am Stück mit: es gibt ein oder zwei Autoren, ein Regisseur, die alle künsterischen Entscheidungen machen. . . . Und das ist eben die Gefahr, ich beim Grips sehe: die Schauspieler sind vom künstlerischen Prozess abgeschnitten worden. Das war gut zu sehen in *Eine linke Geschichte*. Ich habe mir das drei mal angeguckt, weil es auch zum Teil meine Geschichte war. Also mitten drin haben die Schauspieler gewechselt. Aber bis auf'n Schritt, bis auf'n kleinsten Gesichtsausdruck haben die dasselbe gespielt. Das wäre eben bei uns völlig undenkbar. Wir haben das auch ein paar mal gehabt; die Idee des Stückes war zwar mehr oder weniger gleichgeblieben, aber die Figur hatte sich völlig geändert."

23. Ludwig interview. My translation. Original: "Dario Fo gibt's in Deutschland leider nicht!"

CHAPTER 8

1. Miguel Bayón in *Cambio 16,* 22 November 1982, p. 152. My translation.

2. See Toni Mitchell's recently published *Dario Fo: People's Court Jester* (London: Methuen, 1986), pp. 113–15 for an account of this memorable visit.

3. Dario Fo and Franca Rame, *Theatre Workshops at Riverside Studios, London* (London: Red Notes, 1983), p. 64.

4. Dario Fo in an interview with Hannes Heer, in *Dario Fo über Dario Fo* (Cologne: Prometh Verlag, 1980), p. 134. My translation.

5. Fo and Rame, *Theatre Workshops,* p. 2.

6. Ibid., p. 8.

7. Dario Fo, *Mistero Buffo* (Torino: Giulio Einaudi editore, 1977), p. 21. All further references to this work appear in the text. My translation. Original: "Ecco, vieni qua tu, hai la barba, mi piaci, prendi questa corona: tu fai il re. Tu, vieni qua. E tua moglie? Sei simpatica, fai la regina. Che faccia da delinquente che hai tu, tieni . . . fai l'imperatore. E quello . . . che faccia da furbo che ha. . . . Vieni, vieni, to'!, fai il vescovo, vai! A te, guarda, faccio fare il commerciante. A te, vieni, vieni . . . guarda, tutto questo spazio, tutta quella terra che va fino a quel fiume è tutta roba tua . . . mi sei simpatico . . . e tiene tela stretta eh! ! . . . Non mollarla mai agli altri, e falla lavorare per bene . . . E anche a te, prendi questa terra . . . E tuo parente? Bene! così la roba si tiene unita. Ed ora vediamo un po' . . . a te daré tutta la parte sul mare. Il diritto di pesca, invece, è per te. E voi . . . laggiù . . . miseri e striminzitti . . . te e te e te e te, e anche le vostre mogli, lavorarete per lui, per lui e per lui, e anche per lui, e si ve lamenterete vi sbatto all'inferno, come è vero che sono Dio! E lo sono, per Dio!"

8. My translation. Original: "L'hai comandato tu 'sto ammazzamento . . . l'hai voluto tu questo sacrificio in cambio di far venir giù tuo figlio: mille bambini scannati per uno di te, un fiume di sangue per una tazzina! Potevi ben tenerlo vicino a te 'sto figlio, se doveva costarci tanto sacrificio a noi poveri cristi. . . ."

9. My translation. Original: "S'è fatto un silenzio che sembrava di essere in chiesa al Santus, e questo Gesù si è stropicciato un po' le mani, schioccando le dita, e poi ha alzato una mano, con tre dita solamente, che le altre due le teneva contro il palmo, e ha cominciato a fare dei segni sopra l'acqua . . . dei segni che fanno solamente i figli di Dio. Io, che era un po' in là, che ho detto l'acqua mi fa impresione a guardarla, non guardavo, era appoggiato sopra là, ratristato, e di colpo mi sento arrivare dentro i buchi del naso un profumo come di uva schiacciata, non ci si poteva confondere . . . era vino."

10. My translation. Original: "Mi dispiace ma io ti scarico qui e tu fai il sacrosanto piacere di andare a scaricare l'immagazinamento illegale!"

11. My translation. Original: "Gente! . . . Avete ascoltato? Un angelo che mi vuol buttare fuori a pedate . . . a me! Un angelo. . . . *(Aggressivo rivolto verso l'angelo)* Vieni . . . vieni, angiolone . . . vieni a buttarmi fuori a pedate, a me! Che io ti strappo le penne come a una gallina . . . ti strappo le penne a una a una, anche dal culo . . . dal di dietro. . . . Vieni, gallinone. . . . Vieni!"

12. My translation. Original: "Ohi che mestiere da boia fare il papa!"

13. My translation. Original: "Gesù, come va? . . . Gesù, non mi conosci? Sono Bonifacio. . . . Bonifacio, il papa. . . . Come, chi è il papa! Andiamo . . . il pastore, quello che viene da Pietro, con tutti gli altri di fila . . . non mi riconosci? Ah, è per il capellone. . . . Era perchè piove. . . . Magari. . . . *(Rivolto al chierico)* Vieni a levarme tuto . . . l'anello! . . . non far vedere che ho gli anelli."

14. My translation. Original: "Cristo! Una pedata a me?! Bonifacio! Il Principe! Ah, bene . . . canaglia . . . malnato. . . . Oh si lo sapesse tuo padre . . . disgraziato! Capo degli asini!"

15. My translation. Original: "Oh, gente, venite qui che c'è il giullare! Giullare son io,

che salta a piroetta e che vi fa ridere, che prende in giro i potenti e vi fa vedere como sono tronfi e gonfi i palloni che vanno in giro a far guerre dove noi siamo gli scannati, *e ve li faccio sfigurare, gli tolgo il tappo e . . . pffs . . . si sgonfiano.* Venite qui che è ora e il luogo che io faccia da pagliaccio, che vi insegni. *Faccio il saltino, faccio la cantatina, faccio i giochetti! Guarda la lingua come gira! Sembra un coltello, cerca di ricordartelo!"* (My italics.)

16. Heer, "Dario Fo über Dario Fo," p. 124. My translation.

17. The *mundus inversus* structure is obviously related to popular celebrations like carnival, Mardi Gras, and other such public festivals. During celebrations of this kind—to which also the Roman Saturnalia and the medieval Feast of Fools belong—"customary social restraints are abandoned, distinctions of rank and status are turned upside-down, and institutions normally sacrosanct are subjected to ridicule, mockery and burlesque" (*Encyclopaedia Britannica*, 1979 ed., s.v. "Satire," by Robert C. Elliott). During carnival, for a week or more the government of municipalities is symbolically handed over to a locally elected prince of fools who decrees that, until Ash Wednesday, folly shall reign.

18. Dario Fo, *Morte accidentale di un anarchico* in *Compagni senza censura* (Milano: Gabriele Mazzotta editore, 1976), p. 164. All further references to this work appear in the text. My translation. Original: "Ma che cosa avete: un monsone africano personale che passa di qui ogni notte, o è la 'corrente del golfo' che viene su per il 'tombone di san Marco' e vi passa sotto-casa con le fogne?!"

19. My translation. Original: "la gente vi saprebbe perdonare tutte le contraddizioni in cui siete caduti a più sospinto . . . ma se, in cambio, dietro a questi impacci, riuscisse ad intravvedere un cuore . . . due 'uomini umani' che si lasciano afferrare alla gola dalla commozione e, ancorchè poliziotti, cantano con l'anarchico la sua canzone."

20. My translation. Original: "Una crise . . . credo. *(Estrae da dentro un breviario una siringa e si appresta a fargli una iniezione)* Tenetelo, questa gli farà certamente bene . . . è un calmante benedettino. [. . .] *(Con rapidità da cobra gli effettua l'iniezione, poi, estratta la siringa, la osserva)* N'è rimasto ancora un po' . . . ne gradisce anche lei? *(Senza attendere risposta lo siringa con l'agilità d'un banderillero) (Lamento offocato del questore)"*

21. My translation. Original: ". . . il giudice è il meglio di tutti i mestieri! Prima di tutto non si va quasi mai in pensione. . . . Anzi, nello stesso momento in cui un uomo comune, un lavatore qualsiasi, a cinquantacinque sessant'anni è giù da sbatter via perchè comincia ad essere un po' tardo, un po' lento di reflessi, per il giudice, invece, comincia il bello della carriera. Per un operaio alla catena o alla trancia dopo i cinquant'anni è finito: combina ritardi, incidenti, è da scartare! Il minatore a cinquantacinque anni ha la silicosi . . . via, scartato, licenziato, svelto, prima che scatti la pensione . . . per i giudici è tutto l'opposto: più sono vecchi e rinco . . . svaniti, più li eleggono a cariche importanti . . . assolute! Vedi dei vecchietti di cartone tutti impaludati [. . .] traballanti, con delle facce da tappi della val Gardena."

22. My translation. Original: "La tenga pure, ne ho un'altra!"

23. My translation. Original: "si è slacciato il bottone della giacca così da scoprire una croce barocca d'oro e argento fabbricazione rancati, quindi, s'è infilato un anellone con pietra viola enorme."

24. Brendan Gill, "Belasco Fiasco," *New Yorker* (3 December 1984), p. 182.

25. Dario Fo, "Introduction," *Accidental Death of an Anarchist*, adapted by Gavin Richards (London: Pluto Press, 1980), p. iii.

26. My translation. Original: "MATTO: Ma ha idea lei di che cosa sia un operaio? quando arrivano alla pensione, e dalle ultime statistiche ci arrivano sempre in meno, quando ci arrivano, sono ormai strizzati come limoni, delle larve con riflessi ridotti al minimo . . . allo straccio."

27. My translation. Original: "Ho l'hobby di recitare delle parti insomma, sempre

diverse. Soltanto che io sono per il teatro verità, quindi ho bisogno che la mia compagnia di teatranti sia composta da gente vera . . . che non sappia di recitare . . . d'altra parte io non ho mezzi, non potrei pagarli . . . ho chiesto sovvenzioni al ministero dello spettacolo ma siccome non ho appoggi politici. . . ."

28. Franca Rame and Dario Fo, *Tutta casa, letto e chiesa* (Milano: Edizione F.R. La Comune, 1981). My translation. Original: "per proteggermi meglio il primo che mi frega è lui! Mi tine chiusa in casa come una gallina scema, mi prende a sberle . . . e poi subito vuol fare l'amore! . . . Si l'amore! E non gliene frega niente se a me non va, se non ne ho voglia! Sempre pronta devo essere io, sempre pronta! Come il nescafè!! Lavata, profumata, depilata, calda, snodata, vogliosa ma, zitta! Basta che respiri!"

29. Dario Fo, *Fabulazzo Osceno* (Milano: Edizione F.R. La Comune, 1982), p. 82. All further references to this work appear in the text. My translation. Original: "Po' ho comincià a caminare: ambato . . . perchè mi no'savea caminàr de aseno. . . . Po' ho comincià a fare, alternando, cos . . . alora, questo pie ol va avanti, e quest'altro el viene dopo. E a ogni passo che faséo 'sti pirlundún che gh'avevo de cujuni, ghe davo ginugiàdi; un male tremendo!"

30. My translation. Original: ". . . prima te amavo per quel che te eri . . . te, de exexionàle . . . de quel che sempre, voialtri omeni m'avé insegnàt col è potente prìapo . . . cúme dentro un bandieròn . . . un poter grande. Al rovérso, de omeni che parla e che fa' l'amore come ti, ghe n'è tanti . . . De aseni che no' parlava ma faseva l'amor come era ti avanti, no' ghe n'era nisciùno!"

CHAPTER 9

1. Interview with Joan Baixas, Barcelona, 8 January 1978. My translation. Original: "Se cargaron por ejemplo al inspector de policía de San Sebastián y a todo su red de torturadores. Los mataron uno por uno. Y eso comunicó el mensaje muy claro que eso sí se podía hacer. En aquel momento era importante porque parece que Franco ya estaba preparando el traspaso. Parece que su plan era de dejar al rey como figura arriba y entonces mantener el movimiento de su ideología tras sus propios hombres. El representante más grave era Carrero Blanco. El estuvo años preparando a gente como Suárez— gente que se había formado en universidades extranjeras; gente técnicamente buena, ideologicamente muy de derecha y que comprendía que la derecha tenía que cambiar. ETA se encargó del asunto cuando Franco ya era muy viejo para reaccionar. Si no hubieran matado a Carrero Blanco, podía ser muy diferente la democracia española de hoy. Habríamos tenido una democracia sin partido comunista, por ejemplo."

2. Interview with Paco Obregón, Bilbao, 20 January 1987. My translation. Original: "El teatro era como un gesto de libertad en ese momento; era como una ceremonia de libertad. Era un teatro de quiño al publico. Se entendía a veces todo a través de un determinado gesto que no estaba en el texto, ni en el libreto, y que no aparecía en ninguna parte, pero que se hacía en el ultimo momento; porque el teatro era vivo también. Eso le daba al teatro la gran bandera de resistencia anti-franquista y de ceremonia de libertad."

3. Obregón interview. My translation. Original: "Se concretaba esa lucha más que nada en la vida cotidiana, en la vida de la familia, del pueblo, en las formas de divertirte. La libertad que estaba la juventud de Europa creando, aquí era solamente una copia risoria. . . . Yo recuerdo—esto parece una tonteria—en los años 70 todavía estaba multado con 500 pesetas por besarse en la calle. Y en este país hay curas que multaban a la gente o que hacían lo posible para que no se bailase agarrado en la plaza del pueblo."

4. Sam Smiley, "Independent Theatre: 1964–1984" (unpublished paper).

5. See Jerónimo López Mozo, *Teatro de barrio, teatro campesino* (Bilbao: Editorial Zero, 1976) for a detailed description of the *teatro de barrio*.

6. Interview with Guillermo Heras, Madrid, 15 January 1987. My translation. Original: "En Madrid existían pequeños locales que se cerraban periódicamente por la policía. Eran locales que estaban generalmente llenos de mesas de ajedrez o de otros juegos, pero que luego se utilizaban en momentos determinados como locales de discusión política y de difusión cultural con máquinas de cine de pequeño formato en el que se pasaba "El Acorazado Potemkin" y más de estas películas míticas de la Union Soviética. Y luego hay unos espacios muy importantes en el desarrollo del Teatro Independiente y el teatro clandestino: eran los colegios mayores y las propias facultades. Los sectores universitarios trabajaron fuertemente por el desarrollo de ese teatro, que en algunos casos era un teatro directamente político, directamente contra el régimen, pero que en muchos casos era un teatro cultural."

7. Equipo Pipirijaina, *Tábano: un zumbido que no cesa* (Madrid: Editorial Ayuso, 1975), p. 121. All further quotations from this work appear in the text. My translation. Original: "*(Ruido de silbatos. Entra la policía con Lockit a la cabeza. El lord se esconde en un baúl. Macky, detrás de Jenny.)* LAS CHICAS: Redada, redada, la poli, la poli. Qué peligro, etc. LOCKIT: Que nadie se mueva o tiro al aire! TODOS: -Al aire no, al aire no!"

8. The following details are based on information received from Guillermo Heras, who is currently editing an extensive collection of documents on the *Teatro Independiente*.

9. Baixas interview. My translation. Original: "Pasabamos mucho hambre. Nos han llegado a pagar con comida o daban trescientas pesetas para la gasolina. Teníamos una pequeña furmoneta, cuatro focos y alrededor de cinco personas."

10. Interview with Salvador Távora, Madrid, 18 January 1987. My translation. Original: "Por el año en que nace y por sus circonstancias de operar, La Cuadra forma parte del Teatro Independiente Español, pero con un lenguaje estetico singular. Yo, en este tiempo, desconocía totalmente el lenguaje teatral. Con los demas grupos teníamos una afinidad ideologica, claro; eramos anti-franquistas. Pero afinidades estéticas no existían. Teníamos la necesidad de hablar, de expresarnos de nuestra manera. Como la censura en aquel momento nos impusaba muchas limitaciones, creabamos un teatro del grito del canto, del golpe del baile y así, sin decir una palabra, descubrimos un teatro que iba mucho más allá de la palabra. Y lo hacíamos con toda aquella cosa que en nuestra vida cotidiana nos servía para vivir o para subsistir. Con las mismas luces que usabamos para alumbrar a nuestro barrio, con los mismos cantos que conocíamos desde pequeño, con el mismo baile que habíamos conocido desde que nacíamos y con la misma agresividad que teníamos contra ciertas sectores sociales y contra situaciones políticas. Queríamos hacer un instrumento eficaz contra la dictadura, pero más todavía la busca de nuestra dignidad."

11. Obregón interview. My translation. Original: "Aquí se ha dado una realidad política muy fuerte, con muertes, con sangre, con clima de violencia exasperada, con un clima de política que casi no permite formar un gobierno que es lo que sucede ahora. El teatro aquí no ha respondido a esto. Ante esa agresividad tan fuerte el teatro se ha refugiado en hacer un teatro de evasión, escapista—haciendo los grandes autores universalistas. Nosotros lo hemos hecho también. En Euzkadi no tenemos una tradición teatral y siempre hemos seguido la moda. Estamos un poco harto de esto."

12. Ignacio Amestoy Egiguren, *Doña Elvira, Imagínate Euskadi*. In *Primer Acto* 216 (November-December 1986), pp. 80–97.

13. Obregón interview. My translation. Original: "Es realmente la historia de un encuentro de una pareja. La mujer viene de Euzkadi a reunirse con él en Bruselas. Este hombre representa toda una generación de luchadores anti-franquistas en Euzkadi, gente muy joven, ingenua, que inicieron la lucha armada contra el franquismo. En esta obra se ve el encuentro de estas dos personas. No trata de la parte heroica, o política, sino la historia más intima de esos personajes, de los problemas personales, de sus conflictos internos para construirse como pareja, de sus propios errores. El carácter esencial no es

ese héroe o ese martir que ha salido de la cárcel, sino esa mujer que siempre ha estado en la sombra y que nunca ha salido en una revista o un periodico. La obra le da valor humano. Siendo política, muestra otro lado de la historia; el papel sensible que ha tenido y tiene la mujer en esta cultura y sociedad tan rigida que es la nuestra. Dentro de esa generación, la historia de los dos es un poco un microcosmo de lo que pasaba, de una lucha no sólo contra el estado pero que se dió también contra nosotros mismos, contra nuestra propia educación, contra nuestros propios costumbres, contra nuestras tradiciones, contra nuestros padres, contra la familia."

14. Socrates, *Apology* (New York: New American Library, 1956), (sections 29E–32A) p. 436.

15. Heras interview. My translation. Original: "Salen unas viejas védettes a cantar textos más o menos eróticos. Pues llega el hombre serpiente, un mago que hace horribles números de mágia, enanos que salen, o sea, bomberos toreros, 'freaks' practicamente. Pero no se sabe por qué se llama Teatro Chino de Manolita Chen. Manolita Chen era una empresaria que cantaba canciones españoles; era una folklórica. Parece ser que se ligó más que se casó con un chino que no sabemos que era chino de verdad y el chino se llamaba Chen."

16. Tábano, *Castañuela 70*, in *Primer Acto* 125 (1971), pp. 46–60. All further references to this work appear in the text. My translation. Original: *"(Entran DON COSME, que lleva en una silla de ruedas a DOÑA JUANA, muerta.)* Buenas noches, don Cosme. En mi nombre, y en nombre del programa "Reinar después de morir", enhorabuena: su difunta esposa ha sido la ganadora de esta semana. ¿Está usted contento, don Cosme? DON COSME: Si, señor. LOCUTOR: Muy bien, don Cosme, comprendemos su emoción, pero en unos instantes verá la cabeza de su esposa convertida en la de una auténtica reina, gracias a las prestigiosas manos del insigne diseñador de moda capilar Mr. Pierre, de la peluquería Chapital. *(Entra el PELUQUERO.)* Y aquí tenemos ya la lista de regalos para su esposa: en primer lugar, un entierro de lujo con alfombra, tres curas y cuatro velones. Tenemos también brazaletes negros, esquelas mortuorias, una maravillosa tumba de siete cuerpos y globos para los pequeños. DON COSME: No merecemos todo eso. Son ustedes muy buenos."

17. My translation. Original: "recuerden a esa mujer, esposa y madre que como una reina les mira desde el cielo."

18. My translation. Original: "Yo soy Cianón de Oklahoma, pero vivo en Washington, soy un experto estratega y a mí nadie me la pega, porque el dolár es mi dios, y ahora, en su nombre divino, os traigo la salvación."

19. Heras interview. My translation. Original: "Hablábamos de Roma y todos iban con pantalones vaqueros y encima unos sábanas, porque el montaje no sé si costaría diez mil pesetas; nosotros siempre hemos construido el decorado, hemos cosido. . . . En fin, en un momento en este sketch queríamos hablar de bases, pero eso lo prohibía la censura, prohibía la palabra 'bases' y entonces nosotros lo que hicimos fue que en vez de cantar las letras de la cansión, cantabamos solamente 'lalalalalalala.' Y la gente creía que lo habían prohibido porque aquello era tremendo, y entonces aplaudían mucho más porque creían que en las letras originales ya estábamos nombrando directamente a no sé quién."

20. Tábano, *Cambio de tercio* (Madrid: Editorial Campus, 1977), p. 9. All further quotations from this work appear in the text. My translation. Original: "combate entre la ideología burguesa y la ideología proletaria."

21. My translation. Original: "al final se queda sólo, como le suele pasar al que abandona su clase para intentar prosperar."

22. My translation. Original: "Dígame, Vergador, ¿en este tejido se irán fácilmente las manches de sangre?"

23. In Spanish, the verb *cantar* means both "to sing" and "to confess."

24. Interview with Albert Boadella, Vic (Barcelona), 9 January 1987. Translated from the original French.

25. On 12 March 1975, Glória Rognoni, a long-time actress of the company, fell from this tubular structure and broke her back, leaving her paralyzed.

26. Literally, "Civil Guards," the official name for Franco's hated national police force.

27. Annotated from video excerpts (in Spanish and Catalan) that Albert Boadella kindly showed me on 9 January 1987.

28. Boadella interview.

29. Ibid.

30. Ibid.

31. Ibid.

32. Annotated from a video recording of *La Torna* (in Spanish) kindly made available by Albert Boadella. My translation.

33. Boadella interview.

34. Ibid.

35. Els Joglars, *Olympic Man Movement,* in *Pipirijaina* 21 (March 1982), p. 104. My translation. Original: "Estas obras enfermas y degeneradas [que] son consideradas el arte de hoy. . . . Esto no puede hacerse ni patinando, ni conduciendo, ni cocinando, ni bailando . . . que no hace discriminaciones, que puede ser comprendida por todos."

36. Roller hockey is like ice hockey on roller skates and is an extremely popular spectator sport in Spain. The team from Vic, a town located only a few miles from where els Joglars lives, plays in the Spanish professional national league.

37. Moíses Perez Coterillo referred to the play, therefore, as a "ritus interruptus," *El Público* 4 (January 1984), p. 9.

38. Boadella interview.

39. My translation. Original: "qué millor que la música clássica per a simbolitzar la sintesi cultural de la gran Europa?" From *Virtuosos de Fontainebleau* program notes.

40. Els Joglars, Virtuosos de Fontainebleau, documented during the performance in the Teatro Principal of Castellón (Valencia), 11 January 1987. Translation: "Es muy fácil la cultura!" All further quotations are translated annotations from this performance.

41. This is a symbolic reference to the "Tamborolo del Bruc," a legendary Catalan drummer who miraculously succeeded in chasing the French from the Montserrat mountains during Spain's War of Independence.

42. Boadella interview.

43. Ibid.

44. Ibid.

45. Felix Población, "Teledeum: Antes que la cárcel, el exilio," *El Público* 27 (December 1985), p. 10. My translation. Original: "No estoy dispuesto a ir a la cárcel. Quiero que sepa el Gobierno que, de no tomarse una decisión que impida eso, me convertiré en el primer exiliado de la cultura bajo la Administración socialista."

CHAPTER 10

1. This problem should be seen in the context of the increasing deradicalization of unions and left-wing parties in Western Europe since World War II. Many countries had been physically destroyed by enemy and allied bombardment, and most nations had severe economic problems that caused right-wing and left-wing parties to collaborate in different versions of so-called national governments of reconstruction. The class struggle was forgotten. For the reasons mentioned in chapter 3, the sixties revealed a new insight into the more subtle forms of exploitation and repression in the post–World War II era. In

the enormous, international wave of youth protests, the traditionally left-wing parties were often found siding with the national governments; and unions, which throughout the decades that preceded the unrest had been fighting for bourgeois values for their members, refused to endorse the widespread strikes.

2. This was notably true for Dario Fo's collaboration with the cultural branch of the PCI, the Italian Communist Party. But also groups like lo Teatre de la Carriera and le Théâtre Populaire de Lorraine had their share of difficulty with French left-wing parties. On the other hand, the British radical troupe 7:84 still maintains a relatively friendly contact with left-wing organizations in England and Scotland.

3. J. R. Goodlad, *A Sociology of Popular Drama* (New York: Heineman, 1971).

4. Bonnie S. McDougall, *Mao Zedong's Talks at the Yan'An Conference*, p. 80.

5. See Georg Lukács's article, "Zur Frage der Satire" in *Internationale Literatur* 2 (1932), pp. 136–53, for an authoritative discussion of the Marxist view of satire. See also Jürgen Brummack's "Zu Begriff und Theorie der Satire," *Deutsche Vierteljahrschrift für Literaturwissenschaft und Geistesgeschichte* 45 (1971), pp. 350–52, for valuable bibliographical information on Eastern bloc theories of satire.

6. Joseph Bentley called this "the technique of reversing the modus of exclusive perception" in his article "Semantic Gravitation: an Essay on Satiric Reduction," *Modern Language Quarterly* 30, pp. 3–19.

7. George H. Szanto, *Theatre and Propaganda* (Austin: University of Texas Press, 1978), p. 9.

8. See Charles E. Schutz, *Political Humor* (Cranbury, N.J.: Associated University Presses, 1977), p. 32.

9. This is what Northrop Frye calls low norm satire, in which the underdog exposes the folly of the strong man. See Frye's chapter "The Mythos of Winter: Irony and Satire," in *Anatomy of Criticism: Four Essays* (Princeton: Princeton University Press, 1957), pp. 223–39.

10. McGrath interview.

11. It should be kept in mind that in countries like France (at least until 1985) and Spain (since 1982), for example, the subsidies are given out by a socialist government that, in theory, is sympathetic to the objectives of radical troupes.

12. Tordjman interview. My translation. Original: "En fait, dans une certaine façon on ne se bat plus! Peut-être que d'être entré dans l'institutionalisation, d'avoir des moyens qui nous permettent quand-même de vivre sans la crainte du lendemain, ça adoucit les formes parce que ça adoucit les gens. Quand les gens entrent dans des situations confortables, on s'intéresse à d'autres choses parce qu'il n'y plus l'urgence."

13. Ludwig interview. My translation. Original: "Sie erkennen dass Grips ein besonderer kultureller Bestandteil Berlins ist, womit Berlin etwas Spezielles zu bieten hat. Wir sind ein Exportartikel geworden. Wir haben überall auf der Welt gespielt und werden von Goetheinstituten überall eingeladen. Wir sind jetzt so stark etabliert, dass unsere stärksten Feinde . . . jetzt ruhig sind und uns genauso behandeln wie die anderen Theater."

14. Holden interview.

15. Bernard Weiner, "S.F. Mime Troupe's Big 'Establishment' Grant," *San Francisco Chronicle*, 6 September 1984.

16. Flores interview.

17. Holden interview.

18. It should be mentioned here that Catherine Bonafé has also left lo Teatre de la Carriera in the meantime to accept a position as cultural officer with the municipality of Fos-sur-Mer in the fall of 1986.

19. McGrath interview.

20. From an unpublished critique of an earlier version of this manuscript.

21. See my "Theatre and Liberation: Political Theatre That Works (For a Change)," *Illusions* (N.Z.) I, no. 3 (spring 1986), pp. 6–12 for a more detailed theoretical background of Third World theater of liberation.

22. See my articles, "Theatre of Liberation in Action: The People's Theatre Network of the Philippines," *New Theatre Quarterly* III, no. 10 (May 1987), 131–49; "The Theatre of Liberation of India, Indonesia and the Philippines," *Australasian Drama Studies* 10 (April 1987), pp. 3–18; and "Philippine Political Theater and the Fall of Ferdinand Marcos," *The Drama Review* T114 (summer 1987), pp. 57–79.

23. I am aware that Theater of Liberation is quite widespread in Latin America as well and that it also has its practicioners in black Africa. It would lead me too far to discuss their activities in detail in the context of this book. It will, however, receive prominent treatment in my book *Theatre and Liberation,* which is in progress.

Selected General Bibliography

Abs, Dyane and de Graaf, Willy. *Blijf niet gelaten op wonderen wachten*. Antwerp: Soethoudt, 1979.

Amitin, Mark. "Le Living Theatre." *Travail Théâtral* 22 (1976):35–53.

Andro, P.; Dauvergne, A.; and Lagoutte, L. M. *Le Mai de la révolution*. Paris: Julliard, 1968.

Ansorge, Peter. *Disrupting the Spectacle*. London: Pitman, 1975.

Ardagh, John. *The New French Revolution*. New York: Harper and Row, 1969.

Bab, Julius. *Das Theater im Lichte der Soziologie*. Leipzig: Hirschfeld, 1931.

Bablet, Denis. "Rencontres avec le théâtre du soleil." *Travail Théâtral* 19 (1975):5–39.

Barea, Pedro. "Teatro Vasco, 1986." *Primer Acto* 216 (November-December 1986):53–99.

Baumgarten, Michael and Schulz, Wilfried. *Theaterkollektiven zwischen Volkstheater und Animation*. Berlin: Medusa, 1979.

Benach, Juan-Anton. "Una Fuerza natural llamada Claca." *El Público* 7(April 1984):24–26.

Benjamin, Walter. *Illuminations*. New York: Harcourt, Brace and World, 1968.

———. "Programme pour un théâtre d'enfants prolétariens." *Travail Théâtral* 20 (1975):46–50.

Bentley, Eric. *The Theory of the Modern Stage*. Harmondsworth, Middlesex: Penguin, 1968.

Bentley, Joseph. "Semantic Gravitation: An Essay on Satiric Reduction." *Modern Language Quarterly* 30 (1975):3–19.

Birnbaumer, Ulf. "Alternatives Theater—eine kulturpolitische Alternative?" *Maske und Kothurn* 23, no. 1 (1977):58–73.

Boal, Augusto. *Técnicas Latinoamericanas de teatro popular: una revolución copernica al revés*. Buenos Aires: Corregidor, 1975.

———. *Theater of the Oppressed*. New York: Urizen Press, 1977.

Bourges, H., ed. *The Student Revolt*. London: Cape, 1968.

Bracher, Karl-Dietrich. *Zeit der Ideologien: eine Geschichte politischen Denkens im 20. Jahrhundert*. Stuttgart: Deutsche Verlags-Anstalt, 1982.

Bradby, David and McCormick, John. *People's Theatre*. London: Croom Helm, 1978.

229

Bradby, David; James, Louis; and Sharrat, Bernard, eds. *Performance and Politics in Popular Drama*. Cambridge: Cambridge University Press, 1980.

Brandt, Willy. "The Political Significance of Theater." *Comparative Drama* 7 (1973):222–30.

Brummack, Jürgen. "Zu Begriff und Theorie der Satire." *Deutsche Vierteljahrschrift für Literaturwissenschaft und Geistesgeschichte* 45 (1971):350–52.

Buzzi, A. R. *La Théorie politique d'Antonio Gramsci*. Louvain: Editions Nauwelaerts, 1967.

Calandra, Denis. "*Terror*, Rote Rübe." *The Drama Review* 19, no. 2 (1975):114–18.

———. *New German Dramatists*. New York: Macmillan, 1983.

Califona, Joseph A., Jr. *The Student Revolution: A Global Confrontation*. New York: W. W. Norton, 1970.

Cohn-Bendit, Daniel. *Obsolete Communism: The Leftwing Alternative*. London: André Deutsch, 1968.

Copfermann, Emile. *Le Theâtre populaire pourquoi?* Paris: Maspero, 1965.

———. "Quelque chose a changé. . . ." *Partisans* 47 (1969):5–29.

Coterillo, Moíses Perez, ed. *Tábano: un zumbido que no cesa*. Madrid: Editorial Ayuso, 1975.

———, ed. *Anuario teatral, 1985*. Madrid: Centro de Documentación Teatral, 1986.

———, ed. *Guía teatral de España, 1986*. Madrid: Centro de Documentación Teatral, 1986.

Croydon, Margaret. *Lunatics, Lovers and Poets*. New York: Delta Books, 1974.

Dansette, Adrien. *Mai 1968*. Paris: Plon, 1971.

Davis, R. G. "Guerila Theater." *Tulane Drama Review* 10 (1966):131–36.

Davis, R. G.; Schumann, Peter; and Valdez, Luis. "Sur le théâtre guérillero." *Partisans* 47 (1969):87–107.

Demarcy, Richard. *Eléments d'une sociologie du spectacle*. Paris: UGE, 1973.

Dieho, Bart. *Theater op de bres: Vormingstoneel in Nederland en Vlaanderen*. Amsterdam: Espee, 1979.

Dietrich, Margret. "Theater, Wirtschaft und Kulturverantwortung." *Maske und Kothurn* 20, no. 1 (1974):3–9.

Dini, Massimo. *Teatro D'Avanguardia Americano*. Firenze: Vellechi, 1978.

Dort, Bernard. *Théâtre Public*. Paris: Seuil, 1967.

Drillon, Lilyane; Monléon, José; Ortiz, José L.; Távora, Salvador. *Quejío:informe*. Madrid: Ediciones Demofilo, 1975.

Duvignaud, Jean. *Spectacle et société*. Paris: Denoël, Gonthier, 1970.

———. *Le Théâtre contemporain*. Paris: Larousse, 1974.

Elliott, Robert C. *Power of Satire: Magic, Ritual, and Art*. Princeton: Princeton University Press, 1960.

Feinberg, Leonard. *An Introduction to Satire*. Ames: The Iowa State University Press, 1967.

Ferrer, J. M. García and Rom, Martí. *Laberint, La Claca*. Barcelona: Cine-Club Associació Enginyers, 1986.

Fiebach, Joachim. "Werk im werden: Theater der siebziger Jahre in West Europa." *Weimarer Beiträge* 2 (1982):11–38.

Freire, Paulo. "The Adult Literacy Process as Cultural Action." *Harvard Educational Review* 40, no. 2 (1970):205–25.

———. "Cultural Action and Conscientization." *Harvard Educational Review* 40, no. 3 (1970):452–77.

Gaudibert, Pierre. *Action Culturelle*. Paris: Castermann, 1977.

Girault, Alain. "Culture populaire, culture de masse." *Théâtre/Public* 30 (1979):3–20.

Godard, Colette. *Le Théâtre depuis 1968*. Paris: Editions Jean-Claude Lattés, 1980.
Goldstein, Malcolm. *The Political Stage: American Drama and Theater of the Great Depression*. New York: Oxford University Press, 1974.
Gooch, Steve. *All Together Now*. London: Methuen, 1984.
Goodlad, J. R. *A Sociology of Popular Drama*. New York: Heineman, 1971.
Gramsci, Antonio. *The Modern Prince, and Other Writings*. New York: International Publishers, 1977.
———. *Selected Works from Political Writings, 1910–1920*. New York: International Publishers, 1977.
———. *Selected Works from Political Writings, 1921–1926*. New York: International Publishers, 1978.
Hamon, Christine. "Du Théâtre-meeting au réalisme satirique." *Travail Théâtral* 23 (1976):118–21.
Heras, Guillermo, ed. *Nuevas tendencias escénicas: la escritura teatral a debate*. Madrid: Centro Nacional de Nuevas Tendencias Escénicas, 1985.
Herms, Dieter. "Mime Troupe, El Teatro, Bread and Puppet—Ansätze zu einem politischen Volkstheater in den USA." *Maske und Kothurn* 19, no. 4 (1973):342–62.
Horkeimer, Max. *Critical Theory: Selected Essays*. New York: Herder and Herder, 1972.
Ismayr, Wolfgang. *Das politische Theater in Westdeutschland*. Meisenheim am Glan: Anton Hain, 1977.
Itzin, Catherine. *Stages of the Revolution*. London: Methuen, 1980.
———. *British Alternative Theatre Directory*. Eastborne: John Offord, 1982.
Jeanson, Francis. *l'Action Culturelle dans la cité*. Paris: Seuil, 1973.
Jotterand, Franck. *Le Nouveau théâtre américain*. Paris: Seuil, 1970.
Jourdheuil, Jean. *Le Théâtre, l'artiste, l'état*. Paris: Hachette, 1979.
Kernan, Alvin B. *The Plot of Satire*. New Haven: Yale University Press, 1965.
Kirby, Michael. "On Political Theatre." *The Drama Review* 19 (1975):129–35.
Klatt, Gudrun. *Arbeiterklasse und Theater*. Berlin: Akademie Verlag, 1975.
Kopp, A. "l'Art de gauche, instrument de transformation sociale." *Espaces et Sociétés* 1 (1970):15–31.
Kourilsky, Françoise. "Political Theater in France since 1968." *The Drama Review* 19, no. 2 (1975):43–52.
Lebel, Jean-Jacques. *Procès du Festival d'Avignon: Supermarché de la culture*. Paris: Editions Pierre Belfond, 1968.
———. "Notes on Political Street Theater, Paris: 1968, 1969." *The Drama Review* 13, no. 4 (1969):111–18.
Lee, Vera. *Quest for a Public*. Cambridge, Mass.: Schenkman, 1970.
Lenin, Vladimir Ilyich. *On Culture and Cultural Revolution*. Moscow: Progress Publishers, 1966.
Lukács, Georg. "Zur Frage der Satire." *Internationale Literatur* 2, no. 5 (1932): 136–53.
Luzuriaga, Gerardo. *Popular Theatre for Social Change in Latin America*. Los Angeles: UCLA Latin-American Center Publications, 1978.
Lyday, Leon and Woodyard, G. W., eds. *Dramatists in Revolt: The New Latin American Theater*. Austin: University of Texas Press, 1976.
Mallen, Jay, ed. *"Che" Guevara on Revolution*. Coral Gables: University of Miami Press, 1969.
Marcuse, Herbèrt. *Negations: Essays in Critical Theory*. Boston: Beacon Press, 1968.
———. *One-Dimensional Man*. Boston: Beacon Press, 1968.
Maraini, Daria. "Existe-t-il un théâtre populaire?" *Travail Théâtral* 10 (1973):31–38.
Mattelart, Armand and Siegelaub, Seth, eds. *Multinational Corporations and the Control of Culture: The Ideological Apparatus of Imperialism*. Atlantic Highlands, N.J.: Humanities Press, 1979.

McDougall, Bonnie S. *Mao Zedong's "Talks at the Yan'An Conference on Literature and Art": A Translation of the 1943 Text with Commentary.* Ann Arbor: Center for Chinese Studies of the University of Michigan, 1980.

Miller, Judith Graves. *Theater and Revolution in France since 1968.* Lexington, Ky.: French Forum, 1977.

Mnouchkine, Ariane. *l'Age d'or.* Paris: Stock, 1975.

Monléon, José. "El Taller, el cante y el toro." *Primer Acto* 207 (January-February 1985):32–34.

———. " 'Piel de toro,' rito y alegría." *Primer Acto* 207 (January-February 1985):39–42.

Mozo, Jerónimo Lopez. *Teatro de barrio, teatro campesino.* Bilbao: Editorial Zero, 1976.

Oglesby, Carl. *The New Left Reader.* New York: Grove Press, 1969.

Paul, Arno. "The West German Theater Miracle." *The Drama Review* 24, no. 1 (1980): 3–24.

Paulson, Ronald, ed. *Modern Essays in Criticism: Satire.* Englewood Cliffs, N.J.: Prentice-Hall, 1971.

Piscator, Erwin. *Das Politische Theater.* Hamburg: Rowohlt, 1963.

Ramón, Francisco Ruiz. *Historia del teatro Español,* volúmen II: siglo veinte. Madrid: Alianza Editorial, 1971.

Reich, Wilhelm. *Mass Psychology of Fascism.* New York: Farrar, Strauss and Giroux, 1970.

Richards, Gavin. *England Expects.* London: Journeyman, 1977.

Roberg, Dietmar. *Theater muss wie Fussball sein.* Berlin: Rotbuch, 1980.

Robinson, Paul A. *The Freudian Left: Wilhelm Reich, Geza Roheim, Herbert Marcuse.* New York: Harper and Row, 1969.

Rolland, Romain. *Théâtre du peuple, essai esthéthique d'un théâtre nouveau.* Paris: Michel, 1923.

Roose-Evans, James. *Experimental Theater: From Stanislavsky to Peter Brook.* New York: Universe Press, 1984.

Roszak, Theodore. *The Making of the Counter Culture.* London: Faber and Faber, 1970.

Royaards, Rense. *Van wie komen jullie, van God of van de Duivel?* Amsterdam: Latijnse Teaterexperimenten, 1982.

Ryckmans, Pierre. *The Chairman's New Clothes: Mao and the Cultural Revolution.* London: Allison and Busby, 1977.

Sainer, Arthur. *The Radical Theatre Notebook.* New York: Avon Books, 1975.

Schechner, Richard. "An Interview with the Becks." *The Drama Review* 13, no. 3 (1969): 24–44.

———. "Guerilla Theater-May 1970." *The Drama Review* 14 (1970):163–68.

Schevill, James. *Breakout! In Search of New Theatrical Environments.* Chicago: Black Swallow Press, 1973.

Schley, Gernot. *Die freie Bühne in Berlin.* Berlin: Haude und Spenersche, 1967.

Schnapps, Alain and Vidal-Naquet, Pierre. *The French Student Uprising: November 1967-June 1968.* Boston: Beacon Press, 1971.

Schutz, Charles E. *Political Humor.* Cranbury, N.J.: Associated University Presses, 1977.

Shank, Theodore. "Collective Creations." *The Drama Review* 16, no. 2 (1972): 3–31.

———. "The Welfare State Theatre." *The Drama Review* 21, no. 1 (1977): 3–16.

———. *American Alternative Theater.* New York: Grove Press, 1982.

Simon, Alfred. *Le Théâtre à bout de souffle?* Paris: Editions du Seuil, 1979.

Smiley, Sam. *The Drama of Attack: Didactic Plays of the American Depression.* Columbia: University of Missouri Press, 1972.

Spender, Stephen. *The Year of the Young Rebels*. New York: Random House, 1969.
Szanto, George H. *Theater and Propaganda*. Austin: University of Texas Press, 1978.
Tábano. *Cambio de Tercio*. Madrid: Editorial Campus, 1978.
Taylor, Karen M. *People's Theatre in Amerika*. New York: Drama Specialists, 1972.
Terfloth, John H. "Versuche zur Aktualisierung des Theaters in Nordamerika." *Maske und Kothurn* 17 (1971):236–45.
Touraine, Alain. *The May Movement*. New York: Random House, 1971.
Trancón, Santiago. "La Historia de 'la Cuadra' a través de textos de Salvador Távora." *Primer Acto* 207 (January-February, 1985):34–39.
———. "Una reflexión sobre nuestra historia reciente." *Primer Acto* 207 (January-February, 1985):42–48.
Trotsky, Leon. *Literature and Revolution*. New York: Russell and Russell, 1957.
van Berlaer, Dina, ed. *Tot Lering en Vermaak: 9 Manieren voor 10 Jaar Vormingstheater*. Antwerp: Soethoudt, 1980.
———. *Het Politieke toneel heeft je hart nodig*. Antwerp: Soethoudt, 1982.
van Erven, Eugène. "Theater and Liberation." *Illusions* (New Zealand) 1, no. 3 (1986):6–12.
———. "The People's Theatre Network of the Philippines." *New Theatre Quarterly III*, no. 10 (May 1987):131–49.
———. "Philippine Political Theater and the Fall of Ferdinand Marcos." *The Drama Review* (Summer 1987): T114:56–79.
Vilar, Jean. *Théâtre service public*. Paris: Gallimard, 1971.
Vormus, Helga. "Le Festival des groupes libres de théâtre politique." *Travail Théâtral* 17 (1974):123–27.
Wandor, Michelene. *Sexual Politics in the Theatre*. London: Journeyman Press, 1980.
Williams, Raymond. *Marxism and Literature*. Oxford University Press, 1977.
———. *Politics and Letters*. London: N.L.B., 1979.
———. *Problems in Materialism and Culture*. London: N.L.B., 1980.
Zonneveld, L. "De Repetitie van de Revolutie: het theater van Augusto Boal." *Speltribune* 4 (1979):1–2.

This bibliography is far from complete. Many other articles pertaining to the subject have appeared in *The Performing Arts Journal, Theater Work, Canadian Theatre Review, Gambit, Théâtre/Public, Toneel/Teatraal, The Theatre Journal, Gestos,* and *Estreno.*

INDEX